THE QUEST FOR LIGHTNESS IN EQUITATION
by Hilda Nelson
and
EQUESTRIAN QUESTIONS
by Alexis-François L'Hotte
(translation by Hilda Nelson)

Photograph of *Général* Alexis-François L'Hotte taken after his retirement and return to Lunéville in 1890.

THE QUEST FOR LIGHTNESS IN EQUITATION
by Hilda Nelson
and
EQUESTRIAN QUESTIONS
by Alexis-François L'Hotte
(translation by Hilda Nelson)

Dedication
For Burt, who lived through it all.

Original Publication by J.A. Allen 1997
British Library cataloguing-in-publication data
A catalogue record for this book is available
from the British Library

ISBN 0.85131.705.7

Published in Great Britain in 1997 by

J. A. Allen & Company Limited
1, Lower Grosvenor Place
London, SW1 W 0EL

© J. A. Allen & Company Limited 1997

No part of this book may be reproduced or transmitted
in any way or by any means, electronic or mechanical,
including photocopy, recording, or any information
storage and retrieval system, without permission in
writing from the publishers. All rights Reserved.

This exclusive Xenophon Press edition is authorized
by the author.
Copyright Xenophon Press, Franktown, Virginia
All rights reserved 2021
XenophonPress@gmail.com www.XenophonPress.com
Cover design Robert Ashbaugh

Xenophon Press Edition ISBN: 978-1948717342
Edited by Susan Beer
Designed by Nancy Lawrence

Publisher's Introduction

Hilda Nelson's contribution to translating and interpreting the importance of French Equitation through the centuries for the English-speaking equestrian world is monumental. Her earliest translation project reaches the seventeenth-century work of Antoine de Pluvinel: *The Maneige Royal* [Xenophon Press 2010]. Later, she researched French equitation of the nineteenth century including the great polar-opposite schools of François Baucher and the comte d'Aure. In addition, she delved into the heroines of the nineteenth century in the circus with her *Great Horsewomen of the 19th Century in the Circus* [Xenophon Press 2015]. Her work on Baucher: *François Baucher: The Man and His Method* [Xenophon Press 2013] was one of the first books in English to contextualize this French master for the English-speaking equestrian enthusiast. Originally, all of these works were done in partnership with J.A. Allen yet with the loss of this great publishing visionary, the books slowly went out of print and were not appreciated or valued by the acquiring companies.

I discovered that Ms. Nelson had also translated Michel Henriquet's *30 Years with Master Nuno Oliveira* [Xenophon Press 2011] in the early 2000s. Oliveira represented for her, the continuation of the great "French" tradition into the twentieth century. Her translation was part of the archive that Ivan Bezugloff, founder of Xenophon Press, transferred to me. It was on a small floppy disc as a Word Perfect document. Ivan had not published the translation. It took two years to produce that first Master Nuno Oliveira student series book starting with Michel Henriquet's journal and collection of correspondence with the master. During this time, Ms. Nelson approached me to help her preserve all of her equestrian works "long after" she was gone.

So the re-publication of this work is the final equestrian work written or translated by Hilda Nelson to come home to Xenophon Press.

We felt that the original J.A.Allen titling was confusing and did not make enough of the fact that the second half of the book is the only English translation of L'Hotte's *Questions équestres*. Therefore, our Xenophon Press edition clarifies this in our new title. The original index is intact. We hope you will enjoy this important addition to the Xenophon Press Library.

Richard F. Williams
Editor-in-Chief
Publisher
Xenophon Press

Alexis-François L'Hotte (1825-1904)

The French general, Alexis-François L'Hotte (1825-1904) was sent to the Ecole de Cavalerie at Saumur to pursue his equestrian talent. He became the pupil of both François Baucher and comte d'Aure. He returned to Saint-Cyr as commandant of the reopened cavalry section. In 1864 he became *écuyer en chef* of the Ecole de Cavalerie. In 1875 he returned to Saumur as commandant of the Ecole de Cavalerie there. He was considered by all to be the most outstanding *écuyer* of the period. His two works: *Un Officier de cavalerie - Souvenirs* (1905) and *Questions équestres* (1906) appeared posthumously. It was on his personal horses that L'Hotte practiced the teachings of Baucher. But as *écuyer en chef* and commandant at Saumur, he was obliged to follow the teachings and rules of a military establishment. In this respect he was more in the d'Auriste idiom, practicing primarily exterior and military equitation. For not supporting more openly the teachings of Baucher when he was *écuyer en chef* and commandant at Saumur he was, and still is, criticized. However, it was his quest to produce answers to the equestrian problems that he faced that prompted his writing of *Questions équestres*. He provides complete, precise, and definitive answers.

Hilda Nelson (1922-2018)

Hilda Nelson was Professor Emeritus of French Literature and Civilization at San Diego State University in Southern California. She received her Ph.D. from the University of Wisconsin, Madison. She is the author of books and articles on romanticism, dada, and surrealism, and translated Antoine de Pluvinel's classic on horsemanship, *The Maneige Royal*, and authored *François Baucher, The Man and his Method*, and *Great Horsewomen of the Nineteenth Century in the Circus*. She translated *30 Years with Master Nuno Oliveira* by Michel Henriquet; all books are published by Xenophon Press.

Contents

		page	
	Publisher's Introduction		v
	Alexis-François L'Hotte & Hilda Nelson		vi
	List of Illustrations		ix
	Acknowledgements		xi
	Avant-propos		xiii
	Forward		xv
1	The golden thread		1
2	L'Hotte – his life and times		15
3	L'Hotte's teacher: François Baucher		41
4	L'Hotte's teacher: *comte* d'Aure		52
5	Baucher and d'Aure – a comparison		75
6	L'Hotte's spiritual teacher: Rousselet		82
7	*Questions équestres*		88
8	*Amazones* and *écuyères* of the nineteenth century		111
9	L'Hotte's legacy		135
	Translation of L'Hotte's *Questions équestres*		147
	Bibliography		215
	Index		217
	Xenophon Press Library		223

Illustrations

Frontispiece

Photograph of *Général* Alexis-François L'Hotte taken after his retirement and return to Lunéville in 1890.

1	The beautiful Classical building of the former *Ecole de Cavalerie* of Saumur, built in the seventeenth century. It surrounds the *Carrière du Chardonnet*.	page 5
2	The *Manège des Ecuyers*. Also known as the *Manège des Dieux*. Part of the *Ecole de Cavalèrie* of Saumur. (Photograph by Hilda Nelson)	6
3	The duc d'Enghien participating in tournaments such as the *courses de testées et de bagues* in the seventeenth century. (Courtesy of the *Musée National du Château de Versailles*)	8
4	'In tandem' at Versailles. (Courtesy of François Lemaire de Ruffieu, horse trainer, graduated from the *Cadre Noir*, author and artist)	9
5	An example of la *légèreté*, in front of the *Château de Saumur*. (Courtesy of François Lemaire de Ruffieu, horse trainer, graudated from the *Cadre Noir*, author and artist)	12
6	Pluvinel encouraging Louis XIII. (Courtesy of François Lemaire de Ruffieu, horse trainer, graduated from the *Cadre Noir*, author and artist)	14
7	Duc Leopold, the first to make Lunéville the *ville du cheval*.	17
8	L'Hotte presenting the *Cadre Noir* during a *reprise* in the *Manège des Ecuyers*. (Courtesy of the *Musée de Saumur*)	26
9	In 1860 L'Hotte was commandant of the cavalry section at Saint-Cyr. L'Hotte is on his personal horse Zégris in the centre of this gravure.	27
10	L'Hotte riding his horse Sicambre in 1866 at the *Palais de l'Industrie* where he leads the *Ecuyères du manege*.	28
11	L'Hotte on his horse Laruns. (Courtesy of the *Musée de Saumur*)	30
12	Drawing by François Ruaud Gerbéviller, and photograph by Claude Henrard Lunéville of L'Hotte's house, 42 rue Gambetta. Note the door on the right without steps to enable L'Hotte's three horses to enter stables and *manège* (Lunéville).	34

List of illustrations

13	L'Hotte's house, situated centre, back. Photo appeared in an article by J. P. Carciofi. Reproduced as a postcard in 1900 by Edition Quantin (Lunéville).	35
14	Photo taken in 1893. Reproduced as a postcard in 1900 by Edition Quantin (Lunéville).	36
15	*Château de Lunéville*. Photo taken by J. P. Carciofi. The author is grateful to Mr Carciofi and the Office of the Mayor of Lunéville for the use of these illustrations.	37
16	Commemorative plaque placed by the *Cadre Noir* in 1981 on the facade of L'Hotte's house, 42 rue Gambetta (Lunéville).	40
17	François Baucher (1796–1873), a lithograph by Lasalle made for Baucher's *Oeuvres complètes* in 1854.	42
18	François Baucher as drawn by Commandant Margot of Saumur for General Decarpentry, (Courtesy G. Margot)	48
19	*Comte* d'Aure	53
20	*Comte* d'Aure practising exterior equitation. Painted by Philippe Ledieu. (Courtesy of the *Musée de Saumur*)	56
21	*Comte* d'Aure on his horse, Le Cerf.	58
22	A very young Marie-Antoinette astride her fiery black horse. Painted by Louis-August Brun. (Courtesy of the *Musée National du Château de Versailles*)	114
23	How an *amazone* should dismount. (Photo in E. Molier's *L'Equitation et le Cheval*)	115
24	A plate which appears in the book by J. G. Prizeluis, *Etwas für Liebhaberrinnen der Reiterey* (Something for those women who like riding). Leipzig, Weidmann, 1777. Note the astride seat which Prizeluis favoured for women. Most likely this is a portrait of Princess Helena Charlotte to whom the work is dedicated.	116
25	Mlle Yola de Nyss of the *cirque Molier* giving the typical salute of the *écuyère*. (Photo in E. Molier's *L'Equitation*)	117
26	Mlle Blanche Allarty of the *cirque Molier* doing the *cabriole* on d'Artagnan. (Photo in E. Molier's *L'Equitation*)	118
27	Photo of Sarah Bernhardt in the *Bois de Boulogne* by the fashionable father and son photographers Jean Louis Delton. (Appears in *Chevaux et équipages*, Paris, 1878)	120
28	A *manège* in Paris. An *amazone* doing the Spanish walk. (Painted by Edmond Grandjean)	122
29	An *amazone* riding in the park with her spaniels. (Painted by Alfred de Dreux)	123
30	*L'Ecuyère* Kipler riding with her spaniel in the park. (Painted by Alfred de Dreux. Featured on the cover of *L'Express Paris*, June 1988)	125
31	Pauline Cuzent, François Baucher's favourite pupil. (Portrait in Baron de Vaux' *Ecuyers et Ecuyères*)	126

Acknowledgements

I wish to thank the following members of the *Cadre Noir*, the *Ecole Nationale d'Equitation*, and the *Ecole d'Application de l'Arme Blindée Cavalerie* for their cordiality and help:

Colonel G. Margot, former *écuyer en chef* and Commandant of the *Cadre Noir* and the *Ecole de Cavalerie*; Colonel F. de Beauregard, former *écuyer en chef* of the *Cadre Noir*, presently Adjoint Patrimoine of the *Ecole d'Application de l'Arme Blindée Cavalerie*, Colonel Christian Carde, presently *écuyer en chef* of the *Cadre Noir*; General Pierre Durand (ret.) former *écuyer en chef* of the *Cadre Noir* and former Director of the *Ecole Nationale d'Equitation*; Patrice Franchet d'Espèrey, Documentaliste of the *Ecole Nationale d'Equitation*; Antoine Sinninger, Public Relations Officer of the *Ecole Nationale d'Equitation*; Michel Henriquet, *écuyer* and writer, and Catherine Durand Henriquet, *écuyère*, of Bailly, France.

I also wish to thank Caroline Burt, Publishing Director of J. A. Allen & Co. for her patience and guidance.

And last, but not least, I wish to thank Stephanie Weiner for reading the galley proofs and catching countless typographical and spelling errors, inconsistencies, etc. Her help has been invaluable.

Avant-propos

Figure emblématique, 'personnage historique énigmatique, un maître parmi les maîtres, mais qui ne fit pas de disciples, autant de contradictions qui établissent le mystère L'Hotte' et que cet ouvrage contribuera à expliquer, peut-être à dissiper.

Ce qui frappe dans ce visage de ce fils de Lorraine à l'aspect glacial, austère comme la vie qu'il mène, c'est son regard éclatant, ses yeux bleu-clair qui ne quittent pas ceux de son interlocuteur. Dans l'intimité, un sourire révèle la bonté et la gaité. Il est un causeur charmant, érudit sans pédantisme, liseur infatigable. L'Hotte vit comme un spartiate.

Tel est *l'homme* dont Hubert LYAUTEY, Maréchal de France, aide de camp du Général L'Hotte de 1883 à 1887, dit qu'il fut l'honneur de sa carrière, ajoutant, en 1891: 'Je vous assure que votre grande et pure figure est celle que nous évoquons pour restaurer en nous l'idée obscurci de *chef militaire.*' Il est, en effet, la plus haute incarnation de la droiture, du désintéressement, de l'abnégation, de l'austérité, la plus définitive personification de la noblesse de l'état militaire.

Personnalité d'exception, parangon de l'Officier de Cavalerie, le Général L'Hotte est aussi 'le plus savant et le plus complet des *écuyers* de son temps... Son nom doit passer à la postérite.' Ainsi pensait le Général FAVEROT de KERBRECH qui lui écrivit: '... Ayant eu l'occasion, en 1869, de chercher à voir en pays étranger les écuyers les plus célèbres d'Europe, je n'en ai rencontré aucun qui pût vous être comparé... J'en suis revenu bien rassuré pour notre équitation, représenté par vous, mon Général, qui avez su allier la rectitude, la discrétion des aides de l'ancienne école française aux merveilleux résultats que nous donnait l'application des procédés Baucher.'

A ses talents d'écuyer, il joignait enfin ceux d'*écrivain*, compensant ainsi en quelque sorte la concision de son enseignement oral qui confinait au mutisme. Le Général MENESSIER de la LANCE le voyait en proie à un 'conflit intérieur qui a nui à son enseignement'. 'A chacune de ces questions (équestres), le Général apporte une réponse précise, complète, définitive' (Général DECARPENTRY), dans un style qu'admirait GIDE qui prétendait qu'il était le dernier écrivain à savoir manier notre langue avec élégance et pureté.

Le Général L'Hotte s'est hissé à la cime des artisans de l'édification de la chose équestre parce que son tact a été servi par une vaste culture, une intelligence et des facultés d'observation jamais réunies à un tel degré chez le même sujet. Aussi se qualifie-t-il comme 'l'annonceur et le démonstrateur de la connaissance équestre actuelle, voire de la connaissance équestre en soi'.

Colonel François de Beauregard,
Ancien Chef du Cadre Noir
Actuellement, Adjoint Patrimoine de
l'Ecole d'Application de l'Arme Blindée Cavalerie

Foreword

Emblematical figure, 'enigmatic historical personage, a master among masters, who never produced any disciples, full of contradictions, which make up the L'Hotte mystery', and which this present work may explain and perhaps dispel.

What strikes one when looking at the countenance of this son of Lorraine, as austere as the very life he leads, are his piercing glance and his light blue eyes, which never leave those of his interlocutor. In the intimacy of friendship, his smile reveals kindness and gaiety. He is a delightful talker, erudite without being pedantic, a tireless reader. The life L'Hotte leads is Spartan.

Such is the *man* of whom Hubert LYAUTEY, Marshal of France and *aide de camp* of General L'Hotte from 1883 to 1887, said that he represented the honour of his profession, adding in 1891: 'I assure you that the great and pure figure you exemplify, restores to us the obscured ideal of the *military chief*.' Indeed, L'Hotte represents the highest incarnation of rectitude, unselfishness, abnegation, austerity, and the most definitive personification of the nobility of the military estate.

An exceptional personality, the model of a cavalry officer, General L'Hotte is also 'the most learned and most complete of the *écuyers* of his time . . . His name will pass on to posterity.' Thus thought General FAVEROT de KERBRECH, who wrote to him, saying: 'having, in 1869, the opportunity of observing the most famous *écuyers* in foreign lands, I found none who could equal you . . . I returned, heartened by our own equitation which you, my General, represent, you who have been able to bring together rectitude, discretion of aids, which belong to our former French School, with the wonderful results which the application of the procedures of Baucher have given you.'

Added to his talent as *écuyer*, L'Hotte also combined those of *writer*, thereby compensating, in some way, for the concise manner in which he conducted his verbal instruction, which verged on silence. *Général* MENNESSIER de la LANCE saw him as the victim of an 'interior conflict which was prejudicial to his teaching'. 'To each of these (equestrian) questions, the general brought a precise, complete, and definitive answer' (*Général* DECARPENTRY), using a style which GIDE admired, and who claimed that he was the last writer who knew how to use our language with elegance and purity.

General L'Hotte reached the pinnacle of creative craftsmanship in equestrian matters, because his tact and sensitivity were aided by a vast culture, an intelligence, and the faculty of observation, never before combined to such a degree in a single individual. Furthermore, L'Hotte can be regarded as 'the forerunner and demonstrator of present day equestrian knowledge, indeed, of equestrian knowledge as such'.

Colonel François de Beauregard
Former *Chef du Cadre Noir*
Presently, *Adjoint Patrimoine de*
l'Ecole d'Application de l'Arme Blindée Cavalerie

1
The golden thread

France has been fortunate to have had so many exceptional horsemen, not only exceptional practitioners, but men who also wrote manuals on equitation, thus leaving behind precepts and theories for future generations of horsemen and historians to analyse, adopt, or adapt. France was also fortunate to have had several seats of learning in the field of equitation. The *Ecole de Cavalerie* of Saumur, essentially a military establishment, with its famous *Manège des Ecuyers*, and the *Ecole de Versailles* with its *Manège de Versailles* founded by Louis XIV in 1680 for the training of the royal family and pages were two such. To these two schools one must add the names of the *Ecole Militaire* of Paris as well as the *Académie des Tuileries* in Paris, directed between 1715 and 1730 by François Robichon de La Guérinière, but which, unfortunately, did not fare well financially. However, when the former royal stables of the *Manège royal des Tuileries* were vacated and transferred to Versailles in 1680, this establishment was reopened and the direction offered to La Guérinière by his patron, Prince Charles of Lorraine, *Grand écuyer* to Louis XV, who was well aware of La Guérinière's talent as a horseman and helped re-establish him.

As one comes across and examines the many names of famous *écuyers* who go back to the sixteenth, seventeenth, and eighteenth centuries and the many schools of equitation, one discovers a long golden thread that weaves its way throughout France's involvement with and commitment to horsemanship, linking both men and schools. These centuries abound with well-known names, theoreticians and practitioners alike. The names of those *écuyers* who left behind manuals dealing with principles on horsemanship, are, of course, better known than those outstanding *écuyers* who furthered the cause of equitation by word of mouth, passing their knowledge and expertise on to their pupils and disciples. Thanks to the many *mémoires* and anecdotes of some of their disciples, considerable knowledge, emanating from the *écuyers* of Versailles, has been passed down to us. The *Ecole de Versailles*, while it became famous throughout France and Europe, did not produce much in the way of writing. Perhaps court life made it difficult for the riding masters of Versailles to sit down and take up the pen. Nonetheless, the *Ecole de Versailles* became famous, thanks to outstanding *écuyers* such as Louis de Gazaux de Nestier, Vernet Du Plessis (Duplessis),[1] Antoine de Vendeuil, François

---

[1] Du Vernet du Plessis or Duplessis, was considered by many, including La Guérinière, to be the most famous *écuyer* of his age. L'Hotte recounts the following anecdote which he took from Gaspard de Saunier's *L'Art de la cavalerie*, who was also one of Duplessis's pupils:

'I remember when one of France's great lords brought his son to *monsieur* Duplessis who was, at the time, head of all the famous *écuyers* I have mentioned. I remember, I say,

de Salvert, Brunet de Neuilly, and many others.

When L'Hotte refers to the glorious days of French equitation when foreign princes and men who later became important statesmen vied for admittance to the schools of equitation, especially the military schools, he is thinking primarily of the eighteenth century, when men such as Arthur Wellesley, the future Duke of Wellington, William Pitt, and Charles James Fox came to France to further their equestrian education.

An historical outline of the origins as well as the function of the *Ecole de Cavalerie* of Saumur and the *Ecole de Versailles* might be in order at this point.

The *Ecole de Cavalerie* of Saumur has its origins in France's civil wars. During the sixteenth century France was plagued with civil strife of a religious and political nature. It was the penetration of the Protestant Reformation into France, Calvinism, that unleashed these civil and religious wars. At first this Reformation was of a gentle and intellectual nature when in 1523 the scholar Jacques Lefèvre d'Etaples produced a French translation of the New Testament. When d'Etaples and his friend, the Bishop of Meaux and a few other intellectuals, formed what is known as the *Meaux Circle*, matters became more serious. While the king, François I (1495–1547), and some of the members of the royal family, were tolerant of the new ideas, it was the Sorbonne and the *Parlement* of Paris, composed of arch Catholics, that went on the warpath. In a sense it was one set of scholars against another set of scholars. When the Sorbonne and the *Parlement* of Paris began to harass the *Meaux Circle*, Marguerite d'Angoulême, the king's sister, came to its aid. (One should not yet consider these scholars as Protestants, but merely as reformers whose primary concern was translating the New Testament, the Psalms, and other religious texts into French, thus making these works accessible to the layman.) However, matters became more fanatical when Jean Calvin's work, *L'Institution chrétienne* (first written in Latin and then published in a French version in 1540), was eagerly read by a large number of readers, too large a number for the comfort of the arch Catholics. Calvin soon had to flee France and established himself in Geneva. But the Calvinist Reformation began to expand and soon over 600 'established' churches and many smaller, less organized groups, cropped up throughout France.[2]

And so the civil wars of religion began in earnest. However, the religious aspect became political when a large number of members of the nobility, even princes of the blood, joined this new movement. Historians offer a number of explanations for the social composition of the new movement. It can be seen as a protest on the part of members of the nobility who felt strangled by the monarchy's political and economic policies, undoubtedly involving a resurgence of provincial regionalism against the monarchy, especially southern regionalism. It should be remembered that powerful members of the nobility, even princes of the blood, had, throughout the centuries, challenged monarchical power, at times becoming more powerful than the monarch himself.

Eventually François I, tolerant when the movement was of an intellectual nature, changed his attitude when some Protestant fanatics posted abusive manifestos against the

---

that this lord said to him: "I am not bringing you my son so you can make an *écuyer* of him; rather I am asking you merely to teach him how to harmonize his legs and his hands in view of what he wants to do with his horse."

Duplessis answered him in my presence and I had the honour of being one of his disciples.

"Sir, for about sixty years now I have been trying to accomplish what you are honouring me by telling me this; for what you are asking me to do is precisely what I am hoping to accomplish."'

[2] French Calvinists were also known as Huguenots, a more political group.

Catholic mass. One was even posted on the door of the king's chambers. However, during much of the reign of François I and thanks to his sister Marguerite, a modicum of tolerance continued to exist. It was under Henry II (1547–59) that a more violent attack took shape, with the Sorbonne and the *Parlement* of Paris beginning seriously to persecute the Protestants, even decreeing death by burning to the heretics.

When the Queen Mother, Catherine de Médicis, took power as Regent for the three under-age princes, the horrors of the civil war increased. Plots, conspiracies, assassinations, and massacres followed each other, perpetrated on both sides. Many members of the nobility, Protestant and Catholic alike, were killed or murdered. One has only to remember the terrible massacre of Protestants, known as the Massacre de Saint Barthélemy of August 1572. Catholics and Protestants came to Paris to celebrate the marriage of a Catholic princess and a Protestant prince, for this union was an attempt on the part of the Queen Mother to bring about peace between the two factions. Unfortunately things got out of hand. There was an attempt to assassinate Coligny, an important Protestant figure, who had just been included as a member of the royal council. The Protestant noblemen were furious. The young king, Charles IX (1560) tried to assure Coligny that the guilty parties would be punished. But the Protestant noblemen did not believe in the validity of his promise and threatened to take justice into their own hands. Catherine panicked. And the massacre began. Coligny was murdered, as were thousands of other Protestant noblemen. The Parisian populace joined the soldiers in the massacre. Thousands of Protestants were killed without distinction of sex or age.

Wiser heads soon began to prevail and many attempts were made to pacify the Protestants. Edict after edict was passed, allowing Protestants to worship in certain restricted places and have a few 'places of security'. Finally, the assassination of the last of the three direct heirs to the throne, Henry III (1574–89), by a fanatic Dominican monk when the king recognized Henry de Navarre, a Protestant, as his legitimate heir, brought about a change. While not a direct descendant of the French monarchy, Henry de Navarre was now next in line. Catholics objected and the Pope declared him ineligible. But Henry IV (1589–1610) was wise and in 1593 he made a solemn profession to Catholicism. Disapproving Protestants attributed to him the famous statement 'Paris is worth a mass'. Whether he did or did not make this statement, a rather precarious peace came to the land. The Edict of Nantes of 13 April 1598 gave the Protestants freedom of conscience throughout the country; freedom of worship in certain specified areas; the right to have provincial and national synods; the end of discrimination in the distribution of offices and honours; equitable justice was assured; and some 'places of security' or strongholds with forts were granted, such as La Rochelle, Montauban, Cognac and others. It is somewhat ironic that while Protestants were now given certain rights, the Edict of Nantes made of them almost a foreign entity within the nation.

Fortunately for all, Henry IV turned out to be a benevolent and wise monarch whose domestic policy was to bring the two sides together and to repair the economic damage that had occurred in France during the civil wars. While much of the hatred between Catholics and Protestants lay dormant, his assassination in 1610 helped to bring the two sides closer together. The Revocation of the Edict of Nantes in 1685 under Louis XIV rekindled the struggle between certain members of the nobility and the monarchy and persecution of Protestants began again.

Thus it is in the context of these civil wars that one must place the beginnings of the town of Saumur and what eventually came to be known as the *Ecole de Cavalerie*. For

Saumur became one of the strongholds granted Protestants with the Edict of Nantes and could boast a Protestant University with an Academy which included equitation. While academic subjects were taught, equitation was included in the curriculum, for the well-rounded young aristocrat, Protestant or Catholic, was to receive an education in sports (which included horsemanship), as well as in academic subjects. Thus the Renaissance man and *honnête homme*,[3] that is, the well-rounded individual, was to be adept at handling a sword, a compass, a pen, even a dagger, and a horse. The Greek ideal, namely, a sound mind in a sound body, was adopted. Books on the education of children began to appear during this period by such men as François Rabelais, Montaigne, Fénélon, Fontenelle.[4]

The town of Saumur was, like so many towns, initially composed of a castle and houses, surrounded by an impenetrable high wall. When the population increased, houses were built outside of the wall, an area called the faux bourg (faubourg). It was in a section of this 'false burg', the faubourg Saint-Nicholas, along the Loire river, that the Academy of Equitation was installed during the reign of Henry IV. At one end of the Academy was a vast terrain on which were located the stables of the Crown. Equestrian activity occurred in the vast spaces known later as the *Carrière du Chardonnet*. At the other end was situated the church of Saint-Nicholas. Instruction in the art of equitation was given by *monsieur* de Saint-Vual who followed the precepts of Antoine de Pluvinel, *écuyer* to the future Louis XIII. Until the ascension of Louis XIII (1610–43) to the throne, Protestants (who were in the majority) and Catholics lived side by side in relative harmony in Saumur. When Louis XIII became king, Catholicism began to gain the upper hand both numerically and politically. The program of the Academy began to decline, Saint-Vual was dismissed, and a Catholic was put in charge. Which came first, the decline or the Catholic replacement, is difficult to say. However, this change brought about the ire of the Protestants. Eventually *monsieur* de Saint-Vual was re-instated. Unfortunately, not much could be done to save the situation and the decline of the Academy continued. With the Revocation of the Edict of Nantes in 1685 under Louis XIV (1643–1715), many Protestants left Saumur. Matters now appeared even bleaker for the Academy and for the art of equitation.

In 1763, after the disastrous Seven Years War (1756–63), a protégé of Madame de Pompadour, the *duc* de Choiseul, began to reorganize France's military might when he became Minister of Foreign Affairs, as well as Minister of the Army and Navy. Thus, thanks to Choiseul, Saumur was given a second life when he reorganized the cavalry. It was the elite corps, the *Carabiniers de Monsieur* (as the king's brother was called), with its blue uniforms and black horses, that gave Saumur this revitalization. Saumur should also give thanks to the bishop of Angers, the town to which the *Carabiniers* were originally destined. When the bishop heard that Angers was to receive the *Carabiniers*, fearing for the virtue of the young girls of the town, and familiar with some of the antics of the *Carabiniers* in Paris, he used his good offices to prevent their arrival. And so the town of Saumur received the *Carabiniers de Monsieur*. Possibly the young ladies of Saumur were less susceptible to the seductions of these

---

[3] *Honnête homme* is a term already used in the sixteenth century but usually associated with the seventeenth. It is akin to the expression Renaissance man, or the Italian term *virtù*.

[4] Sixteenth and seventeenth-century writers/thinkers of fiction, essays and dialogues expressing their views on the education of the young in view of making an *honnête homme* out of him or, if a member of royalty, a philosopher king. See Glossary to the English translation of Pluvinel's *Maneige Royal*, published by J. A. Allen.

1 The beautiful Classical building of the former *Ecole de Cavalerie* of Saumur, built in the seventeenth century. It surrounds the *Carrière du Chardonnet*.

handsome and gallant young men in blue. Or perhaps a good part of the townspeople of Saumur, only recently converted to Catholicism, were less concerned about the virtue of the young ladies, believing that strict Calvinism had not yet rubbed off. But be this as it may, it was Choiseul who, west of the town, began the construction of the beautiful Classical buildings that one can still see today. The elegant main building with its two wings, became the pride and joy of the *Saumurois*. Also constructed was the famous *Manège des Ecuyers* and its adjacent stables. It is in these buildings that the officers and écuyers of the *Ecole de Cavalerie* made their mark, attracting nobility and royalty from all over Europe. In fact, the *Manège des Ecuyers* became better known than its parent the *Ecole de Cavalerie*.

But the *Ecole de Cavalerie* was to experience yet another setback. In 1788 France was on the eve of a social, political, and economic revolution. During the Revolution of 1789, many members of the *Manège des Ecuyers* went into exile. Some went into quiet exile to await the end of the storm; others left to participate in the counter-revolution by joining the Army of Princes.

After the Revolution of 1789, which underwent several phases, the cavalry was revitalized under the Directory, the Consulate, and the First Empire of Napoleon I. However, while many of Napoleon's generals were outstanding horsemen, the training of the lower echelons was inferior. During the First Empire, the members of the cavalry were so poorly trained that Napoleon was shocked at

2 The *Manège des Ecuyers*. Also known as the *Manège des Dieux*. Part of the *Ecole de Cavalèrie* of Saumur. (Photograph by Hilda Nelson)

the terrible toll his horses were taking. It must be remembered that Napoleon's lightning movement across Europe needed to replenish men and horses as quickly as possible for his *Grande Armée*. Thus the training of men for his cavalry was minimal, which had considerable consequences for men and horses.

After the return of the monarchy in 1814, the aborted return of Napoleon during the Hundred Days, and the second Restoration of the monarchy in 1815, regular equestrian instruction could commence once more.

While the *Ecole de Cavalerie* of Saumur was more inclined to practise military equitation, encompassing the French cavalry as a whole, and included training in artillery and other aspects of warfare, the primary function of the *Ecole de Versailles*, with its *Manège de Versailles* and its *Grande Ecurie* and *Petite Ecurie*, was to oversee the king's stables and to teach the art of horsemanship to the members of the royal family and its entourage, especially the young pages.

When in 1680 Louis XIV moved his whole household and the royal stables to Versailles, it was primarily out of fear of rebellions and an attempt to gather the court and courtiers (especially scheming noblewomen) away from Paris in order to isolate and supervise them. His passion for riding and hunting in the forests around Versailles is, certainly, no mean additional explanation.

The move to Versailles can be explained by the king's experiences of the two *Frondes* when he was still a young boy. The first *Fronde* occurred in 1848/9 and was a rebellion of the Parlement of Paris, soon joined by the people of Paris; some members of the nobility also participated. The second *Fronde* occurred in 1651/2 and is known as the *Fronde* of the Princes, but which also included members of *Parlement*. Both *Frondes* were directed against the Regent, Anne of Austria, mother of the future Louis XIV and her choice of Mazarin, also a foreigner, and under whose spell she had fallen, to head her Regency Council. The purpose of the *Frondes* was an attempt to remove Mazarin from power and limit arbitrary royal power. In this the *Parlement* and the princes failed. All that the *Frondes* accomplished was to turn public opinion more in favour of the king, reveal the weakness of the Princes, and increase monarchical power. Indeed, absolute monarchical power became even stronger during the reign of the next king, Louis XIV.

The *Manège de Versailles* with its stress on *manège* and *haute école* equitation was in keeping with the court life of the seventeenth century and its stress on strict etiquette. This equitation was elitist, elegant, and became part of the education of the nobility. It required considerable training and was spectator oriented. But the *Ecole de Versailles*, perhaps more than the *Ecole de Cavalerie* of Saumur, contributed to the development and fame of French Classical (academic or *savante*, equitation. However, since hunting and military training were also part of court life, it is obvious that training in exterior equitation was also practised.

Instruction at Versailles was very methodical. The most important part of this teaching was to acquire a good seat, which, in turn, served as a point of departure to a good posture. The young pages and other young noblemen who attended, received instruction for three years. They were not allowed to use stirrups or spurs until the third year.

The ideal position of the rider was to sit relatively deep in the saddle, legs hanging down in gentle abandon. The thighs, which inclined to descend, made it necessary to use the stirrup leathers long. The tip of the toe barely sat in the stirrup irons and was often lower than the heel. It was the position that men such as the *comte* d'Abzac, *monsieur* Rousselet, and the *écuyer* P.-A. Aubert had.

The teaching personnel of the *Manège de Versailles* was permanent, as was the head of the *Manège*. This helped considerably, for much time could be devoted to achieving and imparting a degree of perfection to the pupils. At the *Ecole de Cavalerie* at Saumur the personnel of the *manège* was of short duration, for the members were primarily military men and usually sent elsewhere to perform other tours of duty after having served in Saumur. A further important difference between the *Manège de Versailles* and the *Manège des Ecuyers* of Saumur, was that at Versailles, the horse was not only to be well preserved and kept in good shape, but each *écuyer* was to keep his horse for as long a time as possible. It was believed that if the horseman were really instilled with what is known as 'equestrian tact', one could then easily detect the progress the horse made, which was to be constant, limitless, and which took considerable time. This belief is, of course, related to the idea of perfection and its quest. That is why d'Abzac refused to allow the *comte* d'Aure to abandon his horse, Le Cerf. He, himself, kept his school [*manège*] horse for many years.

A number of the *écuyers* trained in Classical or manège riding by members of the *Ecole de Versailles* soon began to feel that there were certain shortcomings with this type of equitation, especially when it involved the training of men pursuing a military career. Some of these *écuyers* began to urge a more simplified and natural kind of equitation which would satisfy the uses to which the horse was to be employed in the cavalry. Although almost all of these men had been trained in *manège* or *haute école* equitation, they urged that this type of equitation, especially training in the high airs, be abandoned. They wanted the horse to have a more horizontal equilibrium, and that the gaits be more natural and extended. This is, of course, what the later advocates of

3 The duc d'Enghien participating in tournaments such as the *courses de testes et de bagues* in the seventeenth century. (Courtesy of the *Musée National du Château de Versailles*)

4 'In tandem' at Versailles. (Courtesy of François Lemaire de Ruffieu, horse trainer, graduated from the *Cadre Noir*, author and artist)

exterior or outdoor riding also urged. Both types of equitation, military and exterior, wanted to see the rider sit more naturally in the saddle, use shorter stirrups and gentler bits. Men such as the *comte* Lubersac de Livron, who as page had received instruction from François de Salvert, then went on to become *écuyer* of the *Grande Ecurie* at Versailles, and was considered one of the early practitioners of military equitation. Jacques-Amable D'Auvergne, a pupil of Lubersac, usually considered the founder of military equitation, followed in the footsteps of his master and further modified the position of the rider, giving him a more natural position. It should be added that, in a sense, equitation also lost some of its elegance. However, while D'Auvergne's reforms made equitation less Classical or academic, thus stripping it of the high and low airs of *manège* equitation and aimed at simplification and making it more daring, he insisted that it was absolutely essential that a horseman know how to school a horse.

There are other names one should also mention in connection with military equitation, names such as Drumont de Melfort, author of *Essai sur la Cavalerie légère* and *Traité de la Cavalerie*, Montfaucon de Rogles, also a pupil of Salvert, the latter having belonged to the Royal Stables. Montfauçon de Rogles' *Traité d'Equitation* eventually became the manual used at the *Manège de Versailles*. All these *écuyers*, urging reforms and whose careers crossed equestrian boundaries, are men of the eighteenth century, directly or indirectly connected with Versailles.

As noted, books on various types of cavalry equitation were being written and published. One has only to think of Gaspard de Saunier (1663–1748), born, raised, and trained in

Versailles by Duplessis, and a contemporary of La Guérinière. Saunier advocated the active life, preferring exterior and military equitation, obstacle jumping, racing, and hunting, to *manège* and *haute école* riding. He was the complete horseman, whose writings include books on hippology and dressage for all kinds of horses and disciplines. Best known is his book *L'Art de la Cavalerie* published posthumously in 1756. It should not be forgotten that La Guérinière (1688–1751), a pupil of Antoine de Vendeuil, also of Versailles, wrote *L'Ecole de cavalerie* in 1733 and *Eléments de cavalerie* in 1740, which also takes into account military and exterior riding.

In the early nineteenth century one encounters Pierre-Marie *comte* d'Abzac, steeped in *manège* and court riding, who, albeit reluctantly, did not totally ignore military or exterior riding. It has been said that he advocated a good gallop for the benefit of the horse after working him in the *manège*. D'Abzac was considered by many *écuyers* as one of France's outstanding horsemen. In his *Souvenirs*, L'Hotte, quoting from the *Mémoires* of the *comte* de Noë, says that d'Abzac 'only got off his horse to enter his tomb'.[5]

D'Abzac could count among his pupils Louis XVI (1774–93), Louis XVIII (1814–24), and Charles X (1824–30), all excellent horsemen who practised hunting with enthusiasm. During their exile, Louis XVIII and Charles X had lived in England and had become proponents of exterior riding and enthusiasts of the thoroughbred. D'Abzac can also count d'Aure as his pupil. Similarly to Gaspard de Saunier, d'Aure received Classical training and, like his mentor, became *écuyer ordinaire* and *écuyer cavalcadour*. Also like Saunier, he had a penchant for exterior riding, racing, obstacle jumping and was a *casse-cou* (dare-devil).

Unfortunately, the *Ecole de Versailles* experienced the same problems as did the *Ecole de Cavalerie* of Saumur during the Revolution of 1789. Here, too, almost all of the *écuyers* went into exile. (The *comte* d'Abzac went to Hamburg where he continued to practise and teach horsemanship.) Likewise, equestrian training did not flourish during the many regimes that occurred after the Revolution. With the Restoration of 1815, which re-introduced the *ancien régime* and placed Louis XVIII on the throne, equestrian instruction took on, once again, a more serious involvement at both Schools. There was, however, a dilemma in deciding which kind of equitation to undertake: *manège* riding, military riding, or the new riding that was being introduced from across the Channel. The *Ecole de Versailles* had barely had time to come to a decision, when it was forced to close its doors with the outbreak of the Revolution of 1830, when the *ancien régime* was finally abolished. A new line of the monarchy was introduced, known as the July or Bourgeois Monarchy of Louis-Philippe.

D'Aure and L'Hotte explain the reasons why the doors of the *Manège de Versailles* had to close. D'Aure in the Introduction to his *Traité d'Equitation* says that Versailles simply did not go along with the changing times. When the *Ecole de Versailles* was re-established with the Restoration, instead of attempting a return to the pre-revolutionary era, that is, the *ancien régime*, the *écuyers* in charge should have tried to go along with the new era and introduce more vigorously certain reforms. Thus Versailles, explains d'Aure, despite its prestige, was unable to acquire new pupils, especially in its attempt to attract many of the officers in the garrisons in and around Versailles. The main reason, says d'Aure, was its refusal to do away with archaic teaching methods, such as the use of

---

[5] Général L'Hotte, *Un Officier de cavalerie – Souvenirs*, Paris: Plon-Nourrit, 1906, 284. (Will be referred to as *Souvenirs*.)

an enclosed and rigid saddle which was to be used by the novice in the initial training stage, and which the potential new pupil considered 'a humiliation'; and the three-cornered hat, the old-fashioned boot, and the long stirrup leathers, which, many felt, 'were ridiculous'. Furthermore, it was inconceivable that 'these old men, who still used powder in their hair, could teach anything'.[6]

In his *Souvenirs* L'Hotte refers to these explanations given by d'Aure, but disagrees with some of them. It is true, says L'Hotte, that the *Ecole de Versailles* 'refused to initiate the rider with the means of developing speed and how to use the horse in the fullness of his actions'.[7] Therefore, Versailles had to close its doors, because contrary to what d'Aure said, the doors of the *Ecole de Versailles* had not been opened widely enough to one and all. Many officers in garrison at Versailles had asked to be admitted to the *Manège* for instruction, but without success. Only the spectator gallery of the *Manège* was accessible to them.

While the doors of the *Ecole de Versailles* remained closed,[8] the *Ecole de Cavalerie* at Saumur continued to operate. During one brief interlude it even functioned in Versailles. It achieved new heights during the nineteenth century with an unequalled number of famous *écuyers*. The experiences of World War I and World War II were felt by the *Ecole de Cavalerie* in Saumur as they were felt throughout France. In 1946 the *Ecole* became the *Ecole d'Application de l'Arme Blindée et de la Cavalerie*. When the *Ecole Nationale d'Equitation* was established in 1972, the *Cadre Noir* continued as its teaching arm; the *Ecole Nationale d'Equitation* served as its administrative arm. Much to the chagrin of the *Saumurois*, the *Ecole Nationale d'Equitation* moved, together with the members of the *Cadre Noir*, horses, and pupils to Terrefort some five kilometres from Saumur. The stables at Saumur have been converted to the housing of tanks.[9]

We have noted that while the *Ecole de Cavalerie* of Saumur, the *Ecole de Versailles*, and the *Ecole Militaire* of Paris stressed different kinds of equitation, more in keeping with their goals, they nonetheless had much in common in that they often shared the same teachers who frequently moved from one school to the other. For example, François de Salvert, one of the early representatives of Classical riding was Lubersac's teacher who, among others, advocated military equitation. And while La Guérinière did not belong to the *Ecole de Versailles*, his connection with it is twofold: firstly, as pointed out earlier, through his patron the Prince de Lorraine; more importantly, through his teacher, Antoine de Vendeuil, who served as the king's *écuyer ordinaire* of the *Grande Ecurie* in Versailles. Later, men such as Cordier and Rousselet, also from Versailles, became instructors at the *Ecole de Cavalerie* of Saumur.

Thus the *Ecole de Cavalerie* and the *Ecole de Versailles* can be considered as embodying what is known as French Classical riding, that is, both schools contributed certain doctrines and principles to the French School of riding. One can say that, although their emphasis differed, both schools were preoccupied with 'la légèreté' (lightness). 'La légèreté' being a

---

[6] *Comte d'Aure, Traité d'équitation et Histoire illustrée de l'équitation*, Paris: Jean-Michel Place, 1987, LXI.
[7] *Souvenirs*, 286.
[8] Michel Henriquet, *écuyer* and writer, Daniel Roche, Professor of History at the Université Sorbonne-Paris I, Catherine Durand, *écuyère* and championne of France for dressage, musical kur, and many others have formed an *Association pour l'Académie d'art équestre de Versailles* in order to revive the *Grande écurie* at Versailles and its past glory and 'bring back the horse'. For further details, see my interview with Henriquet in *Dressage and C.T.* no. 96, September 1994.
[9] Colonel de Beauregard, former *écuyer en chef* of the *Ecole Nationale d'Equitation*, is currently involved in reviving and revitalizing the famous *Manège des écuyers* and some of the former stables surrounding the *Carrière du Chardonnet*. Every summer he presents exhibits and other activities pertaining to equitation in the area.

5 An example of *la légèreté*, in front of the *Château de Saumur*.
(Courtesy of François Lemaire de Ruffieu, horse trainer, graduated from the *Cadre Noir*, author and artist)

concept describing a horse who obeys a rider's imperceptible aids, who is on his haunches, and has an 'équilibre rassemblé' (collected), who moves with ease, fluidity, and harmony, that is, who is capable of moving and executing movements seemingly on his own. He is, so to speak, on parole. Nonetheless, this quest for lightness has been an ongoing one for all horsemen, past and present.

In an extensive pamphlet entitled *La Doctrine de l'Ecole Française d'Equitation* requested by the *Conseil Supérieur de l'Equitation* and approved by the director of sports, général Pierre Durand (former *écuyer en chef* and director of the *Ecole Nationale d'Equitation*) says that *la manière française* (the French manner) owes its equestrian past primarily to three names: François Robichon de La Guérinière, François Baucher, and Alexis-François L'Hotte.[10]

From La Guérinière, explains Durand, the French have learned *la descente de main* (surrender or yielding of the hand), and *l'épaule en dedans* (the shoulder in), that is, that after having been suppled laterally and properly balanced and given what is known as an *équilibre rassemblé*, the horse can be put *sur parole* (on his honour) by means of yielding of the hand, that is, he can be allowed to function on his own.

Indeed, with La Guérinière, we have an equitation that begins to contain theory. La Guérinière believed that this was absolutely necessary if one wished to come as close to perfection as possible. In addition to the shoulder in and haunches in to supple the horse, La Guérinière introduced a more natural and simplified approach in the training procedures of the horse, which allowed one better to preserve the true nature of the horse. He also wanted to make these training procedures clearer to the rider, one of the reasons why he put his concepts down on paper. He wished to explain the nature of certain movements, how one accomplished them, stressing their advantages and how to avoid certain problems. He also introduced changes which involved the use of saddles and bits. Thus La Guérinière tried to get away from strict *manège* and court equitation and combine it with military or exterior equitation.

From Baucher, says Durand, we have the notion of *main sans jambes, jambes sans main* (hand without legs, legs without hand), set down in his *deuxième manière* which appeared in the twelfth edition of Baucher's *Méthode d'Equitation* after the master's death. Baucher's famous and best pupil and disciple, *général* Faverot de Kerbrech, edited and published these later precepts in *Dressage Méthodique du Cheval de selle*. If the idea of using one's aids separately was not totally new with Baucher, at least it was formulated by him and Faverot de Kerbrech in a succinct and detailed manner. This separate use of aids was to be used primarily by novices. The more experienced rider on a more experienced horse could use what Baucher had originally formulated in his *nouvelle méthode*, the idea of *effets d'ensemble* (coordinated effects), which entailed the simultaneous use of leg and hand aids. In other words, the more experienced a rider was and the more confidence the horse had in the rider, the closer could the aids come together. Thus Baucher did not refute his earlier principle of *effets d'ensemble*; he merely left it to the experienced rider.

To Baucher's formulation of the use of aids, one should add his discussion of work in hand whose goal was to supple the horse's jaw and neck.

From L'Hotte, continues Durand, we have the attempt to combine the horse's flexibility and impulsion. Important is also L'Hotte's emphasis that all horses, regardless of the discipline to which they will be employed, must be schooled (*dressé*) along similar formulations. According to a former *écuyer en chef* of the *Ecole de Cavalerie* of Saumur,

---

[10] Général Pierre Durand, *La Doctrine de l'école française d'équitation*, Paris: Crépin-Leblond, 1984.

6 Pluvinel encouraging Louis XIII. (Courtesy of François Lemaire de Ruffieu, horse trainer, graduated from the Cadre Noir, author and artist)

Colonel George Margot,[11] L'Hotte's *Questions équestres* is considered today at the *Ecole Nationale d'Equitation* the *livre de chevet* (the bible) of the pupils and *écuyers* of the *Cadre Noir*. Or, as *général* Decarpentry says in *Academic Equitation*, *Questions équestres* gave 'a corpus of doctrine to that modern French school which owes almost everything to him'.[12]

More importantly, L'Hotte, as a pupil of Baucher and d'Aure, synthesized the two different types of equitation, *manège* or Classical equitation with military or exterior equitation. If L'Hotte was more inclined to follow in the footsteps of d'Aure, this is because L'Hotte, steeped in a military career, and in his capacity as a teacher of cavalry officers and men from the ranks, and the schooling of their horses, could not do otherwise.

---

[11] Letter to me.   [12] Général Decarpentry, *Academic Equitation*, London: J. A. Allen, 1987, 5.

2
L'Hotte – his life and times

Alexis-François L'Hotte, known also as *le sublime muet* (the sublime silent one), was born in Lunéville on 25 March 1825. At sixty-five he retired as a general, returned to Lunéville, and continued to ride his three horses, Domfront, Glorieux, and Insensé. He began to write his *Souvenirs* when he was seventy. Historians and biographers are fortunate to have at their disposal the *Souvenirs* of *général* L'Hotte, for they reveal a great deal of information about French military life, especially, the French cavalry, equitation, Classical and military, and famous *écuyers*.

One may perhaps get the impression, as some have done, that a certain amount of immodesty runs throughout his book as he refers to events in his life, his accomplishments and successes as a young cadet at Saint-Cyr, as a military officer, as *écuyer en chef* at the *Ecole de Cavalerie* in Saumur and at other schools. For example, in the second part of *Les Maîtres Ecuyers du Manège de Saumur*, Jacques Perrier, comparing the works of both Decarpentry and L'Hotte, discusses the modesty of Decarpentry as opposed to the 'the oracle of Lunéville who did not precisely show much modesty'.[1] Yet, one can also explain this 'immodesty' by the fact that L'Hotte, at seventy, was trying to recall his life with honesty (and honest he is, as we shall see) and that if he mentions positive achievements, such as his excellent ranking in examinations, his promotions, or zealousness as a worker who preferred to spend the time working rather than enjoying himself, it is an attempt faithfully to record his life with its successes and failures. Furthermore, the fact that he abruptly ended his *Souvenirs* around 1860, gives one the impression that he did not write his *Souvenirs* with publication in mind – more, perhaps, for his own peace of mind.[2]

There is, however, a certain modesty in the very title of L'Hotte's *Souvenirs d'un officier de cavalerie*, which gives the impression that he wished to avoid the fact that he was a general or a horseman of note. Equally modest is the title of his second book *Questions équestres*, for these equestrian questions are really problems which had, at one time, confronted him and which he tried to resolve. Once these questions or problems were set down on paper, he began to answer them. And once posed, they served as an analysis in his quest for lightness and thus can serve others in their own quest.

Referring to *Questions équestres*, colonel

---

[1] Général Decarpentry and Jacques Perrier, *Les Maîtres écuyers du Manège de Saumur*, illustrated by Lt Colonel G. Margot, directed by General (er) Pierre Durand, Paris: Charles-Lavauzelle, 1992, 103. The first part of this work was written by *général* Decarpentry, the second by Jacques Perrier.

[2] The Appendix was written anonymously, presumably by a member of the family who had access to L'Hotte's notes and journal.

Jean de Saint-André, former *écuyer en chef* of the Cadre Noir says in his book *Le Cadre Noir*:

Questions Equestres is a masterpiece of clarity and style wherein the author's thought neglects the means in order to bring out the value of his principles, underscores the doctrine, and thus arrives at a philosophy of equitation. The art 'to channel the muscular strength of the horse' through the progressive conquest of 'lightness' is the result of the application of the two basic principles of French equitation, namely, 'calm, forward, straight' and that 'submission must be the consequence of the flexibility of all joints and muscles (ressorts).' It is the veritable bible of the present-day *écuyer* who will find in it an answer to all equestrian questions.[3]

The two books, *Souvenirs* and *Questions équestres* complement each other. *Souvenirs* deals with his life as a cadet-pupil at Saint-Cyr, a military man in the cavalry, and an *écuyer* and teacher of horsemanship. But he also devotes considerable time to his two teachers, François Baucher and *comte* d'Aure. Moreover, he gives a portrait of an *écuyer* for whom he had a great deal of respect, namely *monsieur* Rousselet, who will also be included.

One can also say that Lunéville becomes another important character in his book. Lunéville, like Saumur, was known as *la ville du cheval* (the city of the horse) and L'Hotte transmits this atmosphere to the reader in his *Souvenirs*. As one reads L'Hotte's description of the town and its activities, one senses that he had experienced in Lunéville what Lawrence Durrell refers to in his collection of essays *The Spirit of Place*. According to Durrell, 'spirit of place' is a pact or union, a harmony, between an individual and a place. It is something sacred and modern man has, unfortunately, lost this sense of place, this 'spirit of place'.[4]

L'Hotte's *pays natal*, a town so imbued with horses and varied and successive cavalries, was bound to have a considerable impact on his psyche and his choice of career. His family background also had a considerable impact on the young Alexis.

Lunéville became the seat of the *duc* de Lorraine, Leopold, when, in 1698, he installed himself, his household, and some beautiful horses in the city. Not long thereafter, a military academy and a cavalry school were established. Leopold attracted some of the most prestigious *écuyers* to this establishment, Avril de Pignerolle and the baron d'Eisenberg.[5]

After the death of Leopold, Lunéville fell temporarily into a dormant stage. However, around 1738, the ex-king of Poland, Stanislas Leszczinski, father-in-law of Louis XVth, was given the Duchy of Lorraine by the king with the understanding that it would, after Stanislas's death, revert to the king of France.

During this period, Lunéville became again a 'town of the horse', for Stanislas was also an avid horseman and brought with him horses from Poland which he then bred with the horses of Lorraine. Thus, regardless of the changes that took place in Lunéville, horses and cavalry remained a permanent adornment. The court of Stanislas soon acquired a brilliance and, as Voltaire put it when he visited it, became almost the equal of the court of Versailles. Young Lorraine and Polish *Cadets-Gentilshommes* graced the revived equestrian academy.

After the death of Stanislas in 1766, the

---

[3] Colonel de Saint-André, *Le Cadre Noir*, Paris: Julliard, 1981, 46. (The book also contains chapters by *général* de Breuil, *général* Saint-Priest, Col. Lt. (now *général*) Durand.)

[4] Lawrence Durrell, *Spirit of Place*, London, Faber and Faber, 1975, 322–64.

[5] *Baron* Reis d'Eisenberg lived in the middle of the eighteenth century. He was famous as a horseman throughout Europe. He was also known for his *Description du manège moderne*. He was attached to many famous courts of Europe. See *The Classical Riding Master*, The Wilton House Collection, Commentary by Dorian Williams, London: Eyre Methuen.

7 Duc Leopold, the first to make Lunéville the *ville du cheval*.

King of France sent his most prestigious companies to Lunéville, the *Gendarmes Rouges*.

And we can understand and appreciate it when L'Hotte tells us in his *Souvenirs* that 'if an area in which one is born and raised can decide one's vocation, it is clear that I was destined to follow a military career and serve in the cavalry'.[6]

L'Hotte devotes a considerable number of pages to the origin and duties of these companies. Two outstanding *écuyers* taught the *Cadets-Gentilshommes*, Mottin de la Balme and Loubet de Bohan, both pupils of the famous Jacques d'Auvergne of the *Ecole Militaire de Paris*. But the *Gendarmes Rouges* were soon to be replaced by the *Carabiniers de Monsieur* (whose uniforms were blue) until they were sent to Saumur.

It is the background of this city and that of his family that one must consider in order to understand L'Hotte. His family, both on his father's and his mother's side, were not only military men, but also cavalry men. His grandfather was a member of the *Gendarmes-Rouges* and his father belonged to the *Carabiniers*. His nephews, to whom *Souvenirs* is dedicated (L'Hotte never married), had also

---

[6] *Souvenirs*, 16.

opted for the military profession. It is not surprising that as a son and grandson of cavalry officers he readily succumbed to their influence, as well as to the 'spirit of place' of Lunéville.

Horses were always part of family life. Already at an early age, he was 'unable to hear a horse go by without running to the window and following it with my eyes.'[7] First in his life was Sophie and her colt, who, even when the latter reached the age of fourteen was still referred to as *le poulain*.

While the men in his family held important positions and 'were the doers', he seems to have been closer to the women, his mother and grandmother, who always gave him tenderness and moral probity. It was his mother who gave him his first riding lessons on his father's horse, Cocotte.

As a small child, too young to ride, L'Hotte tells us that he always waited in the same place for his father and Cocotte to return from a ride and be raised by his father on to her back. Since Cocotte had a gentle disposition, L'Hotte was soon allowed to ride her on his own.

He received his first serious riding lessons from *commandant* Dupuis who had grown up in Portugal and had received his equestrian training from trainers and teachers of the stables of the king of Portugal. For a while, Dupuis had also been part of the *Manège de Versailles*. In the eyes of the young L'Hotte, Dupuis was and remained a romantic all his life. Dupuis told L'Hotte that as a young soldier in Napoleon's *Grande Armée*, he had been billeted with his regiment in a small village in Portugal. In the bedroom assigned to him, he had seen on the dresser a small gold cross attached to a black velvet ribbon. He had assumed that it belonged to a young girl whose bedroom he was occupying. Before leaving the house with his regiment, he stole the cross, wanting a memento from the girl who, in his mind, he pictured as beautiful and with whom he had fallen in love. As his regiment marched off, he began to feel guilty about the theft. He returned alone to the village, to some extent risking his life, and put the crucifix back on the dresser. Later, back in France, due to his extreme sensitivity, he was for ever fighting duels. During one duel he killed a man, which forced him to abandon his military career. His romanesque nature got him into further difficulties when he continued to wear the *Croix de Saint-Louis* which the new July Monarchy had forbidden.

L'Hotte greatly admired this romanesque and lonely man whose influence upon him was lasting. 'My impressions of him never left me and on several occasions during my life I recalled the memory of this valiant and generous soul.'[8] In many ways, his relationship with Dupuis is repeated in his relationship with another solitary and unhappy master, François Baucher. Thus we see the young L'Hotte already expressing a great love for horses; and his sensitivity and empathy for unhappy and solitary human beings, can, to a certain extent, also make one consider him a romantic. Complementing this romantic bent, we also see in L'Hotte the realist, the successful and ambitious military man. At an early age he had already developed the habit of writing down the essential ideas and precepts imparted to him after each riding lesson. From that time, he tells us 'I began to immerse myself into an art to which I have given such a large part of my life, both in practice and in meditations set down on paper.'[9]

But Cocotte grew old and had difficulty getting up after lying down. The family took special care of her and her dietary needs and tried to make the last period of her life as easy as possible. L'Hotte began to ride and take lessons from Dupuis on other horses from his father's stables, Caïd and Daguet. But these horses were not Cocotte. Then, one day, to

---

[7] Ibid., 27.   [8] Ibid., 32.   [9] Ibid., 32.

his great joy, his grandmother had one of her farmers bring him a little horse whom he named Cosaque. Indeed, says L'Hotte, this little horse 'had the characteristics of our little Lorraine horses, who are so sober, so resistant, and who remind one of those horses of former days, their ancestors, brought over from Poland and the Ukraine by king Stanislas to improve the breed of our horses.'[10]

Like all good and pious Catholics and members of the upper classes, L'Hotte attended what is known as a *collège*, the *Collège de Lunéville*, later the *Collège de Nancy*.[11] At first L'Hotte was not a good pupil at school, preferring to read books on horses and equitation rather than reading his school books. Avidly he read Claude Bourgelat[12] and Antoine de Pluvinel,[13] books taken from his father's library. At school, bored drawing human eyes and noses, which he did with difficulty, he asked his drawing teacher to let him draw a horse. Aware of L'Hotte's poor attempts at drawing, the teacher was both surprised and bemused, but gave in, tired of hearing his pupil's request and believing that by giving in he would satisfy a child's caprice. He was asked to draw the skeleton of a horse. Not only was L'Hotte able to do so without any difficulty, he was also able to name all the bones of the horse. It must have finally occurred to his teacher that this was not a child's mere 'caprice'.

It was at the *Collège de Nancy* that L'Hotte began to make an effort academically, devoting himself to the care and feeding of the mind as well as of the body. 'You can understand how much I had to work during that year. I had so much to learn, so much to make up for wasted time.'[14] A year later, at seventeen, he entered Saint-Cyr, having passed his admission examination thirty-fifth out of more than three hundred candidates. Unfortunately, the curriculum at Saint-Cyr at the time no longer included courses in equitation. To acquire the necessary riding skills in military equitation one had to go to the *Ecole de Cavalerie* of Saumur.

But L'Hotte was proud of wearing the uniform of a Saint-Cyrien. Despite the discipline that existed at Saint-Cyr, L'Hotte worked hard and well and received *les galons de caporal* (a corporal's stripes) within the year. He also excelled in the *salle d'armes* (armory) and the gymnasium. He enjoyed the workouts and found that going three times a week with his own semi-battalion was not sufficient and decided to attend a second round when it was the turn of the other semi-battalion. In this connection he mentions an incident that occurred years later when he was a general attending the funeral of another general. There he met one of his former comrades of Saint-Cyr, *général* Ritter, who had been a rival of his in gymnastics. L'Hotte greeted him, then asked him if he remembered him. 'I can't remember your *name* at the moment', said the general, 'but I remember that you were very good at gymnastics.'[15] L'Hotte was somewhat surprised to think that the only thing the general could remember of him was that he was good at gymnastics.

While he does not speak of homesickness, L'Hotte was happy, after a year at Saint-Cyr, to be allowed to go home to see his family. But this pleasure was soon cut short. The night before they were to go home, considerable disorder had occurred in the dormitory. Since L'Hotte had received his *galons de caporal* he was held responsible for these

---

[10] Ibid., 32.
[11] A *collège* is similar to a *lycée* but run by the clergy.
[12] Bourgelat (1712–1779), a French veterinarian, one of the early founders of veterinary schools in France.
[13] Antoine de Pluvinel author of *Le Maneige Royal*, published in 1623; an expanded version entitled *L'Instruction du roy, en l'exercice de monter à cheval*, was published in 1625. An English translation was published by J. A. Allen in 1989.
[14] *Souvenirs*, 34.
[15] Ibid., 38.

disorders. Instead of going on leave with the others, he had to watch them from his disciplinary cell as they joyfully left for home, for he had been placed in solitary confinement. Food consisted of bread and soup twice a day. It was brought in a bucket and then served on a plate which sat on the floor in front of the cell. And what soup! says L'Hotte. The plate was dirty and numerous hungry cats licked it in the hope of finding something. He could hear them licking the plate by the noise the spoon made as their tongues moved it around. L'Hotte ate only the bread he received. Fortunately for him, the authorities must have felt sorry for him and he was released from his cell not long after the departure of his comrades.

While L'Hotte was successful in his endeavours at Saint-Cyr and proud of being there, he does, however, complain about the rations the pupils received which he considers inadequate considering the large appetites the pupils had. He also makes a comparison between the pupils during his sojourn at the military school between 1842 and 1844 with those he met later when he returned to Saint-Cyr as Squadron Commander. He noticed that the main difference was the kind of spirit that had animated his generation. While less polite and more rowdy, his group expressed greater patriotism and fanaticism about being a professional soldier. They accepted hardships more readily and on military marches increased the load in their haversacks to harden themselves and be better able to resist fatigue. L'Hotte believes that the new generation, while perhaps more 'savvy' and more orderly, did not evince the same degree of military ardour. Furthermore, life had become a little less severe for the new generation of cadets.

L'Hotte, born in 1825, was a witness (albeit a very young witness) to the last years of the *ancien régime* under Charles X which was toppled when he signed the Ordinances in 1830, which took away certain freedoms that had been finally granted to the French people. The monarchy under Charles X had been an arch conservative monarchy and during this period many of the officers who had served during the First Empire under Napoleon, experienced a certain amount of discrimination, even hardship. Matters improved somewhat when the July or Bourgeois Monarchy of Louis-Philippe took over in 1830 and which lasted until 1848.

When L'Hotte came to Saumur to join the *Ecole de Cavalerie* in 1844 he came under the command of officers who had served in the *grande armée* of Napoleon and decorated by him. Unfortunately, most of these men in charge when L'Hotte arrived, while exemplary military men, did not demonstrate much equestrian talent. L'Hotte relates a rather amusing incident that occurred in 1846 when Colonel Selve visited the establishment. Colonel Selve had retired from the French military after Napoleon's attempt to return to power and his disastrous Hundred Days. Selve had taken the name of Soliman Pacha and had become a major-general in the Egyptian army under Mohamed Aly. In Selve's or Soliman Pacha's honour, exercises were performed in the *Manège des Ecuyers*. Colonel Selve, accompanied by Colonel Deshayes, second in command, placed himself next to some pillars rather than be seated in the gallery with the other spectators. Colonel Deshayes had no choice but to follow him. While Selve stood to watch, Deshayes, portly and suffering from gout, sat down on a chair. At the end of the performance, the riders formed a line at the far end of the *manège*, positioning themselves to strike off at an extended canter. The idea was that they were to halt a few feet before reaching the pillars. Unfortunately, someone had left the door to the *manège* open and some of the horses went beyond the line marking the pillars and out of the *manège*. Selve, quick-witted, was able to hide behind one of the pillars and thus protect himself from the onslaught of horses and riders. But

Colonel Deshayes, heavy and awkward, in an attempt to get up, broke the chair in which he was sitting, and found himself lying on the ground in all his length. The noise of the chair breaking gave the spectators the impression that they were hearing Deshayes's bones breaking. Madame Deshayes, seated in the gallery, fainted. Many spectators ran to Deshayes to help him. Deshayes, with great difficulty, managed to get to his feet. No bones were broken, only his ego was hurt.

At this time the *écuyer en chef* and squadron commander was Delherm de Novital. L'Hotte gives a somewhat unflattering portrait of the man who, he says, corresponded to the typical military *écuyer* of the period, possessing an extremely elated notion of military duty and discipline. He was brusque, opinionated, often losing his temper. He completely ignored the civilian *écuyers* who, at that time, formed part of the team. Instead, he exerted his authority over the military *écuyers*. He treated horses with the same harshness. He was considered a fairly good horseman, especially with respect to leg aids, and showed sound judgement in the training of horses. But his horses, like his pupils, showed little or no joy at what they were doing. There was something automatic about how they executed their movements.

L'Hotte gives an outline of the type of equestrian preparation the pupils were receiving at the time when he arrived at Saumur. L'Hotte is quite critical of the kind of training the pupils and horses were getting. The training received was mostly *manège* equitation. The horses were not put to the 'fullness of their capabilities', that is, impulsion and gait extension were not forcefully practised. In fact, the training of young horses was at a minimum. Much of exterior riding was done in the Chardonnet rectangle with Novital demanding a very military exactitude, inconsistent with exterior riding. Work outside the Chardonnet rectangle was limited to riding along roads. Rarely were there any cross-country exercises. The steeple chase was not practised.

According to L'Hotte, Novital preferred to teach the lower echelons, that is, the NCOs. This becomes understandable when one takes into account Novital's frequent outbursts of anger when making observations about someone's riding mistakes. The NCOs were young and more inclined to accept these outbursts. They were, after all, to some extent dependent upon Novital for their future careers. The older officers, who had already begun their military careers, responded with anger. L'Hotte admits that during the two years he spent at Saumur as officer-pupil, he learned more about riding by simply observing others and riding on his own, than hearing his teachers speak and comment. He is quite obviously saying here that almost all of the teachers at the time talked too much and said very little. L'Hotte's main advice to the novice is: acquire a good seat, ride with confidence, daring and energy, and maintain a proper posture. Learning principles and rules come later, after one has become a sound horseman. Like d'Aure, L'Hotte advises that one ride frequently and as many different horses as possible.

After spending a long overdue three-month furlough in Lunéville, L'Hotte joined the 7th Lancers in Valenciennes in January 1847. He had barely set foot in Valenciennes when a Squadron of the 7th Lancers was sent to Bourbon-Vendée to join other detachments sent to quell disorders. A rise in grain prices had provoked these disorders. This was a prelude to the February Revolution of 1848, followed by the June Revolution of the same year which ushered in the Second Republic.

The weather in Bourbon-Vendée was terrible for horse and rider, but listening to the *cliquetis* of his sword hitting his spurs was enough to make him forget the weather. One innovation that L'Hotte experienced on this journey was the transportation of a cavalry detachment by train, travelling from

Valenciennes to Paris and Paris to Tours. From Tours onwards the detachment travelled on horseback. L'Hotte was astonished to discover that when they travelled through some of the villages in the Vendée, the inhabitants shut themselves in their houses and they could hear children crying out: 'Here are the *gendarmes*.'[16] They mistook the cavalry for the militia.

It was during this journey that L'Hotte began seriously to consider the use of the *trot enlevé*, also known as the *trot à l'anglaise*, that is, the rising trot, in the cavalry. Along the route, L'Hotte had noticed a beautiful grey horse who used a racking gait whenever the detachment trotted. Since he had been given permission by his captain to ride the horses of his squadron, he decided to ride the grey horse. He tried the regular sitting trot with him. To his surprise he discovered that the horse had an exceptional trot. When he returned the horse to the stables, he demonstrated to the lancer who had been riding him, this newly discovered exemplary trot. Instead of showing surprise, the lancer replied that he knew that the horse could do a sitting trot, but that he disliked this trot in that it was hard on horse and rider. When L'Hotte asked him how he stopped the horse from trotting, the lancer replied that he did so by using a bell and jerking it whenever the horse went into the trot. L'Hotte was considerably chastened by this declaration. He was struck by the lancer's dislike for trotting and felt that it must also be the experience of other cavalrymen, especially if their horses had a particularly irregular trot. L'Hotte decided that 'from then on, I considered using the rising trot for the ranks'.[17] Indeed, this is precisely what happened when he became part of the *Guides d'état-major*.

After the disorders in the Vendée had been quelled, L'Hotte's detachment returned to Valenciennes. This time they travelled on horseback the whole way to Valenciennes, taking the same route, halting at the same places where they had halted on their way to Bourbon-Vendée. At one of the stops, in the little town of Herbiers, the detachment was assigned to its quarters and L'Hotte was told that he and his horse would be billeted with the same household he had been billeted before. This pleased him, because he and his horse had been very well treated. The only problem was that he could not remember the location of the house. He decided that he would let his horse find the house, hoping that the horse's memory was better than his own. He rode the horse to the main street, then, dropping the reins on the horse's neck, he hoped for the best. Without the slightest hesitation, the horse led the way to the place where he and L'Hotte had been so royally treated six months earlier.[18]

Back in Valenciennes, L'Hotte was given the duty of teaching equitation to junior officers and schooling a number of horses. One horse was a little mare called La Folle (the Madwoman), who actually lived up to her name. Another mare L'Hotte rode at the time was Diane, his commander's horse. While overseeing the grooming of the horses, he learned a great deal about the conformation of horses, their similarities and their differences.

On 11 April 1848 L'Hotte was promoted to 1st Lieutenant. Promotion depended not only upon an individual's earned merit, but also upon there being a vacancy for a particular rank at the time. As there was no vacancy at Valenciennes, he was not promoted. For that he was glad, as the man also up for promotion was an old-timer named Dumont who, had there been a vacancy, would have been passed over because of L'Hotte's arrival and greater merits. But Dumont was a decent chap and did not hold this possibility against L'Hotte. Rather, he helped L'Hotte considerably by showing him the ropes in his new assignment.

---

[16] Ibid., 74. [17] Ibid., 76. [18] Ibid., 76.

The promotion occurred as soon as L'Hotte was sent to Longwy.

With his new place of duty and promotion, L'Hotte was assigned to the newly formed *Guides d'état-major*, a cavalry detachment serving as the *Armée des Alpes* whose function was to quell hostilities that were occurring between Austria and the Piedmont.[19] Another function of the *Guides* was to serve as escort to the high ranking officers and to bring them the necessary orders from headquarters. (A sort of Saint-Bernard perhaps without the cognac.) The *Guides* was the brain-child of *général* Oudinot when he was put in charge of five squadrons, two stationed at Saumur and three at Lunéville. Each of these five Squadrons was administered separately and in no way linked to each other. A Captain, two Lieutenants, and two Second Lieutenants, commanded a squadron. L'Hotte points out that there were thirty-five good horses at their disposal. Furthermore, to L'Hotte's surprise, the men in the ranks could read and write. Quite an achievement, since this was 1848 and universal education had not yet been firmly established in France. *Général* Oudinot, the creator of these squadrons, had asked *capitaine* Buraud, an instructor at Saumur, to take command of one of the squadrons and choose an officer. Since Buraud had been L'Hotte's instructor at Saumur and familiar with L'Hotte's work, he chose him. L'Hotte accepted. Since the Squadron to which L'Hotte was assigned was in Saumur, L'Hotte spent some time there. This was precisely the period when the *comte* d'Aure became *écuyer en chef* at the *Manège des écuyers*. When l'Hotte saw d'Aure on horseback, he says in his *Souvenirs*: 'I devoured him with my eyes.'[20] When the *Guides* left Saumur for Grenoble, L'Hotte left with them. It is at Grenoble that L'Hotte introduced the rising trot to his men, having received permission from his Captain and from *général* Oudinot to do so.

One day, when *général* Oudinot and his *aide de camp* were having lunch with L'Hotte, they heard men on horseback trotting past the window. What was lacking was the terrible clatter of the sabers hitting the spurs. Oudinot asked his aide to determine to which detachment the cavalrymen belonged. 'They belong to the *Guides*', the aide replied. 'Ah', said the general, 'then they are L'Hotte's *Guides*'.[21] The explanation was simple. The rising trot decreased considerably the clatter of the men's arms. Unfortunately, it was still forbidden in the military riding courses at Saumur. While the English saddle was allowed, the course stipulated that only the French principles of equitation were to be considered.

Many high ranking officers were familiar with L'Hotte's attempt to introduce the rising trot. On an earlier occasion, this time at Saint-Cyr, *maréchal* Randon, then Minister of War, called L'Hotte to his office to discuss the rising trot. 'How can you, a horseman, prefer to see a cuirassier trot *à l'anglaise* as you call it, rather than see him remain deep in the saddle as he trots?'[22] As the Minister of War uttered these words, he mimicked grotesquely the rising trot but then imitated correctly the sitting trot. Not in the least perturbed, L'Hotte replied that the *maréchal* was being unfair when he performed the two trots, performing one well, the other one poorly. 'Sir, when you make a comparison between the two kinds of trots, you should perform both equally well, and allow me to indicate the advantages to both rider and horse with the *trot enlevé*.' Without more ado, the *maréchal* quickly dismissed L'Hotte. This kind of criticism was repeated frequently by officers who were against the rising trot. But L'Hotte was never discouraged and patiently

---

[19] Austria at the time controlled a great part of what is now known as Italy. Italy eventually succeeded in establishing its independence.

[20] *Souvenirs*, 85.
[21] Ibid., 87.
[22] Ibid., 88.

kept on mentioning its advantages.

Once again, when L'Hotte was at Saumur and *général* Feray of the *Comité de Cavalerie* visited Saumur, L'Hotte asked the general for permission to demonstrate the rising trot. Reluctantly, the general gave his consent. L'Hotte had a group of farriers, who had never done the rising trot, practise it first for about fifteen minutes. When L'Hotte felt that they had acquired a modicum of familiarity with it, he asked the men to alternate between the sitting trot and the rising trot. Inevitably, when they did the sitting trot, the terrible clatter of swords could be heard. Furthermore, during the sitting trot, the horses slowed down. Whereas, during the rising trot, not only did the clatter of swords decrease considerably; more importantly, the gaits of the horses extended. The general, who had joined the men on horseback, had difficulty keeping up with them when they did the rising trot, since he continued to do the sitting trot all the time. After repeating the two types of trots several times, the general cried out: 'Enough, you have convinced me. But the members of the *Comité* will pluck my eyes out when I plead your cause before them.'[23]

Two interesting events occurred thereafter. An English officer wrote L'Hotte asking him if it were true that the French cavalry was doing the rising trot. L'Hotte, always polite, but not quite sure how to answer this query, asked *général* Feray for help. 'My opinion is still the same, so answer accordingly.'[24] L'Hotte interpreted this statement to mean that yes, the French cavalry was doing the rising trot. Unfortunately, *général* Feray died shortly thereafter and the Franco-Prussian war broke out in 1870 and the *trot à l'anglaise* was put on the shelf for a while.

However, when d'Aure became *écuyer en chef* in Saumur in 1849, where the *trot à l'anglaise* was still forbidden, he, himself, practised it, well familiar with the advantages it had for horse and rider. But both L'Hotte and before him d'Aure knew 'how tenacious routine was'.[25] The higher ranking officers preferred the old ways. L'Hotte spends several pages in his *Souvenirs* discussing the advantages of the *trot à l'anglaise*.

Due to the disorders of June 1848, known also as the first proletarian revolution and which occurred primarily in Paris, L'Hotte's squadron was sent to Lyon where disorders had also occurred. Thus it was in Lyon in 1849 that L'Hotte first encountered François Baucher, 'ce grand maître',[26] as he called him. Once again the habit of taking notes served him well. 'Daily, my discussions with the master were reproduced and the precepts which he gave me orally, were transcribed and commented upon... These notes are so precious and of a rare richness, for Baucher had an unlimited knowledge with respect to equitation. Thus it was that I delved deeply into the treasure of equestrian knowledge which the great artist so generously gave me.'[27] It is his close contact with his two masters and his habit of taking copious notes, begun early in life, that will serve as the chapters in which he deals with Baucher and d'Aure. They will be discussed as separate chapters.

L'Hotte was an exceedingly honest man. He was also a good diplomat, two traits which are not usually compatible. But somehow he managed to combine the two. In 1850 we find L'Hotte once again in Saumur as Lieutenant-Instructor. When he moved from his first to his second year, his ranking should have been No. 1. He was, however, known to be a pupil of François Baucher and this made a poor impression with *général* de Goyon, the current commandant of the *Ecole de Cavalerie*. This was also the period when d'Aure served as *écuyer en chef*.

Requested to appear before the *Conseil d'Instruction*, L'Hotte was told by *général* de Goyon never to admit that he was a disciple

---

[23] Ibid., 90. [24] Ibid., 91. [25] Ibid., 91. [26] Ibid., 95. [27] Ibid., 95, 96.

of Baucher and, more importantly, never to practise Baucher's *nouvelle méthode* at Saumur. It became obvious to L'Hotte that his ranking would depend upon his answer.

L'Hotte was in a precarious position. For not only was his ranking at stake; also in jeopardy was his advancement. He had reached an impasse with his present unit, the *Guides d'état-major*, and was now hoping that his new assignment in Saumur would open up a route for promotion.

Nevertheless, he refused to renounce his master and advance in his career by these means. 'I cannot renounce my first master, nor can I eliminate from my mind what he has taught me. When I first came to Saumur I was quite aware of what I could learn. If, meanwhile, I returned to the *Ecole de Cavalerie*, it was, above all, to be taught in the school of *monsieur* d'Aure.'[28] For a brief moment there was silence and L'Hotte was asked to leave the room. After his departure, d'Aure, who was also present, said: 'I will see to it that L'Hotte adopts my principles.'[29] And *général* de Goyon said: 'Here is a real man.' L'Hotte was ranked No. 1 *ex aequo* together with one of his comrades. *Général* de Goyon made a special notation: 'Outstanding officer, honourable of character, fulfils all the requirements to be promoted to captain at the *Ecole de Cavalerie*.'[30] *Général* de Goyon went even further. He offered him the position of *Capitaine-Ecuyer*. But as a career military man, L'Hotte preferred to be with the troops. In 1851 he became Captain-Instructor with the First Cuirassiers. He was twenty-six years of age.

One should, however, mention that as a result of meeting with *général* de Goyon and d'Aure, there is mention of a letter by d'Aure to *général* Carrières dated 1 September 1851 which states: 'L'Hotte is an officer with whom I am acquainted and whom I esteem and like. It is impossible to give him a better recommendation. But he is a young man who likes action and does not want to be attached to the school. If he is, he will most likely hand in his resignation.'[31]

His assignment as Captain-Instructor with the First Cuirassiers was one of the most active ones of his life. He rode up to twelve horses a day, supervised their schooling (dressage), supervised the introduction of recruits, gave courses in equitation, supervised and participated in *reprises*. He also found time to practise fencing and in 1857 received the degree of master of arms.

It was during these six years with the First Cuirassiers that he began the schooling of Zégris, a grey horse of Breton breed. His duties took him to various places with divers assignments. Again he was offered a position as instructor, this time at the *Ecole Militaire* in Paris. Again he refused. Finally, due to pressure exerted by *général* de Monet, he accepted command of the cavalry section of Saint-Cyr, which had been re-established once again.

His duties were primarily spent as cavalry instructor at the various cavalry corps which had formed and continued to form many generations of officers. He also introduced a number of innovations such as the steeplechase and, in the surrounding woods, he had installed bridle-paths in the form of serpentines, narrow enough for a single horse and rider which would allow for the secure seat and posture of the rider. Carrousels were also organized.

(It should be noted that after 1850 L'Hotte stopped writing his *Souvenirs*. Much of what follows has been entered as an Appendix and written by another hand, presumably a family member.)

The carrousel held in 1860 turned out to be remarkable. Napoleon III was now emperor of the Second Empire, which he had established by means of a *coup d'état* in 1851 and which had toppled the Second Republic. Napoleon III, himself a horseman, who had spent many

---

[28] Ibid., 356. [29] Ibid., 356. [30] Ibid., 357. [31] Ibid., 357.

8 L'Hotte presenting the *Cadre Noir* during a *reprise* in the *Manège des Ecuyers*.
(Courtesy of the Musée de Saumur)

years in exile in England, made one of his infrequent visits to Saint-Cyr. Infrequent because the first time he had set foot in this establishment, the pupils of Saint-Cyr had not given him a very warm welcome. One of the things that had astonished and disturbed the young cadets, was the theatrical uniform the Emperor had worn.

The occasion of Napoleon's second visit to Saint-Cyr was due to the reputation L'Hotte had gained and was continuing to gain. Actually many excellent horsemen visited Saint-Cyr at the time to observe and admire L'Hotte working with his horse Zégris. For example, on 3 May 1860 one could have seen Maxime Gaussen, Jules Pellier and son, Charles, Pellier's son-in-law and other horsemen and *écuyers* of note. On 15 July 1860, *général* Fleury, *comte* d'Aure, and *général* de Monet attended. It was *général* Fleury who had asked *général* de Monet to use his influence with Napoleon and urge him to make a visit. This he did. Napoleon came to Saint-Cyr in the company of *général* Fleury. The two observed many exercises performed by the pupils. Napoleon then asked to see L'Hotte work with Zégris. The emperor was enchanted with everything he saw, especially observing L'Hotte on Zégris. L'Hotte was soon thereafter awarded the *Croix de Chevalier de la Légion d'honneur*.

In 1866 L'Hotte returned to Saumur for the third time. This time as *écuyer en chef*. Once again it becomes clear that he would have preferred to have been assigned to a regiment in Africa. But a military man may request but he cannot choose.

In the same year when L'Hotte returned to Saumur, the *Ecole de Cavalerie* participated in a competition sponsored by the *Société hippique française*. The purpose of this participation was to present French breeds of horses

9 In 1860 L'Hotte was commandant of the cavalry section at Saint-Cyr. L'Hotte is on his personal horse Zégris in the centre of this gravure.

and demonstrate what these horses could accomplish. Present at the competition were the Emperor, his son, the crown prince of Denmark, as were other personages. The programme included a *reprise de manège* with horses using French saddles and bridles. There was also a *reprise de carrière* with the use of English saddlery. And a *reprise de sauteurs en liberté* which used its special saddlery.

After the final performance, *Lt Colonel* L'Hotte rode his thoroughbred Sicambre. Usually, L'Hotte rode this horse when he was off duty and only with close friends present when he executed gaits and airs belonging to *haute école*. But, upon the request of the Emperor, 'he conformed to the wishes of his sovereign'.[12]

Needless to say, the Emperor was ecstatic and asked to greet L'Hotte personally. This time L'Hotte was awarded the *Croix d'Officier de la Légion d'Honneur*. The spectators, the public, and the newspapers were also ecstatic. He was referred to as 'the first *écuyer* in the world' and his work on Sicambre was considered 'a master-piece of equitation'.[13]

This is what was said of L'Hotte's performance on Sicambre:

During the final performance, while the *sauteurs* were regaining their breath, *lieutenant colonel* L'Hotte rode his thoroughbred Sicambre, schooled in *savante* equitation and who belonged to him personally. The artificial gaits and movements had their place in this horse's workout and he was only ridden by the *écuyer en chef* in private and before a few amateurs. But *général* Fleury had made it known to him earlier that the Emperor wanted to see his personal work on Sicambre. Thus the *écuyer* had to conform to the wishes of

---

[12] Ibid., 366. [13] Ibid., 365.

10 L'Hotte riding his horse Sicambre in 1866 at the *Palais de l'Industrie* where he leads the *Ecuyers du manège*.

the sovereign.[14] (This statement first appeared in *baron de Vaux' Les Ecoles de cavalerie*)

What seemed to interest the Emperor most, as well as his entourage and those present, were the *haute école* exercises executed before the Imperial gallery by *Lt Col*. L'Hotte, using an English saddle, mounted on a rather ordinary horse. But he got from this horse all those movements that our most skilled *écuyers* perform in our circuses, the Baucher, the Franconi, get from perfectly schooled horses... (*Le Moniteur de l'armée*, 21 April 1866).[15]

The honours of the day went to *Lt Col*. L'Hotte, commandant of the *Manège*, who practises *haute école* as no one can practise it in France today. He is the best representative of the real principles of the French *manège* and judging by the exercises he performed, he also reminded one of Rousselet, Saint-Ange, Baucher, and d'Aure, as well as old Laurent Franconi. He personified, on horseback, human majesty. (*Le Spectateur militaire*, 15 March 1866).[16]

On 1 July 1890, twenty-four years later, in a letter to L'Hotte, *général* Faverot de Kerbrech had this to say:

I have said, and will continue to say that, after having had the opportunity in 1869 to seek out and observe the most renowned *écuyers* of Europe, I have concluded that I have never met any who can equal you. In Vienna, Saint-Petersburg, Berlin, Hanover, I have seen the most famous horsemen work... and have returned with a feeling of serenity and satisfaction with our own equitation as represented by you, who have

---

[14] Ibid., 365–6.   [15] Ibid., 366.   [16] Ibid., 366–67.

succeeded in uniting integrity and discretion in the use of aids as used by the former French School, with the wonderful results that you give in the application of Baucher's procedures. I regard you, *Général*, as the foremost and uncontested *écuyer* of today.[37]

As an offshoot of the 1866 performance, the Emperor, looking for a suitable parade horse, remembered the event of 1866. During that event L'Hotte had also ridden Laruns at the head of the *reprise des écuyers* and the Emperor had been equally impressed by the harmonious performance of horse and rider. *Général* Fleury was ordered to bring Laruns to the Emperor's stables.

When the horse was brought to the Imperial stables, the Emperor refused to believe that this was the same horse L'Hotte had ridden that day at the *Palais d'Industrie*. Laruns was a small horse and when not mounted had nothing remarkable about him. He appeared elegant only when mounted, especially when mounted by L'Hotte. The Emperor returned the horse. He obviously felt that Laruns did not have the proper presence for an emperor; worse still, that he could not give it the presence that L'Hotte had given him.

In this connection, neither L'Hotte's other horses, Zégris and Sicambre, were particularly well-adapted to perform *haute école*. Yet both were able to perform the artificial airs as well as the natural airs with great flair. They did work on one or two tracks in the *manège*, made lead changes at four, three, and two tempi, and at each stride.

What struck everyone observing L'Hotte on these horses, was the total imperceptibility of his aids. One had the impression that the horses were executing all the movements on their own. In point of fact, they were 'on parole'. And yet no initiative was allowed them. Not only did these horses do work in the *manège*, they were also used for hacking and for military purposes as *chevaux d'armes*.

During the Franco-Prussian War of 1870 and the ensuing civil war between the *Versaillais* (so-called because the government forces had moved to Versailles temporarily) and the Commune of Paris in 1871, L'Hotte was assigned to Tours and then to Paris to command a regiment. Not only did he have to absent himself from Saumur, but also from his horses. Upon his return, the well-known *écuyer* and friend, Maxime Gaussen, asked him to ride Sicambre. In a park at Rambouillet, on uneven terrain, after months of inactivity, Sicambre was able to execute all the movements he had been taught without missing a single one.

After the cessation of hostilities, the year 1873 found L'Hotte on a number of missions in Austria, sent by the Minister of War, *général* du Barail, to observe and analyse the innovations the Austrians were introducing to their cavalry and compare them with the French cavalry which was also undergoing some provisional changes in their regulations. According to L'Hotte, this Austrian cavalry, 'placed under the supreme direction of the famous Edelsheim, was considered, and rightly so, to be guided by regulations that are of the most simple and, from a technical point of view, the best'.[38]

L'Hotte remained in Austria for six months. After his return to France, he began to apply certain aspects he had observed in the Austrian cavalry, first to his regiment in Versailles, then to a few other regiments. Soon a *Comité* was formed but the members of this *Comité* dragged their feet. L'Hotte then presented a programme whose purpose was to demonstrate the results he had meanwhile achieved. Several officers, including the *duc* de Nemours, came to observe the so-called 'Austrian regiment'. They watched movements which used the old method, then, for comparison, the new method. They also watched obstacle jumping. The reaction was favourable among the officers. Even opinion

---

[37] *Ibid.*, 367. [38] *Ibid.*, 373.

11 L'Hotte on his horse Laruns. (*Courtesy of the Musée de Saumur*)

outside the army opted for the new regulations. This positive reaction made the members of the *Comité* finally move. The *Comité* approved the new regulations, but with the proviso that they be introduced only to the upper echelons.

Finally in July 1876 the Minister of War decreed the immediate application of the new regulations and corresponding exercises. He, too, was impressed with the simplicity and clarity of these regulations and the ease with which they could be applied in case of war.

L'Hotte, who had further reforms in mind, decided to hold off introducing them, believing that the time was not yet ripe and that some of them were perhaps too revolutionary for the moment.

It is somewhat ironic that the man who signed the regulations into action, *général* du Barail, gave the impression that he was the one who had fathered the document containing the regulations and spoke only of an unnamed 'collaborator'. This 'collaborator' was, of course, L'Hotte. However, one must point out that in the two letters *général* du Barail wrote to L'Hotte in 1877, he praises L'Hotte for the great work he had accomplished with respect to the French cavalry. 'You have rendered a great service to the cavalry, and no one can contest this.'[19] On 23 January 1904, *général* Jacquemire wrote in *France militaire* that *général* L'Hotte had been the chief mover in the application of the regulations of 1876. He stressed the fact that L'Hotte had insisted that the new regulations be supple, elastic and involve no absolute

---

[19] Ibid., 378.

rules. He added that the main objective of the newly formed instruction was not an end in itself but the means to achieving the procedures. In other words, while prescribing certain goals for the cavalry and ways of achieving these goals, L'Hotte had insisted on working within a large and mobile framework rather than a rigid one. Indeed, the ultimate goal of the training of cavalrymen must, according to L'Hotte, be directed towards mobility and war. And initiative on the part of the individual must be part of this goal.

L'Hotte was sent back to Austria several times after his initial visit. Again he was received with great cordiality, respect, and admiration by the Austrians, including the arch-duke, the Emperor Franz-Josef, who bestowed upon him several orders.

L'Hotte's honesty came to the fore once more in Austria. On his first visit, he had met the *comte* de Chambord, one of the pretenders to the throne of France. The *comte* de Chambord inquired from L'Hotte about common acquaintances and friends in Saumur. Suddenly, Chambord changed the conversation and asked whether the army would follow the white flag of the monarchy should the king return.

'Sire', replied L'Hotte, 'the army only knows the tricolour. Certainly not now when so many officers have shed their blood for the flag which suffered the sadness of defeat [the Franco-Prussian War] would they abandon it. Furthermore . . . if the nation abandoned the tricolour a good part of the nation would hoist the red flag, the flag of insurrection, and that flag is held in abhorrence by all good people.'

'So', insisted the count, 'you do not believe that the army would favour the white flag?'

'Sir', answered L'Hotte, 'I cannot speak in the name of all French officers, but since you are repeating your question, I cannot but give you the same answer.'

A coolness was felt in the room and the count made it quite clear that the interview was over. But before leaving, the count said: 'As an individual I am nothing. I am something only through the principle I represent. Through the symbol of the white flag. I will never abandon it.'[40]

Later, some members of the entourage were curious and wanted to know what the two had talked about. L'Hotte repeated the conversation. They were shocked that L'Hotte had dared talk in this manner to the *comte* de Chambord. One of the members who had listened to L'Hotte's account of the conversation, said: 'If the king has to return to France bearing the tricolour, he might as well be wearing the red bonnet.'[41]

In October 1875 L'Hotte returned once more to Saumur, this time as commandant of the *Ecole de Cavalerie*. He had first seen the town as pupil-officer, then as lieutenant-instructor, again as *écuyer en chef*. However, four years later, in 1879, he was suddenly and unexpectedly relieved of his command due to what became known as the 'Don Carlos Affair'. In October 1879 Don Carlos, Duke of Madrid, and his host, the *marquis* de Maillé, came to visit Saumur. While L'Hotte, as commandant, felt obliged to greet the guests and show them around, he did not provide them with an ostentatious reception. They visited two of the stables, which were mostly empty. A few horses were allowed to run at liberty in one of the *manèges*. That was all.

However, rumours had it, and the press picked it up, that L'Hotte had received Don Carlos and the *marquis* as though they were royalty. A horse blanket lying about became a sumptuous carpet; an ordinary chair, upon which Don Carlos had seated himself, became an armchair, even a throne. The accusations became so vociferous that the Minister of War could not defend L'Hotte. All that L'Hotte had done was show a modi-

---

[40] Ibid., 384–5.
[41] Ibid., 385. The red bonnet, worn by the most radical members of the Revolution of 1789, symbolized liberty, in opposition to the wigs and ornate headgear of the nobility.

cum of courtesy to his guests as commandant of the school. On 12 February 1880, L'Hotte was relieved of his command. Three months later he was assigned to various posts in Verdun, Commercy, then Tours, and promoted to the rank of Division General.

It was primarily when L'Hotte was commandant of the *Ecole de Cavalerie* that he officially proscribed execution of the artificial airs and gaits, even during the *reprise des écuyers* (which he, himself, had executed on a number of occasions, especially when requested by persons in high positions). This became especially a problem since François Dutilh was *écuyer en chef* at the time and had done a great deal of work in raising the horse's neck during the passage which usually terminated each *reprise*. Thus L'Hotte's strict adherence to army regulations prohibiting any methods leading to or executing *haute école* had a detrimental effect on these *reprises* and on Dutilh, who, as *écuyer en chef*, headed the *reprises des écuyers*.

In connection with the method of raising the horse's neck, Baucher discussed this only in terms of how to bring the horse's neck into the vertical position, and then, only in connection with collection. He said nothing about applying it to the extended gaits. In his last teachings, Baucher said that with respect to the canter, the gait should be extended progressively but that the horse's head must not deviate from its earlier position, that is, its position at the slower gaits. D'Aure, as a proponent of cross-country equitation, stressed the importance of the extension of the neck at the extended gaits. This, he said, is a characteristic of the horse in his natural state when he extends his gaits. Unfortunately, he never quite explained how one achieves this. It was *colonel* Guérin, when he became *écuyer en chef* between d'Aure and L'Hotte,[42] who took Baucher's method into account and applied them to his own horses, achieving thereby the more difficult airs of *haute école*. However, it was Dutilh who continued the work of Guérin and presented it in greater detail and with greater precision. He even described a whole set of exercises that would bring about neck extension at the extended gaits. Thus it was the work of Dutilh that L'Hotte was annulling when he prohibited all movements pertaining to *haute école* much to the chagrin of Dutilh.

In May 1881 L'Hotte participated at the Council of Tours where he gave his opinion with respect to certain tactics the German cavalry had used and which he criticized. The chief discussion centred around the question whether the cuirassiers should be transformed into dragoons. L'Hotte spoke eloquently about the glorious position of the cuirassiers and many present praised him. But some members present took issue with him and opted for the transformation.

Then L'Hotte took up the gauntlet and asked those around him: 'If in a war you are charged by a cavalry troop, would you prefer to be charged by cuirassiers or by dragoons?'

'By dragoons', everyone answered.

'And if you are the ones charging, would you prefer to be at the head of a regiment of cuirassiers or dragoons?'

'At the head of dragoons', everyone answered.[43]

L'Hotte had made his point.

At first it was decided to transform the cuirassiers into dragoons. But as *général* de Barail pointed out, 'Common sense finally prevailed and the cuirassiers were retained as cuirassiers.'[44]

Throughout his military career L'Hotte had never asked to be assigned anywhere in particular. But *général* Chanzy, who commanded the 6th Corps, knew that L'Hotte wanted to be assigned to Lunéville. He asked

---

[42] Etienne Guérin, perhaps more than L'Hotte, synthesized the methods of Baucher and d'Aure. It should also be noted that Guérin was the equal of d'Aure in cross-country riding.
[43] *Souvenirs*, 388.
[44] *Ibid.*, 388.

the Minister of War to give him the command at Lunéville. This was denied. This request was brought up once again by *général* Chanzy's successor. Again it was denied. L'Hotte was disappointed, especially considering that he had never asked for any personal favours.

In 1885, the Germans, for the first time, invited French officers to be present during cavalry manoeuvres. This occurred due to the prestige L'Hotte had acquired *as a horseman*. The German press praised the activities of the French section of the mission which demonstrated interest in what the Germans were doing. The old Emperor and the members of the imperial family treated L'Hotte with great cordiality. The Emperor even awarded L'Hotte a decoration. But the French press attacked L'Hotte for accepting this decoration. L'Hotte, always correct, always proud, refused to defend himself from these accusations. But he never wore the eagle.

A year later, in 1886, L'Hotte was appointed to the *Comité de Cavalerie* as its president. What is interesting about this appointment, is that Clemenceau, Minister of War,[45] was behind this appointment. It seemed that Clemenceau did so for political reasons. He wanted to replace *général* de Galliffet whom he disliked. But opposition to L'Hotte's appointment was also expressed. Some accused him of being a monarchist; he is 'the Miribel of the cavalry', they said. Others accused him of being a *Boulangiste*.[46]

Clemenceau was resolved to abide by his decision. 'I have never met *général* L'Hotte but I know that he is neither of the two. He is not interested in politics. Everyone in the cavalry praises him and has great confidence in his abilities. It is he who gave the cavalry its present regulations.'[47] How much truth exists in these exchanges, is difficult to say. What is certain is that *général* Boulanger had attended the Council of Tours and had been greatly impressed with L'Hotte's competence as a cavalryman.

As a member and president of the *Comité de Cavalerie*, L'Hotte was asked to consider a request which was to evaluate a method of the schooling of horses by the well-known *écuyer* James Fillis, of English origin, and who was practising *haute école* equitation in one of the many circuses in Paris. Fillis also happened to be a protégé of Clemenceau. Several meetings were held by the members of the *Comité*, which sometimes included Clemenceau, himself. Mr Fillis was also present at one of the meetings to present the details of his method. Despite Clemenceau's support of Fillis and Fillis's expertise and renown as a horseman and *écuyer*, L'Hotte and the *Comité* rejected the request. While paying homage to Fillis's expertise as an *écuyer*, the members felt that it was not advisable for a civilian to teach equitation to officers and train their horses. L'Hotte, of course, had d'Aure in mind when he voted

---

[45] Georges Clemenceau (1841-1929), was appointed by President Poincaré Minister of War and President of the Council in 1917. He organized and conducted the Treaty of Versailles in 1919. He was also known as the 'The Tiger' for his ferocious arguments.

[46] *Boulangisme* a rightist group of various and sundry malcontents who, between 1887 and 1889, gathered around *général* Boulanger, who was asked by the right to run for various offices, including the presidency. Most of Boulanger's supporters were unemployed workers, thrown out of work due to the economic depression which existed especially in the industrial towns. The supporters also included some Bonapartistes and a few members of the nobility. The party's only programme was the dissolution of the Chamber of Deputies and a revision of the Constitution. A victory in Paris in January 1889 seemed to put power into his hands. However, whereas his followers expected him to use force, he disappointed them by pulling back, giving the government time to recapture its strength. When the government called for his arrest, Boulanger fled to Belgium, and the party collapsed. However, the Boulanger affair brought to the fore a new phenomenon: an authoritarian, superpatriotic, demagogic right.

[47] *Souvenirs*, 391.

12 Drawing (above) by François Ruaud Gerbéviller, and photograph (below) by Claude Henrard Lunéville of L'Hotte's house, 42 rue Gambetta. Note the door on the right without steps to enable L'Hotte's three horses to enter stables and *manège* (Lunéville).

13 L'Hotte's house, situated centre, back. Photo appeared in an article by J.P. Carciofi. Reproduced as a postcard in 1900 by Edition Quantin (Lunéville).

against Fillis's request. He may also have had Baucher's brief experience to teach his *nouvelle méthode* to the officers of Saumur, Lunéville, and Paris. 'It is necessary to have rank in order to command those who have the *épaulette.*' ... 'When subjected to someone not wearing the épaulette, an officer is always ready to rear.'[48]

Before his retirement at the required age of sixty-five, L'Hotte attended the manoeuvres of 1889 where he was the guest of *général* de Galliffet. In front of all the officers present, Galliffet paid homage to L'Hotte's service to the cavalry in the name of the entire cavalry.

A few months later, on 25 March 1890, L'Hotte retired to Lunéville, greatly admired by all, recipient of many orders, including, before his retirement, of the *Grand Officier de la Légion d'Honneur*.

We have few descriptions of L'Hotte. Colonel George Margot has given us a number of aquarelles presenting L'Hotte on horseback. We see him as a man of medium height, thin, elegant, with a mustache. Fortunately, in the appendix to the *Souvenirs*, the biographer gives us a portrait of L'Hotte at the time of his retirement. I will present this portrait in its entirety.

> Despite his sixty-five years, [L'Hotte] was still remarkably vigorous physically. Well-built, slim, elegant in appearance, he looked like a man considerably younger. What almost always struck one as one looked at the energetic soldier's face, were his bright blue eyes which were honest and piercing. And when L'Hotte looked at one, it was impossible for any imposter to uphold his lie.

---

[48] *Ibid.*, 192. D'Aure had been a military man, but had resigned to enter the *Manège de Versailles*.

14 Photo taken in 1893. Reproduced as a postcard in 1900 by Edition Quantin (Lunéville).

In general, his demeanour was cold, even icy. But when one got to know him well, this ice melted and the steely glance softened, taking on a gentle expression under his slightly drooping lids. The smile, which then lit up this severe mask, took on a singular expression, revealing a great kindness which bespoke of joy and a healthy heart.

Général L'Hotte was an exquisite talker. He had a good memory. He was erudite without being pedantic. His habit of being a keen observer, his ability to reflect, his excellent use of language – somewhat old-fashioned at a time when slang was becoming fashionable – gave his conversation a very special charm. His manners were of another age. His politeness reminded one of a grand seigneur of the eighteenth century, and which belonged to the traditions of his family, his upbringing, and memories of his childhood, as did his study of the manèges and écuyers of the past. In short, he was a representative of times gone by.

Despite his cold demeanour and his extreme reserve, he was well-liked in Lunéville. His compatriots were proud to consider him as one of their luminaries, one of the purest. He was greeted by one and all when they saw him passing by in the street, girthed in his jacket which he buttoned in military fashion, his hat slightly to one side and over the ear. He responded with the same politeness whether it was the little bookshop owner or the colonel. His kindness and generosity were without equal. Never did he send away a misfortunate person without offering help; and he did so discreetly and truly, in accordance with the words of the New Testament, that one's left hand ignore what the right hand gave.

When L'Hotte entered the reserves, he had brought with him three horses: Glorieux, Domfront, and Insensé. He rode them every day in a little manège he had built for himself behind the house. At times, he invited friends and

15 *Château de Lunéville.* Photo taken by J.P. Carciofi. The author is grateful to Mr Carciofi and the Office of the Mayor of Lunéville for the use of these illustrations.

officers of the garrison to watch him work. Many a horseman wished for this favour and made pilgrimages to Lunéville from Paris, Saumur, even from foreign countries, to observe the old *écuyer* execute the most brilliant and academic movements on his horses and acquire from them the supreme lightness which had been his constant goal. The spectators were never aware of a single movement of his aids. Those who had the good fortune to observe him at the time, have become the possessors of an unforgettable souvenir.

While preserving his physical vigour, L'Hotte also had preserved his intellectual vitality (greenness). At seventy-five he repeated and applied the words of d'Abzac: 'Despite my sixty years of practice, I still learn something new each day and I never dismount without having made some new observation.'

He spent the afternoons putting order into his innumerable notes on equitation, editing his *Souvenirs*, and reading – he was a tireless reader. His favourite books were *The Imitation of Christ*, the *Essays of Montaigne*, and the *Maxims* of Napoleon. He possessed a considerable library and his military erudition was immense. None was familiar, as he was, with the history of the great Napoleonic Wars. Furthermore, when it was a question of a tactic or a manoeuvre which he defended, he always based his reasoning on examples drawn from these campaigns...

In his retirement, his life was regulated as though he were a soldier or a monk. Dividing his time between his horses and study, he took long walks at fixed hours, usually with his brother, *colonel* L'Hotte, his senior by two years. These two brothers will be remembered for their intimate affection for each other. Everyone respected them.

In October of 1902 *général* L'Hotte experienced the first attacks of the painful illness which was soon to kill him... The death of his brother in

1903 most likely accelerated his own illness and death. He awaited his death stoically . . .[49]

Indeed, L'Hotte no longer felt at home in this everchanging world, and suffered from what he considered the ever-increasing anti-militarism that the nation was experiencing. To close friends he used to say: 'They are demolishing, they are flouting, everything I adored.'[50]

Shortly before his death, L'Hotte was to meet an outstanding horseman belonging to the *Cadre Noir* of Saumur, *capitaine* Jacques de Saint-Phalle. The meeting had been arranged by *général* Faverot de Kerbrech. Faverot de Kerbrech had attempted several times to bring about a meeting between two horsemen he greatly admired, but L'Hotte had constantly refused to do so. His refusal was based on Saint-Phalle's criticism of some aspects of Baucher's *nouvelle méthode*. 'I do not wish to meet this gentleman who denigrates the memory of Baucher so crudely,'[51] he said. But Faverot de Kerbrech did not give up so easily and finally talked L'Hotte into meeting Saint-Phalle. The meeting took place on 7 January 1904.

We know the details of this meeting because Saint-Phalle related the event to his sister, Madeleine (she rode like a *casse-cou*, dressed like a man to shock the people around her), who wrote down diligently what her brother had told her.

The day was cold and it was snowing lightly. Despite the cold, L'Hotte was waiting for Faverot de Kerbrech and Saint-Phalle at the station, looking, himself, very cold. He greeted Faverot de Kerbrech very cordially. When it came to greeting Saint-Phalle, the greeting was very cool. Saint-Phalle was stunned. He had difficulty understanding why L'Hotte behaved this way. Why had he accepted seeing him if the meeting was so unpleasant to him. L'Hotte accompanied them to the hotel and told them that they were to dine with him at his home. Saint-Phalle was still so shaken that he even thought of returning to the station and taking the next train home. But politeness and respect for age made him change his mind. He understood what it must be like for a man of L'Hotte's physical vigour, to be afflicted by bone cancer and have difficulty walking.

That evening, L'Hotte served them a port while he, himself, drank only water. The three men had barely seated themselves at table when L'Hotte attacked Saint-Phalle in the most impolite manner. So vehement was the attack that the maid withheld serving the soup.

'What gives you the authority to criticize Baucher. By what right do you do so? Is it the results you obtained in your experiments? How dare you compare your results with those of [Baucher]?'[52]

It was obvious that these were strictly rhetorical questions and that he expected no answers.

'Your book has some merit, but there is much to be criticized. Tell me, what are your qualifications that give you the right to criticize this prodigious man whom no one will ever equal? Do you hear, nobody. Certainly not you. You, who are not worthy of turning the wheel of his spur.'[53]

By then L'Hotte began to shout so much that he began to feel ill. Saint-Phalle took advantage of the moment's silence to say quietly:

I'm afraid that I have been misunderstood. I did not attack Baucher's personality in my book, but merely some aspects of his method. Besides, Baucher has profoundly changed his method in each of his books and his re-editions. In each instance he repudiated a part of his previous ideas. One is not casting dispersions on his glory to mention this fact. In fact, I, myself, have re-written considerably my book, for I found, when I

---

[49] *Souvenirs*, 394–8.   [50] *Ibid.*, 398.   [51] Perrier, *Les Maîtres écuyers*, 72.   [52] *Ibid.*, 72.   [53] *Ibid.*, 72

re-read it, that I had made a number of mistakes. When you receive the new edition in a few days you will see that I have eliminated a number of useless items and that I have expanded certain topics that I merely touched upon and which now seem to me to be of great importance.[54]

L'Hotte did not once interrupt Saint-Phalle.

He had calmed down considerably. Perhaps the modesty and quiet acceptance of Saint-Phalle had achieved this. It was a different L'Hotte who spoke again. He became the courteous and kind host and even drank the measure of two fingers of wine with the others. Before Faverot de Kerbrech and

---

[54] *Ibid.*, 72–3. I have made a brief comparison between the two editions of Saint-Phalle's work in an attempt to discover what, if any, changes, were made between the 1889 and the 1904 editions of his *Dressage et emploi du cheval de selle*, Paris: Legoupy, Lecaplain et Vidal, 1889 and the 1904 edition bearing the same title, Paris: Legoupy, Floury, Chapelot, Lesoudier.

However, the purpose of this comparison was not to present a detailed analysis of Saint-Phalle's precepts, but merely to compare the two editions and comment briefly whenever there occurred any references to Baucher and whenever changes were made in connection with these references.

The two editions are almost identical, with the exception of some specific references to Baucher which have been either softened or eliminated. Stylistic changes have been made, and the confusion between *descente de main* and *descente de l'encolure* has been rectified in the second edition. There are a number of additions to the 1904 edition.

There is a change in attitude towards Baucher rather than a change in substance when, for instance, in the 1889 edition, he discusses the angle between the horse's withers and the neck. Saint-Phalle believes that the angle between the withers and the neck must not be fixed, for then one would have no useful support in the establishment of the neck's equilibrium and the displacements of the centre of gravity. He then discusses the inconveniences that arise with any lateral play of neck and shoulders 'as stated by Baucher'. 'Indeed, the vice of the Baucher flexion is that it supples the neck in such a way, making it turn to the right or to the left, from the shoulders on. This extreme flexibility weakens the neck, interferes with its direction, and allows the horse to refuse to turn, while still obeying the aids. While the haunches and the neck react to the rider's aids, he loses the means of action.' (49)

In the 1904 edition the substance and text have been retained, but after the name of Baucher, Saint-Phalle has added, 'as the great master taught it in the 13th edition of his works'. (49)

Like L'Hotte, Saint-Phalle was concerned with impulsion and he spends considerable time discussing *la descente de l'encolure* which, in the first edition, he sometimes refers to as *la descente de main*, and impulsion. (While both terms refer to yielding, the former refers to the yielding of the neck, the latter to the yielding of the hand.)

In the first edition, Saint-Phalle says: 'Baucher understood *la descente de main* in a way that brings with it all those dangers which his method entails and which has often been proven wrong.' The dangers are, as Saint-Phalle puts it, when the rider 'lowers his hand on the pommel and abandons the reins and, as a consequence, gives the horse his head without deviating from the position of the *ramener* and without accelerating the gait.' (55–6)

This section has been changed in the second edition. Here Saint-Phalle makes a distinction between *descente de l'encolure*, which can contribute to impulsion and bring about speed acceleration, and the *descente de main* which can impede impulsion and acceleration. He now attributes the *descente de main* to both La Guérinière and Baucher, rather than to Baucher alone, but his criticism is the same. 'This exercise, recommended by La Guérinière and Baucher and much used by them, is executed in the following manner: the horse, now in the position of the *ramener*, and properly engaged, the rider loosens the reins completely and *gives the horse his head without making him change either his position or his gait.*' (56 also 104–5)

What worries Saint-Phalle is that with the *descente de main* the horse can refuse to go forward and that it is precisely the rider who supplies the horse with the best incentive not to do so. Several chapters later, in the second edition, when he discusses lightness and false lightness, he again refers to La Guérinière and Baucher and the *descente de main* and the dangers that ensue with the horse being behind the bit, all to the detriment of impulsion. (Discussion regarding impulsion and lightness occurs very frequently.)

Certainly other topics discussed by Saint-Phalle must have annoyed L'Hotte. For example, Saint-Phalle used spurs sparingly, seeing no great advantage to their use. If they are to be used, he recommends only two quick taps and only if the horse has not heeded the rider's leg aids.

While Saint-Phalle liked the use of the lunge, he does not have much use for work in hand. The only advantage of work in hand, he tells us, is when one is dealing with a nervous horse or when one wishes to correct more energetically certain faults.

16 Commemorative plaque placed by the *Cadre Noir* in 1981, on the facade of L'Hotte's house, 42 rue Gambetta (Lunéville).

Saint-Phalle left their host that evening, L'Hotte offered to accompany then to the station the following morning. But he did not do so. He remained in bed, never leaving it until he died. Whether he read Saint-Phalle's second edition of his work, one will never know.

L'Hotte died on 3 February 1904. After his death his three horses were put down as he had wished it. No one was to ride them and they were spared the uncertainties of old age. They were buried behind the wall of the cemetery of Lunéville, not far from where the one who had loved them was also buried.

3
L'Hotte's teacher: François Baucher

When L'Hotte and Baucher met in 1849, L'Hotte was twenty-four years of age, Baucher was fifty-four. The physical, psychological, and emotional portrait that L'Hotte has given us of 'the most exceptional equestrian genius of all times',[1] is one of the very few we possess. We have numerous drawings, even caricatures, of Baucher, but it is mainly thanks to L'Hotte that we have a detailed and, above all, sympathetic description of Baucher.

The physical description that L'Hotte gives us is of a Baucher of medium height with a somewhat heavy torso and slightly bow-legged. This, says L'Hotte, is an advantage in equitation. But, he quickly adds, one should not give too much credence to this. After all, d'Aure's legs were shaped in the opposite direction and he was an outstanding horseman.

L'Hotte is especially impressed with the way Baucher's eyelids fell slightly over his eyes giving him, as L'Hotte puts it, a sense of perspicacity. And, L'Hotte believes, perspicacity was what Baucher possessed to a considerable degree. After all, explains L'Hotte, he can personally attest to this trait, having frequently witnessed it, especially when it came to Baucher's equestrian knowledge and ability to deal with horses.

Baucher's skull was well-shaped, his nose prominent (which Lorentz has caricaturized), but well-formed. He had a scar on the right side of his jaw caused by a kick from a horse. The expression of his face revealed the thinker, an accurate assumption, since Baucher constantly meditated on his art. When he considered publishing his *nouvelle méthode*, he was so greatly absorbed in what he was writing that he began to suffer from monomania. He was very intelligent and possessed sound judgement. Like L'Hotte, he always carried with him pencil and paper to write down the correct word. He was for ever seeking the word which had no synonym.

Baucher was averse to the amenities of society and often ignored them. It is interesting that L'Hotte, always courteous and polite, seems to consider this a positive trait. He relates how a member of the *Comité de cavalerie* had voted against Baucher teaching his *nouvelle méthode* to members of the French cavalry, because Baucher had had the audacity to sit down before having been asked to do so. In many respects Baucher reminds one of another writer, Jean-Jacques Rousseau, who also disliked society and behaved somewhat boorishly when introduced into the world of letters by his more mundane colleagues, men such as Montesquieu, Voltaire, Diderot, and other *philosophes*.[2] This aversion to the amenities of society on the part of Rousseau and Baucher

---

[1] *Souvenirs*, 231. M. Maxime Gaussen, a well-known *écuyer*, knew both d'Aure and Baucher personally, and had been a pupil of Baucher.

[2] The term *philosophes*, whose French spelling is also used in the English language, refers to writers and thinkers of the eighteenth century and includes men such as Voltaire,

17 François Baucher (1796–1873),
a lithograph by Lasalle made for Baucher's *Oeuvres complètes* in 1854.

can perhaps be explained as a means of self-defence, a way of disguising their feelings of insecurity, for both belonged to the *petite* bourgeoisie and, while aware of their background, resented it. Both were suddenly thrown into the limelight. Rousseau as writer and *philosophe* entered a field that, in the eighteenth century usually belonged to the bourgeoisie, middle and upper, and, to the aristocracy; Baucher entered a field that in the nineteenth century, still belonged to the aristocracy and the *haute* bourgeoisie.

While L'Hotte, as we have seen, appreciates and praises Baucher, he also points out some of his weaknesses, namely that Baucher believed his method to be of such tremendous import that the others were fools not to understand and appreciate its importance. Yet, it was not so much the method that was criticized, but the fact that Baucher saw little good in the works and precepts of his predecessors and was convinced that he alone was now finally filling certain existing lacunae in equitation. It was this following statement, taken from his *Méthode d'Equitation*, that aroused much anger in many *écuyers* and horsemen:

Unfortunately one looks in vain at works on equitation written by past and present writers. I

Montesquieu, Diderot, d'Alembert, Rousseau, Helvetius, and many others. They were not 'professional' philosophers like Descartes, Leibniz, Kant, *et al.*, who were creators of world views; rather they were thinkers who criticized religious bigotry, excesses of the monarchy, often by means of satire.

won't say for sound rational principles, but simply for the presentation of ordinary data pertaining to the strength of the horse. All of them have spoken well of *resistances, oppositions, lightness, equilibrium*; but no one has been able to tell us what causes these resistances, how one can combat and destroy them, and thus obtain this lightness, this balance which they recommend so incessantly to us. It is this serious lacuna which has brought about so much doubt and obscurity with respect to the principles of equitation; it is this lacuna which has brought this art to a standstill; it is this serious lacuna which I have finally succeeded in filling.[3]

When L'Hotte met Baucher in 1849, Baucher's *nouvelle méthode* had undergone an eighth edition and a ninth one was being contemplated. Yet Baucher complained about the way society was treating him. He felt that despite the success of his work, he and his method were still being misunderstood and not given their full value.[4] In 1849, Baucher had already behind him the unpleasant experiences with the Army which had first asked him to teach his *nouvelle méthode* to the various cavalry corps in Paris, Saumur, and Lunéville, but then decided to cancel the agreement. Baucher often attributed this rejection by the Army and fellow horsemen to his low social status and his work in the circus. L'Hotte remembers how he had once said to him: 'What can I do? Establish a *manège*? This can ruin one financially. Above all, one must be able to make ends meet. In the final analysis, I am a *saltimbanque*, a circus entertainer. I live with those who sleep on straw and I make an appearance for ten sous.'[5]

There is, undoubtedly, an element of truth in this complaint by Baucher. Baucher would most likely have been regarded as the great equestrian lion had his origins been different. Unfortunately, the death of the dauphin, the *duc* d'Orléans, his patron, and his replacement by the *duc* de Nemours, a fervent supporter of d'Aure, contributed greatly to a change in Baucher's fortune.

Baucher's daily schedule was filled with work and meditation. He rose early to ride his horses in the *manège* of the circus. He liked to work without being disturbed or even observed. It actually took a while for him to notice and then accept the quiet and unassuming presence of the observing young L'Hotte who often came in the morning to observe Baucher riding. At first Baucher was annoyed by these visits. But when he realized that this observer was animated by the same passion he himself possessed, his reserve melted and little by little the master gave L'Hotte his confidence and intimacy.

Baucher worked until eight in the morning, got off his horse, and drank a cup of cocoa. He then gave a lesson to either a horseman or an *amazone* of the privileged classes. In the afternoon he gave several lessons to groups of pupils. He made a point of not taking on novices, making it very clear that his pupils had to have some experience in equitation. In fact, it was essential that a pupil be a relatively experienced rider for his *nouvelle méthode* to be of any use. His course usually lasted six weeks which, according to the master, sufficed to initiate the pupil to his method.

Twice in the evening he performed in the circus. He devoted his other evenings, seated in his study, to meditating and writing. He worked so intensely at night that his mind continued working when he tried to fall asleep.

While the general public admired and applauded his *tours de force* on his horses in the circus, the former *écuyers* of the Manège de Versailles laughed at his posture, for his torso was short, his thighs rather fleshy, and his head was bent over forward almost touching his chest. His legs and feet were thrust back. It was a horseman, the baron de Cornieu, who

---

[3] François Baucher. *Oeuvres complètes*, Paris: 1854, 104.
[4] It is obvious that he wanted approval of the *Versaillais*.
[5] *Souvenirs*, 99

once said that 'd'Aure rode on his back, Baucher on his stomach.'[6] The caricaturist Lorentz has given us an amusing portrait of Baucher performing on the famous Partisan. Critics reproached him for moving in his seat when he had his horse execute lead changes at the canter. General Decarpentry, whose book *Baucher et son école* is very laudatory, also says that Baucher's 'legs always gripped his horse's flanks (jambes plaquées) and placed so far back that his torso was pushed forward, where the weight of his head already inclined it to go'.[7] According to L'Hotte, Baucher cared very little what the former *écuyers* of Versailles, such as d'Aure and other *Versaillais*, thought of his seat and posture. But he was extremely sensitive as to what his critics said about his *nouvelle méthode*, especially when they said that his method was not that new.

Baucher's main principle in his *nouvelle méthode* lies in the destruction of the instinctive strength of the horse and replaced by a transmitted strength, transmitted by the rider. (At first Baucher used the term 'to destroy', which he then replaced by 'annul', then by 'reduce'.) Baucher's goal was to suppress any initiative on the part of the horse and acquire the complete possession of the horse's strength so that the rider can dispose of it at will. This is the fundamental precept behind Baucher's quest, namely, lightness. During lessons, L'Hotte often heard the master call out to a pupil 'léger, léger'. This, says L'Hotte, indicated to him that the master was reminding his pupil that the horse's jaw was not sufficiently flexible. For the flexibility of a horse's jaw meant a submissive horse which, in turn, meant lightness.

It is interesting to note that while lightness was Baucher's constant aim, the means of achieving it often changed during his lifetime. It was his constant quest for lightness and perfection that was at the basis of these changes. These changes, this search for different methods and means, was not, according to L'Hotte, the mind of an unschooled rider or a dilettante, flitting from idea to idea simply for the sake of change or out of ignorance. Simply stated, as L'Hotte points out, Baucher's mind was too mobile for it to remain in a rut. And the quest for perfection, regardless of whether one can ever find it, necessitates modifications and changes, whether the direction is the right one or not.

In this connection, L'Hotte remembers how on one occasion he had struggled to perfect a movement Baucher had just shown him, only, on the following day, to discover that Baucher was now working out a different and supposedly better movement. He had completely discarded the one he had only recently shown L'Hotte.

L'Hotte tries to explain the reason for these frequent modifications or the discarding of a previously used method on the part of Baucher. Aside from his quest for perfection and a mobile mind, this trait was perhaps due to the fact that Baucher had never been the recipient of any precise academic and methodical equestrian training and had never followed a well worked-out path. On the other hand, this may have worked to Baucher's advantage. He could thus build his

---

[6] Ibid., 146.
[7] Decarpentry, *Baucher et son école*, Paris, Jean-Michel, Place, 1987, 36.
[8] René Descartes believed that by creating a *tabula rasa*, that is, by refuting past knowledge and experience and making a clean slate, he could prove the existence of God by means of logic and the deductive method. He used as his premise: 'I think, therefore I am.' Being equipped with memory and intelligence, he could obviously not dismiss the past, neither could he prove the existence of God through logic and deduction. Blaise Pascal was quick to point this out, believing that the existence of God could only be based on faith. Similarly, Baucher, with his own *tabula rasa*, even if he wanted to, could not completely disregard or refute the past. For example, as Michel Henriquet points out in my interview of him, Baucher was practising the shoulder in, but never acknowledged doing so, that is, he never referred to it (see *Dressage and C.T.*

new method on something akin to Descartes' *tabula rasa*.[8] To some critics, building something out of nothing and making modifications or changes may denote genius; to others it may denote a restless or an over enthusiastic mind, or even an insecure mind. One should also add that this is not always good paedagogy, for frequent modifications or changes can be disturbing to a pupil who is not as quick or as skilled as was L'Hotte. This kind of teaching certainly necessitated a great deal of discernment on the part of the pupil. Even L'Hotte found it sometimes difficult to keep up with Baucher's modifications and changes.

L'Hotte, however, justifies Baucher's methodology by saying that the master, in his quest for perfection, had to be excessive and push ideas and methods to extremes before he could discover the correct limits of a new method. 'No matter how much he modified or changed, the end result was always wonderful', says L'Hotte. 'He sensed instinctively when something was right.'[9] He knew when a particular movement could cause a certain resistance in a horse and knew immediately how to correct this resistance or, as L'Hotte puts it, 'counterbalance it'.

The following explains how Baucher attempted to counterbalance a horse's resistance. Usually the unskilled horseman reacts in an exaggerated and continuous manner when a horse resists, that is, he usually over-reacts. This over-reaction immediately brings about the horse's further resistance. Thus, according to Baucher, instead of opposing resistance with another resistance in order to subdue the horse, the rider, if he fails at the first attempt, should try to subdue the horse in limited or small doses. Should this remedy also fail, the rider should then modify the general strength of the horse by altering his own position and movement. Only then can the rider react more directly with the horse's resistance.[10]

But this method did not always work well. Baucher continued to use it with his own horses. If for some reason it did not work out for him, Baucher was always able to remedy the problem right away. Unfortunately, this was not always possible for the average horseman.

In his quest for lightness, Baucher introduced flexions of the jaw and neck. The aim of flexion of the jaw is the total relaxation of its muscles and its ability to remain loose and supple. However, L'Hotte believed that Baucher's flexion of the jaw 'went beyond what was necessary'.[11]

With respect to Baucher's lateral flexions, the neck was to become elastic and soft. Once more L'Hotte believed that these flexions 'went beyond what was necessary' and 'softened and weakened the neck too much'. Bending the horse's head until it reached his shoulder during work in hand, was detrimental to the horse, once he was put into motion. In other words, ultimately, it affected impulsion. It was detrimental to the strength of the horse. It also predisposed the hocks to engage more heavily under the mass rather than push it forward. Furthermore, it tended to make the horse back. To compensate for some of these undesired effects, the rider was to make a constant and energetic use of legs and spurs.[12] In fact, Baucher's use of leg aids (spurs) was considerable and frequent. Baucher, himself, later recognized the abuse of the spur on his part.[13]

During the first half of his life Baucher used what he called the *effets d'ensemble* (coordinated effects) that is, the simultaneous use of leg and hand aids. This use of leg aids, whether constantly attacking or legs

---

No. 96, September 1994.)
[9] *Souvenirs*, 105.
[10] Ibid., 106.
[11] Ibid., 107.
[12] Ibid., 107–8.
[13] Ibid., 110.

gripping the horse's flanks, could easily make a horse immune to these aids. And the rider, himself, could experience certain ill-effects from this. L'Hotte explains that Baucher, himself, was obliged to wrap his thighs tightly with wet linen bandages when he got off a horse. For a while, to spare his legs, Baucher used a crop with a certain amount of force to bring about the necessary impulsion.[14]

Years later, when talking to L'Hotte, and after he had introduced the precept of *main sans jambes, jambes sans main*, Baucher wondered how in the past they had managed to misuse their legs to such an extent.[15]

L'Hotte gives us a portrait of the 'baucherized' horse as of the year 1849 when he first met Baucher. According to L'Hotte, the 'baucherized' horse was the consequence of holding or compressing the horse between leg and hand aids, which tended to bring together the two extremities of the horse, that is, his forehand and his hindquarters. This resulted in an artificial equilibrium and made the horse well adapted for movements such as the piaffe, the passage, pirouettes at the canter, and successive changes of lead at the canter. However, the horse was not able to move his mass forward easily and freely. And the rider, while not necessarily carrying the weight of the horse on his arms, bore it with his legs. But, adds L'Hotte, true lightness consists in having the horse light on the legs as well as on the hand. In other words, the horse must flow forward easily and freely, barely being touched with the heel or spur and with the hand not opposing the forward movement in any way.[16]

It should, however, not be forgotten, that Baucher schooled his horses for a very specific purpose, namely circus performances, and that the space in which he performed was limited. It is also important to remember the kind of horses Baucher was obliged to work with.

L'Hotte spends several pages discussing Baucher's horses, their origins, conformation, disposition, schooling, and what kind of schooling he gave each one of them.

When one looks at the list of these horses, one realizes that they were horses who had been abandoned, cast off, or neglected.

Baucher found Kleber abandoned in a stable, unattended, and looking very forlorn. Nobody wanted to ride him due to his unsound gaits. He was a light grey stallion, tall, with long legs. His neck was well set and he carried his tail well which gave him a certain majestic presence. Baucher trained him for approximately four weeks before presenting him to the public.

Stades was a bay mare, afflicted with a bad case of vertigo, who violently shook her head from side to side. After training her for a while, the vertigo disappeared, showing up only rarely. Baucher bought her for 150 francs and, after training her, sold her for 6,000 francs. She died shortly after he had sold her.

The four horses with which Baucher made his reputation were Partisan, Capitaine, Neptune, and Buridan.

Partisan was a thoroughbred, elegant and light. Baucher bought him for 500 francs, after his initial owner, who had paid considerably more for him, had discarded him and made him totally unsound in his gaits and disposition. Unskilled hands had spoiled the rich qualities with which Partisan was endowed. But Baucher was able to exploit these positive attributes of the horse and turned him into a noble looking, elegant and beautifully cadenced horse. Partisan was able to piaffer, first fast, close to the ground, then at a reduced speed, legs elevated. He did this with a wonderful rhythm and looked extremely noble. When L'Hotte met Partisan he was not a young horse but still elegant and noble looking. Baucher told L'Hotte that if Partisan had the gift of language, he would have said much about the

---

[14] *Ibid.*, 110.   [15] *Ibid.*, 110.   [16] *Ibid.*, 111.

misuse and poor treatment he had received previously. It is most likely that it was during the period when he was training Partisan that he got the idea of writing his *Dialogues*.[17]

Baucher's acquisition of Géricault is rather amusing if not quite cricket. Géricault was known to have unseated many a horseman, even some of the best. His unpleasant disposition and his defences were so bad that his owner, Lord Henry Seymour, a rich Englishman living in Paris and founder of the Jockey Club, decided to give him to the horseman who could ride him around the Bois de Boulogne. L'Hotte's sources for this story are many. It was related to him by one of the participants, *comte* Lancosme-Brèves. It was also retold, with modifications and probably more accuracy, by a witness to the incident, Maxime Gaussen, who described it in the *Revue des Haras* of 1884 and 1885. It has also been described by baron d'Etreillis in his book *Ecuyers et Cavaliers, d'aujourd'hui et de hier*.

The opening act of the event occurred one night at the circus where Baucher was performing. Lord Seymour had positioned himself near the entrance to the stables of the circus, surrounded by a group of horsemen, including Lancosme-Brèves. Baucher had barely dismounted from the horse on whom he had been performing that evening, when Lord Seymour, in a loud voice, said that he had in his stables a three-year-old thoroughbred whom nobody could ride; not even Baucher, despite his talent, would be able to remain seated. He was willing to bet on it. When Lancosme-Brèves heard this, he came forward saying that, as a pupil of Baucher, he, himself, would take up the challenge and that there was no need to disturb the master himself. And so the bet was made.

Lancosme-Brèves soon regretted his foolhardiness, suddenly concerned that it might have dire consequences, not only for himself, but for the *comtesse* de Lancosme-Brèves who was pregnant at the time. But, being a man of honour, he could not go back on his word.

The first one to accept Lord Seymour's challenge and attempt riding Géricault was the *vicomte* de Tournon, one of d'Aure's most skilful pupils. He failed abysmally.

Then it was the turn of Lancosme-Brèves. He more or less won the bet. When he got on Géricault, a group of his followers surrounded the horse so that he was unable to do anything but move forward, thereby making it impossible for him to execute any of his defences. They went around the Bois in this manner. One should also add that Lancosme-Brèves had once been a pupil of d'Aure and had only recently gone over to Baucher. But be this as it may, Lancosme-Brèves gave Géricault to Baucher who set out to train him not only to do certain movements, but also to perform under bright lights, with a loud orchestra, and the applause of the public.

Baucher trained him two and three times a day, for twenty-eight days. He allowed no one to observe him. Of course, rumours abounded. Some said he was tranquillizing the horse, others that he was depriving the horse of food, water, and sleep. And so it went.

The great day arrived and one and all made their appearance at the circus. The former *écuyers* of Versailles and of the *Manège royal de Paris*, all *d'Auristes*, were present. So were *général* Oudinot, Baucher's patron, and writers and artists such as Eugène Delacroix, Eugène Sue, and many others. The writer, Théophile Gautier, considerably stouter, wore the famous red gilet he had worn in 1830 during Victor Hugo's controversial play, *Hernani*, which had caused a riot. Almost all the artists and writers were *Bauchéristes* with the exception of Alexandre Dumas who was a

---

[17] See 'Dialogues on equitation', in H. Nelson, *François Baucher, The Man and his Method*, London, J. A. Allen, 1992.

18 François Baucher as drawn by Commandant Margot of Saumur for General Decarpentry.
(Courtesy G. Margot)

d'Auriste. *Tout Paris*[18] was present to see the great horseman on Géricault. The *duchesse* d'Orléans and her children were also present in their loge. Only the *duc* d'Orléans had not yet made an appearance. The performer before Baucher was just finishing his act when the *duc* d'Orléans made his entrance and as discreetly as possible made a sign to the public not to acknowledge him.

When Baucher made his entrance on the

---

[18] The rich and the famous.

by now famous Géricault, there was complete silence in the circus. He was dressed as an officer of the National Guard. At his side hung a sabre. Géricault advanced at a rather fast walk. He did not waver and his stride was straight and sure. When the two reached the centre of the ring, Géricault stopped and Baucher raised his *bicorne* enriched with the plume of a cockerel. He saluted, his hat raised, lingering especially in front of the loge of the royal family. Then all broke loose. The public applauded loudly and lengthily and the orchestra began a loud march. Géricault showed neither surprise nor fear. To resist was farthest from his mind. Everything he did was correct. At first he executed very simple movements, movements belonging to a military drill. Only then did Baucher seem to give the horse more rein and allow him to relax in his gaits. Géricault did not even show fear with respect to the clicking of Baucher's sabre against his spurs. He then did several voltes then the half pass. He halted swiftly at each command, then struck off at the canter with a flowing movement which became more cadenced when he went into several pirouettes. Géricault terminated the performance with two direction changes and lead changes at a rapid pace. Then he halted with great presence in the middle of the ring. Baucher saluted, this time with greater confidence. The applause of the audience was deafening when Baucher and Géricault left the ring with a precise and determined reinback. It goes without saying that the *Bauchéristes* were delirious, while the *d'Auristes* appeared rather muted. They applauded, to be sure. Not to have done so would have shown a lack of etiquette. But the applause was also muted. Baucher returned to bow once more, this time on foot.

L'Hotte discusses the training Baucher's horses received in order to show to what extent he was able to size up each horse and train him in accordance with his disposition and abilities. Each horse had a weakness but also a strength. The perspicacity of the master made it possible to take advantage of each weakness and each strength and make use of them wisely and skilfully. Thus not all his horses did the same work or executed the same movements. For this he was criticized. After all, said his critics, did he not maintain that his method could be applied to all horses regardless of conformation or temperament?

Yet only a judicious horseman like Baucher with much experience and sound judgement could immediately discern the problems a specific horse has and find the way to remedy them or, better still, how to take advantage of them. And, adds L'Hotte, one must not forget that as a circus performer, to prevent a spectator's interest from flagging, he had to vary the work and movement for each horse.

L'Hotte tells us that he had succeeded in getting work from his own horses that had a richer quality than Baucher was ever able to obtain from his own horses. But L'Hotte had infinitely better horses at his disposal than did Baucher. And L'Hotte only trained those with the right disposition and, if not perfect, at least those who had acceptable conformation so that they could be schooled and perform the artificial airs. And L'Hotte did *manège* riding as a hobby, for his own personal gratification, and not as a profession. He trained his own horses to the artificial airs and only when he was off duty. Baucher had to train his horses for the circus and lacked the necessary funds to purchase good horses. Thus it is to his credit that he was able to accomplish so much with horses who had been misused, spoiled, and neglected. Some were almost impossible to train. Buridan, for example, was a nag, heavy and lazy. As a matter of fact, Baucher chose such diverse horses to prove that his method could be used with any horse. That is why he took both Partisan, the noble thoroughbred, and Buridan, the nag, to Saumur in 1843 when he was asked to demonstrate his method.

There is no question that L'Hotte greatly and unwaveringly admired Baucher's honesty and his ability to modify and advance both his intellectual and his practical abilities. To make his point, L'Hotte tells us how on one occasion, when he was dismounting one of Baucher's current horses, the latter said to him: 'If you had been riding my former horses, Partisan, Capitaine, Neptune, or Buridan, horses greatly admired at the time, you would not have found them adequately schooled (dressés). The difference between them and my present horses is tremendous.' And, Baucher added, as an afterthought, 'I had my arms full with Partisan. Capitaine was a little lighter.'[19]

L'Hotte explains this seeming inconsistency by saying that in actuality Baucher's former horses had been well trained, but that it was the talent of the master that had advanced since then, making it possible for him to realize more and more what perfection meant and how difficult it was to achieve it.

This, of course, is what happens in all artistic endeavours. As one improves one finds dissatisfaction with one's previous work. It is also possible that the master now understood what perfection really meant; that perfection lay in purity – the purity of a simple movement rather than the execution of complicated movements that 'thrill' the philistine.

'This purity of movement', underscores L'Hotte, 'depends upon the rider's ability to put into action that strength that is useful to the specific movement and, also, how the horse is able to make use of this strength.'[20]

But, adds L'Hotte, to achieve this purity with any perfection at all, all opposing and useless contractions must disappear, that is to say, all the horse's resistances must disappear.

During the latter part of his life, after the accident he had experienced when a lustre fell on him and pinned him down, resulting in his inability to perform in the circus, Baucher insisted on simple and pure movements. It is also at this time that Baucher introduced his *deuxième manière*, that is, the concept of *main sans jambes, jambes sans main*, a system, says L'Hotte, more to be used in ordinary equitation. To critics who complain that Baucher is now no longer Baucher and consider his use of separate hand and leg aids a radical transformation, L'Hotte retorts that this is an indication of the flexibility and complexity of the mind of this genius. Furthermore, Baucher was not replacing one method with another, that is, *l'effet d'ensemble* by *main sans jambes, jambes sans main*, but was saying that each method has its validity and use, depending upon the experience of the rider and the type of equitation that is being practised.

'In the past', Baucher once said to L'Hotte, 'I often opted for movements that were complicated. Today it takes me six months just to get my horses to walk straight and turn well . . . When total lightness is achieved by making a horse walk straight and become well-balanced, the feeling that the rider gets is the sense of complete accord with the horse's strength. One then hesitates to pass on to any other movement which will modify the combination of forces and destroy this feeling of harmony.'[21] When he noted that L'Hotte did not respond, Baucher continued: 'You will have the same experience. After having attempted all the difficulties of the equestrian art, you, too, will find great joy in achieving perfect lightness, no matter how simple the movements are.'[22] Baucher was now replacing the artificial equilibrium imposed upon the horse with the horse's natural equilibrium. Baucher now also believed that the less one interfered with the horse, the more one could accomplish.

Years later, remembering his master's wise words, L'Hotte added, as if as an afterthought: 'I have reached this stage for some time now.'[23]

And, reflecting on this point, l'Hotte says that when all the energy reserves and joints

---

[19] Ibid., 125.   [20] Ibid., 126.   [21] Ibid., 127.   [22] Ibid., 127.   [23] Ibid., 127.

and muscles of a horse become active due to one's actions, when they can be put into play and are able to vibrate at the slightest touch of one's aids, then there is no need to look for complicated movements in order to experience pleasure.

It is from this flexible elasticity and softness, found in a horse's joints and muscles and animated by impulsion; it is from the harmony of movements, due to the correct use of one's aids, that lightness is ultimately achieved. 'It is this lightness that gives to *savante* equitation, to high equitation, its veritable distinction and, to the *écuyer* involved, the true nature of his talent.'[24] Indeed, artistic equitation demands possession of all of the horse's joints and muscles, as well as their perfect submission.

And just as Baucher, during his early years, had observed in d'Abzac (and perhaps Mazuchelli) certain qualities and secrets and had hoped to glean something from them, so did L'Hotte, likewise, observe the master as he practised in the early hours, alone, on his horse, in the hope that he, too, could enter into and understand the equestrian secrets of the master who had pushed this art to such a degree of perfection.

---

[24] *Ibid.*, 128.

4
L'Hotte's teacher: comte d'Aure

Before L'Hotte became d'Aure's pupil, he had frequently observed him when he had come to Saumur for the second time with the *Guides d'état-major*. 'From then on', says L'Hotte, 'it was my fervent desire to study at his school...'¹ As with Baucher, L'Hotte became a pupil of d'Aure and a close confidant. As he had done with Baucher, L'Hotte, likewise, recorded carefully his relationship with d'Aure, taking down copious notes which pertained not only to equitation, but also to d'Aure's life as a page and as an *écuyer ordinaire* and *cavalcadour* for the king and his entourage. Fortunately for us, he also recorded the many anecdotes which enliven his *Souvenirs*. With his usual diligence, L'Hotte listened and recorded carefully. He studied under d'Aure during the two years he was at Saumur and, once again in 1960 when he became commandant of the cavalry section at Saint-Cyr.

L'Hotte was a diligent note taker. He was also known to be a man of few words and soon became known among pupils and colleagues as *le muet sublime*. L'Hotte knew how to listen carefully to advice given him, whether coming from his teachers or from colleagues. It is to his credit when he tells us that he often asked other horsemen to judge his work with his horses and give their candid opinion, especially if they felt that some of his work was imperfect.

Both Baucher and d'Aure mention this ability of L'Hotte to listen carefully and ask brief and pertinent questions.

Baucher once said to him: 'You will go far in equitation, not solely because of your aptitude and will power, your love of the equestrian art, but also because you know how to listen.'²

The master paused for a while and added: 'For quite some time now I have been struck by your attentiveness. You heed my words carefully and desire to understand their significance. You never bring up an inopportune observation.'³

D'Aure once made a similar observation when his son, Olivier, reproached him for giving a more complete analysis and explanation of a movement to L'Hotte rather than to him.

'Of course', d'Aure replied, 'that is because L'Hotte has confidence in my words. He knows that I have more experience than he has and when I give him advice, he applies it right away without discussing it. You, on the other hand, when I give you advice, you always have first to find some objections.'⁴

Antoine Cartier d'Aure was born in Toulouse on 30 June 1799. He went to Saint-Cyr and emerged from it as Second Lieutenant of the Infantry. However, he left a military career in 1817 to become a pupil-*écuyer* at the *Manège de Versailles*.

L'Hotte presents d'Aure as having a very expressive face, frequently animated by a

---

[1] *Souvenirs*, 138. [2] *Ibid.*, 130. [3] *Ibid.*, 130. [4] *Ibid.*, 131

19 *Comte d'Aure.*

smile that had a somewhat mocking air, a trait which was also visible on his lips. He used tobacco in the form of powder which he kept in a *tabatière* (snuffbox).

Unlike Baucher, d'Aure was not a reflective and secretive individual; rather, he was open and usually acted intuitively and with great initiative, sometimes even impulsively. He was quick to assimilate new ideas and showed an inventive mind. He was far from being the pedant and he disliked routine activity. He was a delightful talker, a man of the world. He possessed what the French call *l'esprit gaulois* (gallic wit, a down-to-earth humour) and loved to joke and tease people, but in a charming and endearing way, which was never taken amiss even when it was directed at royalty. At times he was disdainful, verging on crudity, when things or people crossed him, but this was only on the surface. Basically, he was decent, generous, and kind.

He was well-built, above average, just not exceeding the proper height for an *écuyer*. While his neck and torso were rather long, this served him to an advantage as a horseman, giving him suppleness and grace.

Indeed, he was a very elegant rider, but never showed any affectation when he rode. But it was obvious to all who observed him that he belonged to those few privileged riders. It was not for nothing that he was named 'a centaur' by Baucher who admitted that he was an excellent rider.

It was, however, outdoors, riding cross-country, jumping obstacles, that he really excelled as a rider. He rode with ease, never gripping with his legs to the horse's sides. When he went into a rising trot, which he did with grace and suppleness, one had before one the ideal horseman. His legs harmonized gently and perfectly with his mount.

L'Hotte points out one or two flaws that were visible when one observed him closely, especially when he worked with his horse in the *manège*. He sat deep in the saddle but his thighs did not come down sufficiently which inclined his knees to rise. L'Hotte explains that this imperfection was due to the hernias he got at Versailles when he rode as page and *écuyer* using very flat saddles. But contrary to the habit at Versailles, d'Aure even then, wore his stirrup leathers very short for which he was frequently admonished. While it was considered elegant, at least for a while, to hold the position that was accepted and admired at Versailles and which men like d'Abzac, Aubert, Rousselet, and many others adhered to, it should be remembered that this worked well when one rode well-schooled horses and worked in a *manège*. But when one rode all types of horses, as d'Aure did, and rode in all types of terrain, long stirrup leathers were dangerous. When one looks at drawings of the placement of the legs of d'Abzac and other *Versaillais*, they denote a certain amount of abandon compared with d'Aure's legs which are more in harmony with his mount in that they are placed closer to the horse's sides, less abandoned. While never closely held to the horse's sides, d'Aure's legs were always ready to react to a given situation and could always determine the amount of freedom that should be given to the horse's forward movement.[5]

D'Aure's use of hands and reins were legendary. While remaining fixed, they were extremely light. He only used the pressure of his fingers, which were always gentle, and played with the reins as though they were light ribbons he feared could break.

His hand had a constant rapport with the horse's mouth and the degree of tension on the reins corresponded to the energy of the gait. He also allowed the neck to extend or retract swiftly and easily, depending upon whether he desired extension or shortening of a motion.

D'Aure's horses always went forward positively, free in their gaits, which were always in accord with the rider's hand and legs. Impulsion was of prime importance to d'Aure. The horses he trained were always sought and appreciated by other riders because he trained them so that they could be ridden by others. L'Hotte tells us that when he rode with the king or other horsemen he always gave them the better and easier side of the path, choosing the side with ditches or ruts, thereby making his horses more skilful and used to all kinds of terrain. It was for this reason that his horses were sought by the king's entourage, especially by those horsemen who accompanied the king on hacks or hunts, for they knew that since they had to cede the better side of the path to the

---

[5] *Ibid.*, 146.

king, they felt more secure with a horse trained by d'Aure, for they knew how to cope with difficult terrain.

D'Aure was greatly liked at the court due to his grace, charm, and wit. He also had the ability of saying things in such a way so as not to offend people, not even the royal princes and the king. The story goes that one day, as d'Aure accompanied the *comte* d'Artois (the future Charles X) on a hunt, d'Artois, after having made his horse jump over a fairly wide ditch, turned to d'Aure and said: 'Well, Sir. This is how a prince jumps.'[6] Most likely d'Aure bowed, smiled, acknowledging d'Artois's prowess in horsemanship.

A little later, d'Artois and d'Aure came to a fast flowing river with steeply sloping banks on either side, presenting an obstacle that was considerably more difficult to jump than the ditch d'Artois had jumped.

D'Aure dashed forward and jumped over the river and its banks. He then jumped back and joined the prince, saying to him: 'Sire, and this is how an *écuyer* jumps.'[7] Most likely it was now the turn of the prince to smile and acknowledge this feat. Obviously, d'Artois did not take amiss this act of bravado, which could have been construed as a put-down.

D'Aure was also the favourite pupil of the *comte* d'Abzac, who was considered the dean of *écuyers* of the *Manège de Versailles*. He also received training from *comte* d'Abzac's brother, the *chevalier* d'Abzac who, while like his more successful brother, also taught *manège* riding, was more adept at and interested in exterior riding.

It was in *manège* riding that the *comte* d'Abzac trained the young d'Aure. But already at that early stage of his equestrian education, one finds that d'Aure was disposed to exterior riding. While he received many an admonishment from d'Abzac for violating the precepts taught at Versailles and for being a *casse-cou*, d'Aure found it difficult to restrain his predilections.

Despite his training at Versailles in court and *manège* riding, L'Hotte sees d'Aure rather as a representative of military riding going back to men such as d'Auvergne, Lubersac, Chabannes, Boideffre, Montfaucon de Rogles and many others who, while almost all were trained in Classical and *manège* riding, had opted for military equitation as a means for training the French cavalry corps. It was their desire for simplicity and utility that d'Aure now sought and practised. Added to the military equitation of the eighteenth century, a more or less new kind of riding was emanating from across the Channel and was influencing French equitation, namely exterior riding or cross-country riding, with the steeple chase and obstacle jumping and which was part of this Anglomania that beset both royalty, the aristocracy, and the haute bourgeoisie. It should not be forgotten that members of the royal family and many a nobleman had sought refuge in England and had returned to France in 1802 when the amnesty act for émigrés was put into effect by Napoleon I. Anglomania continued during the second half of the century with the return of Louis Napoléon (who had also spent some time in England), who first as president of the Second Republic then, by means of a coup d'état, made himself emperor as Napoleon III.

It is interesting to note that after the upheavals of 1789, the *Manège de Versailles* adopted the book written by Montfaucon de Rogles, *Traité d'Equitation*, a proponent of military equitation, rather than the more complicated book by La Guérinière, *Ecole de Cavalerie*. Yet, the kind of equitation that continued to be practised by the *Versaillais* still did not satisfy d'Aure's temperament, who felt that there was still something incomplete and static in some of their teachings. He wanted to adapt some of their methods of equitation to the changes that were occurring in the society of the nineteenth century.

---

[6] Ibid., 151. [7] Ibid., 151.

20 *Comte* d'Aure practising exterior equitation. Painted by Philippe Ledieu. (Courtesy of the Musée de Saumur)

For d'Abzac, the talent of an *écuyer* lay in making the horse go straight, supple him, and regularize and perfect his natural gaits. An *écuyer* was also capable of analysing and, above all, of sparing a horse's strengths. All this must be accomplished by seeking and finding the necessary *stride* (animated and cadenced movements, elegant and elevated) which would give the horse elasticity and movement. To a certain degree, the ideas of the two schools of riding were not very far apart when it came to the basic schooling of horses.

D'Aure, instead of following in the wake of others, or even accepting the changes that were occurring at Versailles, decided to head a new school. Yet he did not totally ignore the past. He still used the old methods of schooling the horse, to make the horse obedient and regularize and perfect his natural movements. But he went beyond what his teachers were doing; rather he used the methods of 'provoking and maintaining the clarity and freedom of the horse's gaits and, above all, developing speed. In other words, he wanted to make the horse keen and sharp in every respect.'[8] In no way did he want to limit impulsion.

---

[8] *Ibid.*, 157.

D'Aure also advocated cross-country riding, obstacle jumping, hunting, and racing. For him *manège* riding was not an end in itself, but a means of preparing the horse for the new age. He wanted his horse to be a *manège* horse in winter, a hacking horse in summer, and a hunter in autumn. For d'Aure the ideal *écuyer* must try to make the best use of every horse, but limit his demands with respect to the horse's potential. The most important thing was to leave the horse his natural energy.

The equitation he prescribed was an equitation that was mostly instinctive. Yet it was to be orderly and regularized. It was not random as some of his critics claimed. The aim was to develop riders, that is, competent amateurs, rather than perfect the talent of the *écuyer*. Like his own riding, d'Aure wanted to instil in others a combination of ease, daring, and elegance. Unlike Baucher, he did not want to rid the horse of resistances essential to executing and perfecting *manège* exercises. Rather, d'Aure wanted movement that was easy, movement in itself, rather than acquiring movement within a given position and achieving perfect lightness.

In the preface to his *Traité*, d'Aure believes that critics accused him of having taken advantage of ideas of the past and interpreted them falsely. 'But they were wrong,' says d'Aure, '(truth was falsified), in that they judged the *Ecole de Versailles* on the basis of my *manège* in Paris. How could they compare an institution whose instruction was organized, whose young pupils were under a teacher for several years, with a commercial venture which taught pupils of all ages, with different kinds of abilities and strengths, and who wanted to become riders in twenty lessons. How could they compare a venture that was independent and subject to many obstacles with a *manège* that was supported by "royal munificence"'.[9]

D'Aure knew how to control the horse's haunches and play with his resistances by using the rein of opposition. He knew also how to make concessions to these resistances, oppose them to each other, and thus obtain the desired movement, not only despite the resistances, but, often, by combining them. As was the case with Baucher, much of what d'Aure did was instinctive and improvised, not always correct and regular, but nonetheless, achieving something positive. These very traits seem to denote, as they did with Baucher, a great artist who, in his own field, creates a new path, building upon the past, but bringing to it something new and different.

According to L'Hotte there are certain inconsistencies in d'Aure's method. On the one hand he wanted the horse to be trained in such a way that anyone could ride him. On the other hand, instinct and improvisation are very personal tools, effective when a horse and rider are used to each other. But d'Aure's goal was also to instil the quality of improvisation and instinct in the rider. L'Hotte also brings out these very inconsistencies when he discusses Baucher's claim that his *nouvelle méthode* could be used with any horse, horses with poor conformations or with resistances. Yet a rider was usually successful with Baucher's method on a horse with which he was familiar. Not any horse.

While still at Versailles, d'Aure was often asked to buy horses for the king's stables. The outstanding ones were destined for the king's stables and went under the name of *brides d'or*; the others, also excellent horses, were designated as *brides d'argent* and were destined for the king's courtiers. D'Aure went to the great fairs of Normandy, Guibray, and others, to select these horses. It was, indeed, for the people at these fairs, a sight to behold, to see an *écuyer* of the *Manège de Versailles* get on these young horses, horses who had been left to themselves in pasture and who had never been saddled or ridden.

---

[9] D'Aure, *Traité d'equitation*, VI.

21 *Comte* d'Aure on his horse, Le Cerf.

When d'Aure got on these young horses, he not only remained seated without difficulty, but soon made them move at all three gaits. Of course, d'Aure was not doing *haute école* equitation with these horses. But mounting these Norman horses was quite a change from riding and training young thoroughbreds.

At the Haras du Pin between 1818 and 1840, d'Aure mounted a great number of young thoroughbreds. This included Tigris and Eylaw, two thoroughbred stallions who were born and raised at the Haras du Pin. After five days of schooling, Eylaw was presented at a *reprise de manège*.

When L'Hotte became squadron chief at Saint-Cyr, he visited the Haras du Pin with d'Aure. On this occasion d'Aure related to L'Hotte his earlier experiences, especially the races in which he had participated on young unschooled stallions.

'Those are the kind of horses you should get hold of', he suggested to L'Hotte. 'They are generous and giving.' And, he added, 'I attribute my rapid success to the high quality of these stallions.'[10]

D'Aure was so popular and successful with the people at the Haras du Pin, that there exists a painting representing d'Aure mounted on Eclatant posing in front of *Madame la Dauphine* (the Dauphin's wife) who had come to visit the haras.[11]

In his sections on Baucher, L'Hotte discussed some of the horses Baucher had schooled in order to give an idea of the different methods he used with different horses. Likewise does he discuss some of the horses d'Aure had schooled to give an idea of his methods used with different horses.

Le Cerf was a bay stallion from the Limousin. While at the *Manège de Versailles*, d'Aure used Le Cerf to execute very complicated movements. Le Cerf was so agile that while cantering, he could execute a series of lead changes that became tighter and tighter and eventually arrive at lead changes at three, then two, then a single one 'a tempo'. These are some of the movements that Baucher later executed in the circus on some of his horses. Despite the agility, skill, and generosity of Le Cerf, d'Aure, on one occasion, wanted to exchange Le Cerf for a different horse, merely for the sake of change and a dislike of routine. But d'Abzac made him keep Le Cerf. Sound advice which d'Aure later recognized. Many drawings of d'Aure present him on Le Cerf, with horse and rider looking very elegant.

Later, when the *Manège de Versailles* closed its doors in 1830, Le Cerf was sold to a certain Kuntzman who rented him out to Sunday riders. D'Aure was now in Paris, the proprietor of his own *manège* in the Rue Duphot.[12] One day, at the request of Lord Seymour, d'Aure rode his former horse. Lord Seymour was so impressed by the harmony that horse and rider exhibited, that he afterwards bought the old horse and had him put down, not wanting to see him used ignobly and suffer the fate that all rental horses eventually suffer.

One particularly outstanding movement that d'Aure executed was called *le tête à queue* (the head with tail movement), in which he struck off at a fast canter, then whipped around (slued) at a fast pace. One other horse named Maître de Dance, who belonged to Lord Seymour, also executed this movement with tremendous speed and energy. Like Géricault, Maître de Dance was considered untrainable.[13] But d'Aure was able to make of him a good school (*manège*) horse which was ridden by his pupils.

During this period of d'Aure's career, the trot became the rage and d'Aure, having chosen the path of modernity, had to follow

---

[10] *Souvenirs*, 163.
[11] Ibid., 163.
[12] Ibid., 165. One wonders why d'Aure did not keep Le Cerf in his own *manège*.
[13] What was there about the stables of Lord Seymour that contained so many 'untrainable' horses?

the times. His temperament made it easy for him to do so. So d'Aure experimented with the trot. He executed, what at the time was the fashion, namely, a disconnected and disorganized trot. He also took the trot to a tremendous speed. For this purpose he used another of Lord Seymour's horses, Madame Putiphar. Quite obviously, when one does a very fast trot, it tends to degenerate rather rapidly. Harmony and clear cadenced movements no longer exist. Not to speak of what it does to the poor horse if this kind of trot is sustained for any length of time. When he executed this fast trot, d'Aure used a snaffle rather than the bit he usually used with the double bridle, so that the horse could find more easily the necessary contact which corresponded to the tension of the neck that this fast and energetic trot required.

L'Hotte considers this disconnected and fast trot (the canter was also abused in a similar fashion), a perversion, detrimental to the beauty of the horse's natural movement. And, emphasizes L'Hotte, it also leads to his premature ruin. These 'perversions', as L'Hotte calls them, are surprising coming from a horseman who always sought free, positive, and natural movements and who criticized Baucher for making his horses execute unnatural movements and give them an unnatural equilibrium.

L'Hotte relates an incident which has a bearing on d'Aure's 'experimentations'. Général de Brack, who felt that the *Ecole de Cavalerie* was somewhat behind the times, invited d'Aure to spend a few days at Saumur for the express purpose of showing the *écuyers* to what extent riding had evolved in the new age.

On that occasion, d'Aure rode several times, singly and at the head of a *reprise des écuyers*. Each time he was greatly admired by the spectators who sat in the spectators' gallery of the *Manège des Ecuyers*.

He was then asked to ride the famous stallion Sans-Pareil, a tall, elegant, sorrel. Sans-Pareil had been schooled by *commandant* Rousselet and was considered one of the best-schooled and brilliant horses of the *Manège*. Rousselet could ride Sans-Pareil with only a simple ribbon instead of a regular bit. There is a drawing of Rousselet riding Sans-Pareil with this simple ribbon.

Hardly seated in the saddle, d'Aure gave Sans-Pareil's neck two blows with his crop. The poor horse had never experienced such treatment, certainly never from Rousselet, the most gentle of trainers. And Sans-Pareil was of a generous disposition, although at times he could be somewhat irritable.

The two blows Sans-Pareil received for no reason at all had exasperated the poor horse and he reacted with anger and refused to obey. D'Aure, of course, did his best to make the horse obey. The duel went on for a while. Eventually d'Aure managed to get Sans-Pareil to execute some successive lead changes in the middle of the *manège*. But he had hardly accomplished this feat when Sans-Pareil once again refused to co-operate and another struggle commenced between man and horse. Finally the rider succeeded in bringing the horse once again to the centre of the *manège*. D'Aure dismounted and caressed Sans-Pareil, saying: 'Indeed, you are a noble creature and I bungled the whole thing.'

In the background one heard a voice saying: 'Indeed.'[14]

It was the voice of the *sous-écuyer* (second in command), Michaux, to whom Sans-Pareil had been assigned.

The following morning d'Aure mounted Sans-Pareil once again. This time he exhibited all the delicacy that a good *écuyer* should have. At first Sans-Pareil was apprehensive, remembering the treatment he had received the previous day. But d'Aure soon got the better of the horse's nervousness in a manner that was the direct opposite of the way he had treated the horse the day before.

---

[14] *Souvenirs*, 170.

This time d'Aure was able to bring out the excellent qualities of the horse. Horse and rider executed movements in harmony. When he dismounted, the applause was unanimous.

L'Hotte ponders as to what made d'Aure act so despicably with Sans-Pareil in the first instance. What did he want to prove? Was it to impress the spectators seated in the gallery of the *manège*? Prove to them that he, too, could ride a well-schooled horse, make it execute the required movements, but also make this horse move in different ways, modern ways? L'Hotte can find no explanation.

But L'Hotte notes that although d'Aure had behaved with brutality on that particular day, one should not assume that he was always brutal with his horses as some of his opponents have claimed. Furthermore, adds L'Hotte, show him the horseman who has not at some time lost his temper with a stubborn horse and behaved in a way that later made him feel ashamed. Perhaps he can come up with only one, says L'Hotte, and that is *commandant* Rousselet. Even d'Abzac, one witness has claimed, once hit a horse on the head with the handle of his lungeing whip. At the *Manège de Versailles* it was considered very poor taste to treat a horse with brutality. But D'Aure, already at Versailles, had always sought difficult horses and, as such, may, at times, have been rough with them. And when he rode these young unschooled horses at the fairs in Normandy or at the Haras du Pin, he most certainly must have used force, even violence with them. After all, riding these horses was dangerous.

While d'Aure was always ready to get on difficult horses, he did not like to be the butt of a joke. And he was quite annoyed when Lord Seymour did so on one occasion.

D'Aure and Lord Seymour were riding in the Bois de Boulogne. D'Aure rode a pony belonging to Lord Seymour whose temperament was so ambitious that he became violent if he did not have the lead. Lord Seymour, fully aware of the pony's aggressive disposition, rode ahead at a very fast pace. At first, d'Aure tried to hold back the pony. But he gave him his head, letting him go as fast as he wished. The bridle paths of the Bois were made for that very purpose.

But the pony soon tired and began to slow down and pant. But d'Aure, digging his spurs into the pony's sides, forced him to continue his fast pace. The pony was now completely out of breath with little or no strength left. His grey coat was by now bluish, so much was he sweating. D'Aure, now riding beside Lord Seymour, said in a mocking tone: 'Your pony must now walk. First he ran to please himself, then he ran to please me. I must say, he gallops well. If you wish, we can make a good horse out of him – for a woman.'[15]

L'Hotte does not tell us what kind of reaction Lord Seymour had. Fortunately for this pony the consequences were not harmful. All he experienced was fatigue. However, the consequences were considerably more serious when d'Aure was given another horse to ride.

On this occasion, when d'Aure got on the horse, it began to leap and bound forward. D'Aure's first thought was that it had been trained as a *sauteur en liberté* (jumper at liberty). He, himself, had schooled many a *sauteur* at Versailles. But none had jumped quite like this one. He then noticed that the owner of the horse and his friends were giving each other knowing smiles. D'Aure knew that he was the butt of another joke.

He then called out to his servant of long standing: 'Pierre, hand me my stick.' Pierre handed d'Aure a heavy stick. Then, turning to the owner, he said to him: 'Sir, your horse has jumped for your benefit. Well, he will now jump for mine.'[16] D'Aure made use of spurs and stick so extensively that the horse later came down with pneumonia and died.

It was incidents such as these that gave

---

[15] Ibid., 172–3. [16] Ibid., 173.

d'Aure the reputation of being brutal with horses. Yet, says L'Hotte, during the two years he was at Saumur as Lieutenant-Instructor taking lessons from d'Aure, he had never seen him behave in a harsh or brutal manner with a horse. Only once, but that was to serve as part of their instruction. It was to explain how the lunge could be used to punish a recalcitrant horse. With the horse's head bent slightly into the circle, the lunge must be undulated, the hand raised, then quickly and violently lowered. Depending on the force used, the tug the horse experiences on the caveçon would serve as punishment. On this occasion one of the most mediocre horses was used for the demonstration. Some of the pupils felt pity for the horse, but L'Hotte believed that this rather harsh treatment was justified in that it served as a lesson.[17]

D'Aure has been judged diversely with respect to his personal equitation. Much, of course, depends upon which of the d'Aures one is analysing. Is it the young d'Aure of Versailles, the man of the world d'Aure of Paris, or the more mature d'Aure of Saumur?

There is the young d'Aure, the *casse-cou* of Versailles as d'Abzac often referred to him. But at Versailles there were other outstanding horsemen, men like d'Abzac, Rousselet, and many others to keep d'Aure's excessive exuberance and daring in check. But even after d'Abzac's death and when d'Aure replaced him as *écuyer ordinaire* and *écuyer cavalcadour*, his reputation as a dare-devil continued to follow him.

After the Revolution of 1830 and the closing of the doors of the *Manège de Versailles*, d'Aure was in great demand when he opened the doors to a successive number of *manèges* in Paris. His reputation as an *écuyer* of the *Manège de Versailles* had followed him. He was also lucky to have been able to transfer to Paris some of the best horses for his use.

His background stood him so well that many pupils left the *manèges* run by other *écuyers* such as Jules Pellier to take lessons from him. Especially important to his new business was the acquisition of Lord Seymour as a pupil, whose name and fortune brought him other names with titles and fortunes.

This was now d'Aure as man of the world, the d'Aure who mingled with the rich and the great of the equestrian world and the Jockey Club and who was greatly admired by them for his background, his riding ability, his ability to improvize, as well as his seat and posture. It was this d'Aure who taught equitation to the *jeunesse d'orée* (gilded youth) of Paris.

When in 1847 d'Aure came to Saumur as *écuyer en chef*, it was the mature d'Aure whom one saw. Gone, or almost gone, was the brilliant and improvisational riding that he practised in Paris and which instilled in his pupils praise and admiration. As L'Hotte points out, these daring and brilliant improvisations of the Paris period did not have and could not have dire consequences for the dandies and *amazones* he taught. For their goals were limited. All they wanted was to acquire certain equestrian skills so that they could show themselves in the Bois de Boulogne on a beautiful and expensive thoroughbred, followed by the appropriate hound.

But at Saumur, the goals were different. While the officers and NCOs admired d'Aure's background, reputation and skill, and were fully aware of his skill and daring and would have been delighted to emulate him, d'Aure himself held back, and held them back. As L'Hotte puts it, 'he was far too fore-sighted not to be aware of the consequences'.[18]

At Saumur he was still an energetic and

---

[17] The question comes to mind whether the horse was chosen for this particular purpose because he was mediocre? Was a beautiful horse too good for this purpose? Did a mediocre horse feel less pain? Or, if it did feel pain, did it matter less because he was mediocre?

[18] *Souvenirs*, 178–9.

skilled rider, but he was also a wiser rider and used sound judgement. He still occasionally used the exaggerated and disconnected way of trotting, but without the speed. But, in general, he acted in such a way that could and did serve as an example to the young officers.

L'Hotte also compares the various teaching methods d'Aure used during the different stages in his career.

At Versailles, d'Aure's teaching method was methodical since he was under the constant supervision of d'Abzac. Here, as we know, the seat was of the utmost importance and served as a point of departure to a good, overall posture.

After the death of d'Abzac in 1827, d'Aure was given the directorship of the Manège de Versailles. However, it was the comte de Boisfoucaud, the oldest écuyer who had replaced de facto d'Abzac as instructor. According to an official document which can be found in the archives of the grande écurie at Versailles, d'Aure was given the directorship because 'he was at the moment the only one with real talent'.[19]

D'Aure's teaching methods changed considerably when he opened his own manèges in Paris. His teaching was now no longer methodical. Mostly, the rich pupils were taking lessons from d'Aure for their benefit and pleasure and not because they were to pass on to others the instruction they were receiving, as was the case at Versailles and Saumur.

Whereas the pupils at Versailles spent three years of methodical and progressively graded training, the dandies and amazones who came to d'Aure wanted to learn to ride as quickly as possible. D'Aure complied, giving them sufficient knowledge to make of them energetic, enterprising, even daring riders, that is, riders who could use a horse cross-country in relative safety. It should be mentioned that, according to L'Hotte, d'Aure in no way flattered the sons and daughters or wives of the rich and great; rather, it seems that he was severe with them.

We have seen that d'Aure's equestrian experiences, as well as his contact with diverse people, were extensive: Versailles with its court and manège instruction, and sports equitation with its contact with the rich and great. Yet, despite his contacts in Paris with the rich and famous, his manèges did not prosper financially. Quite obviously, d'Aure was not adept in the world of business and administration. He took his failures to heart and for a while wanted to leave France and seek his fortune elsewhere in equitation.

That he was superbly qualified to serve in foreign climes goes without saying. His background and experiences, and the list of his publications dealing with horse-breeding, equestrian instruction, even equitation for ladies, critical works, and his two books attest to this.

L'Hotte, comparing d'Aure's two works, Traité d'Equitation and Cours d'Equitation, considers the latter one superior. L'Hotte felt that d'Aure, in the later work, had acquired greater experience and maturity and could speak with greater confidence and authority. His early work, L'Hotte believes, represents the thoughts of a somewhat immature individual. A person 'to write with conviction, certitude, and authority',[20] needs experience. And d'Aure in 1834 lacked this experience. The third edition, published shortly before he took command of the Manège de Saumur, despite its few changes, differs very little.

L'Hotte says that he understands why nothing new came from d'Aure's pen. During his Paris period, he was too much the man of the world, surrounded and involved with the fashionable equestrian world. The kind of life he led was not conducive to meditation and writing.

Furthermore, only after much of the dust had settled after the Baucher/d'Aure contro-

---

[19] Ibid., 180. [20] Ibid., 188.

versy could a new book emerge from the pen of d'Aure. Six years before the publication of *Cours d'Equitation*, d'Aure had come to Saumur to take command of the *Manège des Ecuyers*. It is 'from this great centre of horsemen and *écuyers*' that d'Aure was able to acquire considerable experience. 'Horses', says L'Hotte, 'from all over, in large numbers, passed daily before him, were evaluated by him and ridden by him'.[21]

D'Aure was thus able to assimilate much and take advantage of what he saw and experienced. Unlike at Versailles, where he had very inexperienced pupils, or in Paris where he had mostly dilettantes and amateurs, here, at Saumur, the pupils were of a different sort. They were experienced riders, eager to learn more. It is of great advantage to an instructor when the pupils are curious and eager. Many were older. There were many officer-instructors who were able to discuss and analyse certain problems with him. Even beneficial were those who opposed him. There were some who did not like the dazzling background which came with him to Saumur.

While L'Hotte shows great admiration and praise for d'Aure as a horseman and as a person, he has one important reservation with respect to d'Aure's position at the *Manège de Saumur*. What d'Aure lacked, says L'Hotte, was the necessary rank to serve well and efficiently as *écuyer en chef*. According to L'Hotte, 'to take orders from someone who does not have rank, an officer is always ready to rebel when the one he must obey wants to impose his authority'.[22] L'Hotte may also have had Baucher in mind. Yet, when Baucher and his son came to Saumur (as well as Lunéville, and Paris), to present his *nouvelle méthode*, the reaction of the officers and NCOs, while at first somewhat negative, soon became receptive to what he had to offer and almost all evaluated him positively.[23]

D'Aure had difficulty supervising the direction of the *Manège*. As we have seen, he was not a good businessman. Neither was he a good administrator. He was not always consistent in his orders. Nor was he always firm. Thus discipline suffered. A certain *colonel* Jacquemin who was second in command at the *Ecole de Cavalerie* was asked to make certain observations about the nature and functioning of the *Manège*, the regularity of service, and discipline. D'Aure was extremely hurt by this. The whole affair was compounded by the fact that Jacquemin had been at Versailles at the time when d'Aure had been there and the differences in position and status between the two men at the time was considerable. D'Aure had been the darling and spoiled child of the king and the court, the brilliant *écuyer*, and Jacquemin had merely been an NCO. At Saumur, the relationship between the two men was a hostile one. On one occasion d'Aure was particularly upset by some observation Jacquemin had made to him. Later he said to L'Hotte:

Don't do what I did. Never resign from a military career. In order to enter the *Manège de Versailles* I sacrificed my position as an officer. Had I remained in the army, I would now be Jacquemin's superior. And instead of him making remarks to me, I would be making them to him. When he hurts me, I go home, throw myself on the bed, close my eyes, and relive the past. I then see myself at the court, as *écuyer cavalcadour* of the king, and see Jacquemin in his barracks.[24]

However, remarks made by *colonel* Jacquemin to d'Aure never dealt with the teaching of equitation. D'Aure always directed instruction the way it was intended to be taught at Saumur. But his personal instruction was, nevertheless, influenced by his status as a civilian *écuyer* which, ultimately, did not give him the unquestionable authority he would have had as an *écuyer* with rank.

To aggravate the situation even further,

---

[21] Ibid., 189. [22] Ibid., 192. [23] See Nelson, *François Baucher*, for more detail. [24] *Souvenirs*, 194.

d'Aure's character was such that he did not like to impose his opinion on others, whether they were *écuyers* or *sous-écuyers*. During a discussion d'Aure would give his opinion, which was never dogmatic, then retreat from the discussion if he saw that he was getting nowhere. He would then become silent or broach a different topic, thus maintaining his 'man of the world' manner, or, at times, take on a good-natured but mocking air.

But if he did not interfere with or impose himself on the *écuyers* or instructors, he felt very much at ease with his pupils and gave them all the help and care he could. He gave special attention to the lieutenant-instructors who were sufficiently experienced horsemen to be able to appreciate the value of his instruction. They, like L'Hotte, had come to Saumur to complete their equestrian training so that they could eventually become captain-instructors in charge of equestrian and military training as well as the schooling (dressage) of horses in their own specific regiments.

D'Aure not only taught practical equitation; he also took charge of theory, giving them also the history of equitation. It was through these lieutenant-instructors, who would then go and teach others, that his precepts and ideas were transmitted. Indeed, men like L'Hotte, the *baron* d'Etreillis, the *baron* de Vaux, who had been his pupils, did write about d'Aure and his precepts. D'Aure also staged the *reprise de manège* at the end of the year with the lieutenant-instructors rather than the *écuyers* which had always been part of the tradition. When d'Aure had to be absent from his duties, it was the lieutenant-instructors who were asked to take over and whose duty it was to school the horses. At the time L'Hotte was one of the lieutenant-instructors assigned to ride and take care of these horses. It was always a pleasure for L'Hotte to give special attention to these horses so that d'Aure would, upon his return, find them in as good a shape as he had left them.

L'Hotte also presents us some of the horses he rode at the time in Saumur.

Marcellus was a dark chestnut bay, tall, elegant, light, with a nice top line and a well-set head. He moved forward with ease as soon as he was ridden. His impulsion was excellent. 'Impulsion', said d'Aure, 'is like vapour. The rider holds in his hand the outlet valve of a boiler and allows the vapour to escape but at a constant rate.'[25]

As with many of the horses d'Aure had trained, Marcellus' obedience rested on a free and positive impulsion. The joints of his hocks were pliant but, at the same time, firm and tempered like steel, increasing, as the speed and energy of his gait increased. They maintained their elasticity, never presenting the stiffness or dryness that is often characteristic of cross-country riding.[26] Marcellus was obedient to aids and conformed to all the requirements of a cross-country horse. He moved beautifully in those wide spaces, both at moderate and at fast gaits. He went by or jumped over all types of obstacles with the greatest of ease. The speed at the different gaits could be easily regulated. Speed increases could be achieved smoothly, without precipitation, which he accomplished through extending his gait. His equilibrium changed easily to accommodate his new speed. He never gave the impression of rushing or wanting to go fast. But fast he could go. He simply did everything so easily and smoothly. Decreasing speed as well as increasing it was also achieved smoothly. While Marcellus' trot was extremely fast, he was always attentive to the rider's slightest move of the hand or pressure of the fingers. Then his gait slowed down and his neck became flexible once again.

There were, of course, other horses L'Hotte rode during that period.

Endymion was a very elegant light bay,

---

[25] Ibid., 196. [26] Ibid., 197.

light on the forehand, with a highly set neck. He had great action, especially at the gallop. At times he was inclined to bolt. He was d'Aure's favourite horse for a while.

While Endymion was light on the forehand, Chasseur was heavy on the forehand, making the rider carry his weight. D'Aure changed this horse's equilibrium and transferred his weight to the haunches.

Angevin, in turn, was heavy on the hindquarters. His gaits were irregular, his movements disconnected, especially at the trot. Heavy hands, trying to cope with his natural action, were responsible for these problems. At first d'Aure made use of the kind of martingale that was divided by a ring above the horse's chest, as well as using a fixed martingale to make the horse lower his head and transfer some of the weight to the forehand. To accomplish further putting the horse on the forehand, d'Aure also had the horse walk down steep inclines, all the while caressing his ears, thereby moving his body forward to put weight on the forehand. The improvements were considerable, says L'Hotte. He was especially aware of this when, one day, they were riding in the countryside of Saint-Florent near Saumur, going down the side of a hill. Angevin's equilibrium had been re-established, his trot was regular. Above all, so was his well-being.

As d'Aure and L'Hotte approached the area that led to the school's stables, d'Aure and Angevin left L'Hotte and his horse to return home. L'Hotte was continuing on his way to the stables when he heard a commotion. Angevin, also wanting to return to the stables, had pressed himself against a wall, scraping the pavement with his hoof, refusing to turn around. L'Hotte turned back, without rushing, so as not to frighten Angevin. Meanwhile, d'Aure had succeeding in dominating Angevin and had extricated himself and the horse from the wall. D'Aure, very upset, said to L'Hotte: 'When I was thirty years old this would never have happened.'[27]

An analysis of some of the horses d'Aure had schooled and ridden at Saumur when he was *écuyer en chef* indicate some of the procedures and goals d'Aure pursued with respect to exterior riding.

As has been stated, d'Aure wanted the horse to go forward freely and positively, distribute his weight well on his legs in order to acquire an equilibrium and movement most propitious to him, regularize and develop his gaits, make him turn to the left and the right with ease, and regulate the uses of his strength so that he could move outdoors safely and easily. This, in summary, was d'Aure's method.

D'Aure was more concerned with a good distribution of the horse's weight than making him overly flexible. He was also concerned with making the horse go straight, that is, having the horse's haunches follow the line of the shoulders, and often said that many riders had difficulty doing this. This weakness became evident when, one evening, L'Hotte and d'Aure were attending a circus performance. During the performance of horse and rider, d'Aure pointed out to L'Hotte that the performer allowed his horse to be thrown out of line. This, he added, would have been immediately apparent had he been performing in a rectangular *manège*. In a circular area this fault was barely visible.

The kind of training d'Aure gave his horses was, of course, what was expected from an average, but sound, horseman who wants his horse to be serviceable, safe, and pleasant to ride. And, adds L'Hotte, for the horse to be long-lasting. This is good average training. But it does not prepare the rider for *haute école* where the use of the horse goes beyond the serviceable and the safe. Pleasant and safe to ride is, of course, always a constant. While the average horseman with a certain amount of skill can ride horses with average training, in general, only a horseman with special

---

[27] *Ibid.*, 200.

preparation and who has given his horse special schooling, can ride a *manège* horse.

Even when d'Aure schooled *manège* horses for *haute école*, while he expected greater obedience and submission, he never sought perfect lightness. D'Aure was fully aware that almost all the horses in the *Manège des Ecuyers* could never be compared with those he had ridden earlier at Versailles. L'Hotte is of a similar opinion.

While d'Aure was skilled at bringing out certain positive qualities in a horse, or eliminating certain flaws, he needed high quality horses such as Le Cerf, Maître de Dance, Tigris, Eylau, horses generous with their rider, to exploit and nurture these qualities.

D'Aure frequently criticized the *manège* horses, especially after they had participated in a long *reprise*. In his book *The Horse Industry in France*, which appeared in 1840, d'Aure says: 'Officers, luckily, will no longer have to come in contact with routinized and broken horses for the remainder of their careers.'[28] He is, of course, referring to horses trained the new way, his way.

L'Hotte then gives us an example of a horse, Néron, trained by d'Aure with his method, that is, stressing the proper or natural equilibrium rather than the overuse of suppling, but a horse who is, nonetheless, able to cope with the demands of a *reprise*.

Néron was a particularly special stallion whom d'Aure had schooled. His coat was grey, of average height, with a well set neck. His problems were as follows: he was heavy on the forehand and, consequently, weighed heavily on the rider's hand.

Another problem was that Néron was sensitive to the curb-chain. To spare Néron's barbs, often made sore and bloody by the curb-chain, d'Aure placed some of the bit's action on to the area above the nose by putting a tight noseband on the upper part of the curbs. He then provided the noseband with a little metal blade encased in leather which rested in the area above the nose. The ends of this noseband crossed under the hollow space within the lower jaw area, the right end ending in the left eye of the left curb, and *vice versa*. Thus the action of the noseband made itself felt as soon as the bit was tilted under the tension of the reins.[29] L'Hotte notes that Néron, despite the frequent bloody mouth he got, was still eager to leave the stall and be bridled.

Néron's resistances were considerable. His exceptional energy was compounded when he found himself behind other horses. D'Aure often made him appear at the head of the *reprises*. Eventually d'Aure succeeded in getting him to accept being at the end of a *reprise*.

L'Hotte then discusses one of the remarkable qualities of Néron. During the *reprises* Néron was the only horse who could canter and change leads without throwing himself out of line. Thus the rehabilitation of Néron lay more in the proper equilibrium of his mass rather than in his suppleness, thus preventing his mass from being thrown out of line when performing lead changes at the canter.

D'Aure usually ended a *reprise* with a few successive lead changes executed in the centre of the rectangle. While Néron did not perform these lead changes gloriously, he performed them well. Neither did he shine when he was to execute the passage.

While the artificial airs were usually forbidden at the *Ecole de Cavalerie* of Saumur, L'Hotte feels that d'Aure should have, in private, broached with greater vigour and interest the difficulties that some of these movements entail. For to excel in them would have given him greater authority when he had to proscribe them. As *écuyer en chef* he either had to follow the rules or submit his

---

[28] Ibid., 202.
[29] Could this be similar to a flash noseband, usually used to keep the bit stable in the horse's mouth as well as to keep the mouth closed?

resignation. Had he attempted on a personal basis to introduce some *manège* movements, it would have stopped critics from saying that he forbade them because he could not do them, rather, than out of principle.[30] That is why L'Hotte, when he was *écuyer en chef*, made considerable effort always to school one of his horses in *haute école*.

However, L'Hotte makes it very clear that d'Aure did revolutionize the equestrian world and succeeded in changing many of the old traditions by introducing exercises such as using obstacles of graduated difficulties for the steeple chase, or the rising trot. The schooling of young horses took on a more developed phase and became more practical and natural. Training in horse-racing began. As of 1850, the *Ecole de Cavalerie* began to participate in many of the town's events.

In the past, horses used for exterior riding were often mediocre mounts. D'Aure changed this by seeing to it that they were of the same quality as were the *manège* mounts.

In the past exterior riding consisted mainly of a simple hack. Now exterior riding became varied and accompanied by specific exercises. This was especially important when riders went out together and set out to trot. Since the fast trot was then fashionable, each rider went into a fast trot without any concern for the other person. Not only was this discourteous, but it was also dangerous and did little for the preservation of the horse.

D'Aure put an end to this individualism. By means of advice and special exercises, he reformed this aspect of equitation. He divided the riders into groups of four, making them ride abreast. If someone's horse moved faster, he had to moderate his pace, or if a rider fell behind, he had to quicken his horse's pace. The riders also had to leave the line, sometimes extending the gait of the horse, sometimes shortening it.

The riders sometimes competed with each other: who could walk the fastest, who could trot the fastest, who could canter the slowest. These contests did not last long so that the horses would not tire too much.

To show the difference between horses destined for exterior riding and *manège* riding, d'Aure had his pupils do *manège* work with horses used for outdoor riding. This made them aware of the kind of work that had to be accomplished in order to succeed in schooling a *manège* horse. They learned simple things at first, such as what it takes to make a horse go forward, to direct it by acting on both ends, how to use the rein of opposition to dominate and win over the haunches, what aids to use when turning a horse.

One of his first demands was to make the rider sit relatively deep in the saddle and chase the buttocks under him, but as far forward as possible. He wanted the rider to sit with ease so that the rider's suppleness could become united with the horse.

'Let yourself go like a sack of flour'[31] he always told those who exhibited stiffness. Stiffness in the saddle not only means a lack of solidity, but also brings about fatigue which is communicated to the horse. Suppleness in the rider, says L'Hotte, in agreement with d'Aure, is of the utmost importance. Not only can the rider be in harmony with his horse, he can determine the intensity of the horse's actions, coordinate these actions, and obtain harmony in the horse's movements.

In the following anecdote, l'Hotte relates how d'Aure, several years earlier, had circumvented stiffness in a rider.

About 1833 Louis-Philippe chose Laurent Franconi to give lessons in equitation to his two older sons, the *duc* d'Orléans and the *duc* de Nemours. Laurent Franconi was a circus *écuyer* of great renown and popularity, belonging to the famous Franconi family and with whom François Baucher was closely connected. At the time when L'Hotte was writing his *Souvenirs*, Victor Franconi,

---

[30] D'Aure defends himself from these accusations in the preface of his *Traité*, VI.   [31] *Souvenirs*, 208.

Laurent's son, was directing the circus of the Champs-Elysées.

Laurent was known for his severity with his pupils. But when it came to his newly acquired royal pupils, he reversed himself, for he was in constant fear that an accident could occur to his high-born pupils. As a result his pupils showed extreme timidity and stiffness, which hampered their progress.

The king, one day, wanted to be present at one of the lessons. A good horseman himself, he was immediately struck by what was happening. Most likely the presence of the king had aggravated the situation even further. He later mentioned the problem to the *comte* de Cambis who was in charge of the stables of the young *duc* d'Orléans and had accompanied the king to attend the session.

'If this goes on', said the king, 'while my sons are well built to ride, they will never be able to appear to their advantage in front of the troops. They must be placed in the hands of another teacher. But who?'[32]

The *comte* de Cambis did not have to ponder long. 'The *écuyer* who is the most able and who can give the princes the confidence they lack, is the *comte* d'Aure who taught many pages at Versailles. Since the doors of the *Manège* have closed, he has been keeping himself in the background and has ceased to have any relationship with the service of stables. If one made some advances to him, he may perhaps accept to giving lessons to the princes.'[33] And d'Aure, forewarned, accepted.

To eliminate quickly and without difficulty, the stiffness and lack of confidence of his new pupils, d'Aure had a path constructed in the park at Saint-Cloud, in which were placed here and there branches sufficiently low so that a rider would have to bend over the neck of the horse to avoid them.

When this was accomplished, he took the two princes with him for a ride. At first, to distract them, he told them a few anecdotes. As we know, d'Aure excelled in story-telling and he soon captured the interest of the princes. They then moved at a faster pace and reached the path that had been prepared for them. All the while d'Aure continued talking.

To avoid the branches, the riders had to bend, first on one side, then on the other. These repeated movements were done unconsciously by the princes who were also listening intently to the words of their teacher. In the process, much of their stiffness diminished. Much of their confidence mounted.

It was the *duc* de Nemours who, much later, insisted in placing d'Aure at the head of the *Manège de Saumur*. He had never forgotten what he owed his former teacher.

While L'Hotte has already discussed many of d'Aure's precepts, especially that of impulsion, it is in his final chapter on d'Aure, that L'Hotte discusses more fully his main precept, impulsion, which can be summarized as follows: 'Forward! Forward! Push the horse forward into the hand!'[34] For d'Aure it is the horse who must seek the hand, and not the hand the horse.

It is in this free forward movement that serves as a basis for the use and exploitation of the horse. To ask for a movement without first having provoked impulsion is like wanting to direct a boat without wind in the sail. Impulsion must remain constant and energetic, necessary to maintaining speed when changes in direction occur, which would then be difficult and ungainly as soon as impulsion begins to weaken. According to both L'Hotte and d'Aure, the cause for disobedience and defences on the part of a horse is when one does not obtain this free and forward movement. And for the rider to be always in control to provoke impulsion and maintain it, d'Aure wanted the rider to use spurs. However, he wanted the rider to use them sparingly; but, if the occasion necessitated their use, they should then be used

---

[32] *Ibid.*, 210.   [33] *Ibid.*, 210.   [34] *Ibid.*, 212.

vigorously and only to push the horse forward. 'Spurs', said d'Aure frequently, 'must make the horse go through fire.'[35]

D'Aure wanted the rider to give the horse a great deal of initiative. 'The rider', he said, 'always does too much. His demands often go against the goal he is pursuing.' Thus one can summarize another percept of his: 'The less one does, the better one does.'[36]

For example, Angevin was a horse who was not always easy to put to a walk. He was sometimes also obstinate at the trot. He was being especially obstinate one day when *lieutenant* Deshorties and d'Aure were riding side by side. For a while d'Aure left the poor man to his own devices in attempting to get Angevin to walk. His efforts were in vain. Finally d'Aure said to him: 'Now stop worrying about your horse and tell me about the ball you attended the other day in Angers?'[37]

Deshorties talked about the ball and when he finished he was astonished to find that the horse was actually walking. D'Aure explained that 'When I asked you about the ball I was sure that as soon as you began to think about the ball your aids would become inactive. You then allowed yourself to move freely with your horse which made it possible for you to get the results you wanted. Whereas all your earlier efforts went against the horse.'[38]

When d'Aure was teaching in Paris one of the horses he owned always became frightened whenever he saw an omnibus. So d'Aure had one of his pupils get on this horse. He made a point of not telling the pupil the name of the horse. Neither did he mention the horse's fears. Actually, this pupil was not one of his best pupils. He used him only because he was corpulent and easy-going.

D'Aure and his pupil proceeded to the Bois de Boulogne. In the process the horse crossed one omnibus after another but expressed neither preoccupation with nor fear of them.

'Even with me', d'Aure pointed out to L'Hotte, 'this horse exhibited uneasiness at the approach of the huge buses. Why? Because whenever one approached us, I instinctively used my aids more protectively which the horse immediately felt. But throughout our ride through the streets of Paris, he felt only the total abandon of this rather heavy and unskilled rider. Upon our return, after dismounting, I told him which horse he had just ridden. He became white as a sheet, for he knew the horse from hearsay.'[39]

L'Hotte gives another anecdote to illustrate the idea of by doing less one does more.

A Lieutenant-instructor was riding his horse in the *Manège des écuyers* when d'Aure arrived unexpectedly. He observed the lieutenant for a while, noticing that he was having problems. The officer came to d'Aure and said to him: 'My commandant, what must I do to get my horse to distribute his weight correctly and make him walk straight? I cannot do so.'[40]

D'Aure called out to Père Le Camus, an old and worthy servant. 'Bring us a feedbag of oats and give it to the horse and make him walk. But first remove the bridle.' The horse stuck his head in the bag and walked. 'There', said d'Aure to the officer, 'your horse is now walking straight.'[40]

The story about how the *écuyer en chef* had made a horse go straight soon circulated among the other officers. It served as a lesson to the lieutenant-instructors who would later, as Captain-instructors, school young horses in the regiments, aided by riders who had very little experience or talent. D'Aure hoped that this would serve as an example and convince others that by doing too much they can often prevent a horse from being straight and balanced. By doing less the horse could regain balance and straightness of his own accord, resulting in freer and regularized gaits.

---

[35] *Ibid.*, 213. [36] *Ibid.*, 213–14. [37] *Ibid.*, 214. [38] *Ibid.*, 214. [39] *Ibid.*, 214–15. [40] *Ibid.*, 215.

D'Aure rejected force on principle; rather, he wanted the rider to place the horse in the proper position and allow him to execute the movement on his own.

L'Hotte had a similar experience when he was trying to execute lead changes on a young inexperienced horse. 'You are using ten times too much force', d'Aure told L'Hotte. 'Simply place your horse in the proper position for lead changes and let him do them on his own instead of forcing him. You will succeed the moment you limit your actions when the haunches straighten out. You don't have to go beyond that. The straight position of the haunches will imperceptibly make your horse change leads on his own.'[41]

That, says L'Hotte, is precisely what happened. 'Think of the movement you want to execute and you will find it being accomplished of its own accord.' Instinctive actions on the part of horse and rider were frequently part of d'Aure's methods. L'Hotte found this suggestion to be true. With the thought of turning to the right, the rider automatically looks in that direction and the body makes the appropriate and imperceptible movement to the right. L'Hotte then considers the importance of the direction of a rider's look and the bearing it has on the body. He finds that it is also true that if one wants a rider to sit straight in the saddle, he must look straight ahead. But should the left side refuse to straighten out, he must look to the right to do so.

L'Hotte explains how even in daily encounters the body instinctively follows the direction of the eyes' glance. You wish to avoid bumping into someone, but if you look at the person you wish to avoid, you will, indeed, bump into him, or at least move in that person's direction. And if that person hesitates in trying to avoid you, you will actually follow that person's very hesitations. As soon as you stop looking at this person, you will avoid bumping into him. For that very reason if a rider has to pass through a narrow passage, he must look at the centre and not at the edges of the passage. Likewise, an acrobat fixes his eyes on a point in the direction of the taut rope in order not to lose his balance.

D'Aure knew horses intimately and made a point of examining the horse carefully before mounting so that he could determine the kind of action to expect on the basis of conformation, what could be demanded of him, what concessions one could and should make. He constantly reminded his officers on the importance of doing so. 'Know your horse', he told them, 'so that you can ride him better; ride him so you can know him better.'[42]

L'Hotte remembers what d'Aure used to say about the conformation of a horse. 'He must be built like a wheel-barrow and a grasshopper.'[43] That is, adds l'Hotte, he must become thinner going from the hind-quarters to the chest. There must also be a great distance between the point of the hip to the hock. Whosoever knows horses, knows how important it is to have a horse with a sound conformation.

According to d'Aure, the ideal age of the horse destined to serve on a regular basis is seven to eight years of age. At that age one can ask of a horse all that he is capable of giving. He has acquired the maximum of extension and support of which he is capable. At this age he has also become attentive, wise, and his disposition has now been formed and become assured. If he had the good fortune of experiencing good hands, he can function on his own. The rider has now discovered that he is more comfortable in the saddle because it has now found its place on the horse's back, for the back has now lost its youthful roundness, often uncomfortable for the rider.

D'Aure was in favour of using horses who

---

[41] Ibid., 216. [42] Ibid., 218. [43] Ibid., 218.

have preserved their strength[44] for harnessing. Harnessing is also beneficial to young horses, for it disposes them to carry their weight on their shoulders; furthermore, it pushes them forward and preserves their hocks.

D'Aure's knowledge of horses was challenged when he was the *écuyer* and inspector of stables of the emperor, Napoleon III during the Second Empire. At that time, L'Hotte was squadron chief at Saint-Cyr and had the opportunity of frequently visiting d'Aure.

The occasion was as follows. The Empress Eugènie, after visiting the Duke of Hamilton in Scotland, wanted to send her host a thank you present. The Duke of Hamilton was known to be a great amateur of horses. But he did not have in his stables any Percherons. It was decided to send the Duke four Percherons. Naturally, the very best were to be sent. *Général* Fleury, who served as *grand écuyer* to the Emperor, informed d'Aure (who was in charge of the Emperor's post-horses and riding horses) of this wish.

D'Aure immediately sent off Lendormy, a man of considerable experience, to poke around Le Perche, Normandy, in search of good horses. The four Percherons were found, examined, and accepted by d'Aure. Fleury was informed and it was at Saint-Cloud that he saw the four Percherons as they were being worked on the lunge.

But *général* Fleury was not impressed. What he wanted were, as he put it, those beautiful horses who pull omnibuses. D'Aure tried to convince him that the Percherons were superior to the ones he was referring to.[45] To prove the superiority of the Percherons, d'Aure asked the *Compagnie de l'Ouest* known to have the most beautiful omnibus horses, to send two of their best. The end result proved d'Aure to be correct.

Fleury's error lay in the fact that he remembered the omnibus horses of Paris adorned with their beautiful harness decked with brilliant copper and moving under the hand and whip of skilled drivers who brought out the best in them. Since they were stallions they were also animated by the other horses passing near them. But these very horses, seen away from their usual milieu and on the lunge, appeared to be inferior. Thus it is true that things are better and more beautiful in their place of origin and the milieu that is appropriate. As d'Aure said: 'Work hard and you will find.'[46]

D'Aure's tenets were often simple and to the point. Like his precepts, he made them known to everyone. He had no secrets. He was open. He was never furtive when he rode, trying to hide some of his secret aids or movements. His goals were achievable and the means used were not complicated. His methods did not always require great talent.

For example, d'Aure suggested the following simple tips: when getting on a horse one does not know and could present problems, make a knot in the snaffle reins to which one could have recourse without much difficulty should the need arise. Place yourself in the saddle quietly and with ease so as not to risk stiffening the horse and arousing possible susceptibilities.

Should the horse ignore the leg aids and refuse to go forward, do not insist. Click your tongue instead. Or use your weight to make him go forward by leaning lightly forward and lengthening his neck. You do the latter by either swaying the neck lightly back and forth between the reins, which makes the horse move or sawing lightly on the snaffle. To deviate the haunches should they not react through leg pressure, immediately use the rein of opposition. To calm a horse who is too active or whose movements are too disordered on the way

---

[44] Presumably he is referring to older horses who have preserved their strength.
[45] Presumably the *Boulonnais* who, with the *Percherons*, pulled omnibuses in Paris in those days.
[46] *Souvenirs*, 220.

back to the stables, do the following: begin your hack at a walk, go into an open and coordinated trot, use a by-path which leads back to the stables. Make sure that the whole course is sufficiently long to tire somewhat the horse. As you near the stables go into a walk, first as you come close to the stables, then farther and farther away from them. This technique, says L'Hotte, worked very well with Soleil, a cross-country horse known for his impatient behaviour as he neared the stables.

To make a half-turn at the canter, recommends d'Aure, with a horse who is not easy to manage, come almost to a halt at the half-turn and then proceed. This movement is easier and faster to execute than if one moved without interrupting the canter.

To make a horse who is trotting go into a walk, reassure the one who frightens easily, and calm the one who is irritable or too impressionable. Above all, the rider must not tighten his aids and restrict the horse; rather, he must use them as gently as possible and let himself go with a certain abandon. The use of voice and caresses is also important, but one must not insist in using them if no result is forthcoming or too late in coming.

To re-establish the equilibrium of the horse and to regularize his gaits if his weight is too heavy on the haunches, d'Aure recommended riding him down inclines, all the while caressing the horse's ears which makes the rider bend his body slightly forward, bringing his weight closer to the horse's shoulders. And, finally, to make a horse's trot become regular, quick changes of direction are useful.

All these useful hints, says L'Hotte, can be easily used by the average rider.

But, says L'Hotte, really to appreciate d'Aure's equestrian precepts in their totality, one should read his *Cours d'Equitation*.[47] Reading this work, says L'Hotte, while there are certain imperfections in it, one is, nonetheless, struck by the tremendous equestrian feeling and correctness of ideas that it contains, especially by the atmosphere it reveals. It is also important for the sound advice expressed with respect to the regular use of the horse and riding (those 'hints' mentioned earlier).

The *Cours*, says L'Hotte, is not a scientific work; neither is it a methodological work. Rather, it bears the imprint of a man's enormous experience in the field of equitation and an exposition of what is necessary in modern equitation. It addresses itself primarily to a rider's sensibility, for in it one finds those images that are typical of the master's thought. One finds also examples of equestrian perspicacity, at times, even inspiration. And the great practitioners of equitation have been blessed with a great deal of perspicacity and inspiration.

L'Hotte remembers how in 1867, when he was *écuyer en chef* at Saumur, d'Aure's editor, Le Neneu, asked him to write a treatise on equitation. L'Hotte has often said that only a man's constant and consistent observation, reflection, long and reasoned-out practical work, and experience joined by study, were necessary before an *écuyer* could write about an art with any certitude and authority.

All of L'Hotte's contemporaries were unanimous in recognizing in d'Aure a most privileged and talented horseman, a horseman of the highest equestrian aptitude. Unfortunately, says L'Hotte, his outbursts and pranks, his little flights of fancy, caused some horsemen to challenge his abilities as a teacher.

L'Hotte makes it quite clear that he does not share these negative opinions. Rather, he has only praise and respect for him. After all, almost all great equestrian practitioners had weaknesses. But they have acquired a lasting place in the history of French equitation.

---

[47] L'Hotte prefers the *Cours d'équitation* to his *Traité d'équitation* and which Baucher ridicules. See Nelson, François Baucher. D'Aure's *Cours* and the *Ordonnances* of 1826 were combined and used at the *Ecole de cavalerie*.

L'Hotte's gratitude to d'Aure is enormous when he thinks how much he has learned from this great master. D'Aure was the most admired and the first horseman of his age. He was the creator and head of a school that wanted to combine the traditions of the past with the demands of the new age. L'Hotte is not stinting with praise when he says that d'Aure will leave a legacy that is deeply embedded in the equestrian art, and that the annals of French equitation will register a name that is brilliant.

Equal to L'Hotte's unstinting praise of d'Aure as a professional horseman, we also see how deep and sincere was his personal attachment and friendship for d'Aure.

5
Baucher and d'Aure – a comparison

After discussing and analysing, in separate and alternate chapters, his two teachers, Baucher and d'Aure, L'Hotte devotes an interesting chapter to specific comparisons between the two men as riders and writers. While he has already accomplished this in his earlier chapters, here he summarizes their accomplishments and differences.

It is interesting to note that at the end of the chapter on d'Aure, L'Hotte becomes aware of, and apologizes for, the fact that he had perhaps devoted more time and space to d'Aure than to Baucher.

That he spent more time on d'Aure's equestrian origins, the positions he held in the equestrian world, his numerous anecdotes, often cited to illustrate a point in his character or one of his precepts, becomes obvious as one reads his *Souvenirs*. To remedy this lacuna, L'Hotte now devotes an additional chapter to Baucher, wherein he discusses Baucher's origins, his equestrian background, his books, his work at the circus, the controversy between Baucher and d'Aure, his accident, and his last years spent in seclusion, some of which have already been alluded to.

Although of different backgrounds and although following different paths, the two men dominated the equestrian world towards the middle of the nineteenth century. Each one in his own way contributed to a rebirth in the field of equitation.

Horsemen of different backgrounds and laymen, circus-goers, artists, and writers were quick to side either with one or the other, often expressing more fanaticism in their support of the two horsemen than did the two men they followed. A great deal was written, for or against them, in the newspapers and magazines of the day. Pamphlets abounded.[1] Indeed, all this interest and activity in equitation gave new life to a field that had begun to founder. The circus was now frequented by all social classes who rented loges much as they did at the opera and the theatre.

Unfortunately, the two men became rivals and their followers so vociferous, that it became impossible to bring the two together. This should and could have been possible, says L'Hotte, for the two men were not involved in the same kind of equitation. L'Hotte had hoped to serve as intermediary and had tried to do so, but things had gone too far for the two men to make any concessions and agree to seeing each other.

They did, however, meet on one occasion and Maxime Gaussen was a witness to this meeting. The story of their meeting is told by Maxime Gaussen in *La Revue des Haras*, March 1878. It is also retold by the *baron* de

---

[1] *Général* Jacques-Léonard Thomas (Clément-Thomas), wrote *De l'Equitation militaire de l'ancienne et de la nouvelle école*, published in 1846. In this pamphlet he defends François Baucher. See Nelson, *François Baucher*.

Vaux in *Equitation ancienne et moderne*, Paris, 1888.[2]

Maxime Gaussen, an *écuyer* and teacher of equitation of renown, met d'Aure one day at Tortoni's. Upon the invitation of d'Aure, Gaussen sat down at d'Aure's table. After a few exchanges of politeness, they began to talk about their passion: the equestrian world. D'Aure knew that Gaussen was one of Baucher's excellent pupils and began to talk about Baucher in a most laudatory manner. He admitted that they had never met.

My dear and illustrious *maître*, you just don't know *monsieur* Baucher. He does not obtain results by simply choosing the right subjects, which is what you seem to believe, having been told that . . . He possesses a method which is ingenious, new kinds of movements that are very powerful and which permit him to obtain extraordinary things. It is regrettable that you have not had the opportunity of seeing him and talking to him; you would have a different opinion of him.

Gaussen then added that he would find the opportunity to get the two together. 'Baucher is at the moment looking for a fairly refined horse, not too expensive, to make it into a circus horse. Do you think you have something like that you could propose to him?'

D'Aure said that he happened to have such a horse. Gaussen then suggested that the two meet the following afternoon in the *manège* Rue Duphot.

As already noted, Baucher was an extremely proud man, as well as a very sensitive man. And when Gaussen approached him, he did not want to appear too eager to meet the *comte* d'Aure, the man with the illustrious reputation, who was leading the challenge against his *nouvelle méthode*. On the other hand, this may give him the opportunity to explain his precepts to him. Thus the meeting was on. Baucher and Gaussen arrived at the *manège* in the Rue Duphot at the appointed time.

A few minutes after their arrival, a groom opened the heavy door to the *manège* and d'Aure appeared. Baucher made a few steps towards him and the two rivals shook hands, each one giving the other an appraising and curious look. Each one told the other that they had heard too much about the other not to want finally to meet.

D'Aure said to Baucher: 'I understand that you are looking for a horse to use as a *manège* horse. I have here a nice little mare you can have for a reasonable price. She may be just the right horse for you.'

When Baucher replied that he would, indeed, like to see the horse, d'Aure asked his groom that she be bridled and brought to them.

A pretty little bay mare appeared and d'Aure remarked on her elegant conformation.

She was then put to a walk, then a trot by the groom and d'Aure asked Baucher if he wanted to ride her. 'The creature has not been properly schooled but she is quite meek', said d'Aure.

'No, no', said Baucher, 'I am not properly dressed to ride her.'

D'Aure then stated that he had not ridden for a few days due to this, and he pointed to his groin, presumably alluding to his hernias. But each man kept on insisting that the other should ride the little mare. Then d'Aure asked the groom to saddle the mare and return her to them.

When the mare returned to the *manège*, one glance at her and it became obvious to Baucher that she was far from pleased at having had a saddle placed on her. The vigorous swishing of her tail attested to her displeasure and indicated that she was a difficult and irritable creature. D'Aure then asked for his crop. D'Aure asked Baucher once more whether he wanted to ride her. Once again Baucher refused. Then d'Aure

---

[2] The description and conversation have been taken from (and rewritten) the *baron* de Vaux, *Ecuyers and écuyères*, Paris, J. Rothschild, 1893, 359–64. Also presented in Vaux's *Hommes de cheval*, 181–90.

got into the saddle with his usual ease. Horse and rider went around the *manège* several times, reins loose, first at a fast walk, then at a trot. D'Aure's posture lived up to expectations. However, an experienced and perceptive eye could tell that leg and hand aids, although well dissimulated, were operating quite vigorously.

Then, changing direction, d'Aure and the mare went around again. It became more and more obvious that the poor creature had had no training whatsoever. D'Aure then struck off at the canter. After a turn around the *manège* at this gait, he made the horse execute a lead change. D'Aure then surprised the mare when they reached the opposite side of the *manège* by a vigorous opposition of hand and leg, most likely aided by contact with the right spur, forcing her to execute a very brusque flying lead change.

The swishing of the mare's tail continued. Quite obviously she found it difficult to submit to this kind of treatment. Furthermore, the lead change just executed had been poorly performed, shoulders and haunches far from being straight. The rider then attempted another lead change, achieved with even greater difficulty.

The 'brilliant horseman of Versailles' should have stopped at this moment and dismounted. But his confidence was not disturbed, all the more since he was performing in front of a serious judge, and his rival to boot. He probably also hoped that he would be able to execute a decent lead change. So he tried a third time near the *manège* door which had not been properly closed. Here the mare fell back on her four legs as though to regain the strength that was gradually dissipating and, like lightning, reared. She then pushed the door open and, with great authority, disappeared with her rider into the adjoining cobbled courtyard.

Baucher stood quietly near one of the pillars of the *manège*, waiting for the dénouement of this scene.

A few minutes later, the door opened wide this time to let the mare and her rider enter – in leaps and bounds. D'Aure's seat and posture were still irreproachable. But he was furious and his menacing voice could be heard saying: 'Has one ever seen anything like this? What a creep! It's the first time she's done this.' A slight smile of incredulity appeared on Baucher's face which, heretofore, had been impassive.

Thus d'Aure, his back braced, his legs light on the horse's flanks, struck off at a fast canter, executed a rein change, then a lead change at the end of the *manège*. This time the lead change was executed at a more or less fast gait. The power of the rider, his stamina and his skill were able to triumph over the mare who was fast beginning to sweat and whose swishing tail became more and more forceful.

Once again they came to the door of the *manège* at the moment when d'Aure asked for a lead change. At this point the mare began to slow down and, despite receiving a rather forceful attack of the spurs, she halted then and there. Once again she began to rear, fell back on all four feet, then rose again and walked on her hind legs for four or five metres, raising herself like an I. She then leaned her front legs against the door (which had been improperly closed once again) and pushed it open. Horse and rider were once more in the courtyard.

A struggle ensued between man and beast. One could hear the noise of her shoes as they scratched on the cobblestones, mingling with the angry voice of d'Aure. The mare then came to a halt and refused to go either forwards or backwards. She then reared again then went forward in violent leaps and bounds.

D'Aure, still master of the situation, did not budge from his initial posture. He seemed one with the horse. Finally, he managed to make her go forward. Once again they entered the *manège* with the same leaps and bounds, the mare, ears flattened, eyes haggard, her coat wet and shiny. She seemed to be totally immersed in a powerless fury. But d'Aure made her execute a rein change and a lead change on the spot where she had expressed her earlier defences. This time the movements were well executed but with violence. The poor creature was no longer able to defend herself. Finally she executed a quarter of a volte to arrive in front of Baucher to whom d'Aure said: 'I assure you this is the first time that she has acted like this.'

Baucher replied coldly: 'Since this is the first time that she defends herself, she doesn't do it badly. One would think that she is used to it. But she is too difficult for me. And since I am looking for a horse with a good disposition, she does not suit me.'

D'Aure dismounted with his usual ease. The two men exchanged polite words, shook hands in the most ceremonious manner, and these two remarkable men separated never to see each other again.

Later, whenever someone mentioned the director of the *manège* of the Rue Duphot, Baucher always said: 'That man is a real butcher; moreover, he is a slick horsetrader. I thought him to be quite different.'

Both men passionately loved the equestrian art. Both, as L'Hotte tells us, were outstanding in their own way. L'Hotte was one of the few men who, as pupil and horseman, had witnessed their riding abilities and the way they could handle and dominate horses. It is to his credit that he was able to serve as an impartial recorder dealing with the lives and passions of these two men with great understanding and sympathy.

That he seems to have spent more leisure time riding with d'Aure, conversing with him, listening to his many stories, not solely as pupil and teacher, but also as friend, is understandable. L'Hotte's contact with Baucher was principally in the *manège*, for Baucher seldom, if ever, left the *manège* to go riding cross-country. Furthermore, d'Aure and L'Hotte had similar backgrounds. Both were Saint-Cyriens. They belonged to the same social milieu, they spoke the same language.

D'Aure was a flamboyant rider and his background, his contacts, contributed to further a brilliant career. And yet, at certain moments, when his successive *manèges* failed, he seemed to despair of himself and his abilities and even wished to leave France to seek fame and fortune elsewhere.

Baucher's origins were modest. He grew up in Versailles where his father was a wine merchant. His background in equitation is rather obscure. We know that as a child he used to observe and admire d'Abzac on the parade grounds. At thirteen his uncle, who provided mounts and personnel for the stables of Prince Borghese, who had married Napoleon's sister, Pauline, took him to Milan where he became involved with horses and riding. He also tells us that he used to watch men like Mazuchelli train horses. It is obvious that he acquired much knowledge about equitation to be able, later on, when he returned to France after the downfall of the First Empire, to serve in various capacities in the stables of noblemen. While the career of d'Aure was effortless, Baucher 'in order to make himself known to the equestrian world, for his genius and talent to be revealed, was forced to give his all.'[3] He also had to work relentlessly in the circus, 'showing himself for two *sous*', as he put it. And while the two men were rivals, L'Hotte says that he heard each one praise the other – with reservations. D'Aure admired Baucher for being able to exploit horses who were to function in a restricted space. Baucher said of d'Aure: 'He is a centaur, and nature has showered him with gifts. Had he accepted my principles he would have surpassed me in their execution.'[4]

But often, each one spoke of the other in derogatory terms. D'Aure spoke of Baucher with a certain amount of disdain. Baucher claimed that d'Aure was a butcher of horses.

---

[3] *Souvenirs*, 249–50.   [4] Ibid., 250.

L'Hotte claims that Baucher talked more willingly about d'Aure than the other way around and felt that the animosity that existed between them sprang from the exaggerations and passionate words of their disciples and pupils. Except for the meeting related earlier, they made a point of keeping away from each other.

While L'Hotte has throughout the pages of his *Souvenirs* analysed the precepts of his two teachers, in this final chapter he presents them once more in summary. Once again does he set down the advantages and disadvantages of the kind of equitation they practised and taught and how these precepts affect horse and rider.

D'Aure's type of equitation is simple, practical, and easily transmitted to the horseman with average skill. Yet, its goals are limited. It is a matter of getting the horse to go forward, freely and positively, by the simple pressure of the rider's legs. If the horse leans somewhat on the rider's hand that is in accordance with its purpose and function. This works well, says L'Hotte, if all one wants is for the horse to move forward. But, if a rider wishes to control the strength of the horse and play with this strength at will, it is Baucher who succeeds in this.

Baucher wanted the total possession of the horse. To achieve this, the horse must be placed behind the rider's hand, but at the same time, he must flow in front of the rider's legs. It is only when the horse is contained between legs and hand, that the rider becomes complete master of the horse, for now no force can escape him and the rider can deal with all the difficulties that Classical or *savante* equitation entails.

Yet, to accomplish this, the rider using Baucher's method must be skilful or else he will affect the horse's impulsion, make him uncertain, and have him function behind the legs of the rider. This will handicap the horse in his chief function: to move forward.

But, to repeat, the rider must be skilful. And if he manages to overcome the problem of having the horse behind the legs and lacking impulsion, but, rather, succeeds in achieving Baucher's goal, he will find this type of equitation pleasant and rewarding. He will equally satisfy the demands made by d'Aure's type of equitation. Whereas d'Aure's more limited type of equitation cannot solely be used if the goal is Classical or *savante* equitation. Much more is necessary.

Comparing the two types of equitation, L'Hotte says:

'Baucher is opting for what one can call the poetry of equitation. It is towards that kind of equitation that Baucher directed the aspirations of horsemen who sought to learn at his school. But not everyone can go to Corinth. D'Aure's only ambition was to make good prose writers (that is, riders) out of his pupils.'[5]

Thus a horseman must decide in advance which kind of equitation he wants, pleasure riding or cross country or *manège*. Once decided, he must follow the principles of either d'Aure or Baucher.

Whereas with cross-country riding, submission of the horse's strength is limited, with *manège* riding total possession of the horse's strength is required which finds its main characteristic in perfect lightness.

While lightness is also a trait in d'Aure's type of equitation, it is neither perfect nor complete lightness, for to be so would make it incompatible with the prolonged exercises that involve outdoor equitation and the constant attention of putting the horse freely forward.

L'Hotte states that when he adds up all the horses he had ridden and trained, it is mostly in the idiom of d'Aure's riding, and that the horses that had been confided to him had only to satisfy the equitation taught in military schools at the time. Using d'Aure's method was especially true when he was with

---

[5] *Ibid.*, 246.

the First Cuirassiers as Captain-instructor for seven years, a period in his career when he rode daily the greatest number of horses.

The young horses and the horses belonging to officers which he schooled or mostly reschooled, had many faults such as lack of obedience to the aids, lack of regularity or extension of gaits, etc. which made them unacceptable as military horses.

L'Hotte had to make these horses move forward, freely and positively, carry their weight on their shoulders, and alter whatever irregularities they had acquired through too severe hands. Or, conversely, he had to put the weight on their haunches when some horses fell heavily on the forehand or abused contact.

To accomplish this L'Hotte needed only the equitation of d'Aure. The same held true when he had to school (dresser) horses for military use at the *Ecole de Cavalerie* of Saumur.

But when L'Hotte schooled his *manège* horses, it was to Baucher's method that he had recourse. And the *manège* horses that L'Hotte used, that is, his personal horses, were able to do the artificial gaits and movements in the *manège*.

While he schooled these horses with the gaits and movements based on the precepts of Baucher, these very horses were also schooled following the precepts of d'Aure. They could also function well outdoors. None of L'Hotte's horses was limited. Thus, like d'Aure, he, too, wanted his horse to be a *manège* horse, as well as a cross-country and military horse.

L'Hotte quotes a friend, a Captain Paul de Courtivron, a remarkable horseman who, after having ridden L'Hotte's horse, Zégris, said to L'Hotte: 'He flows under the action of one's legs like a cherry kernel which slips away under the pressure of one's fingers; and the mobility of his jaw communicates to the hand a feeling of softness which makes one think how it would be were one to dip one's hand in beaten egg whites.'[6]

L'Hotte makes an interesting comparison between the great masters by giving the key word or phrase which characterized the basis of each one's precept:[7]

D'Aure: 'En avant' ('Forward')
Baucher: 'Poussez' ('Push')
D'Abzac: 'Assis' ('Seated')
Rousselet: 'De l'aplomb' ('Straight and proper distribution of the equilibrium')
L'Hotte: 'En avant, calme et droit' ('Forward, calm, and straight')

'Assis' summarized the ideal seat at Versailles, that is, deep in the saddle, legs abandoned, for a good seat led to good posture.

'De l'aplomb' meant a good deep seat; but it also implied that a horse be straight and that his equilibrium be well distributed. Rousselet had been trained at Versailles.

'En avant', with d'Aure, meant, of course, the free and positive forward movement of the horse, that is, impulsion.

'Poussez' also meant impulsion, but impulsion with Baucher was not a free and forward movement desired immediately. The rider had first to control the horse's strength and obtain his complete submission. Thus with the horse contained between legs and hand, it was often difficult always to attain impulsion. Thus to push with the legs was necessary.

When one analyses these key words or phrases as they represent the underlying tenets of each *écuyer*, one realizes that, in the final analysis, they are not very far apart.

L'Hotte says frequently that horsemen, past and present, arrived and arrive at certain principles by means of empirical data and discoveries. But since men and horses have not changed much psychologically and physically, and men are imbued with a certain amount of logic and a sense of observation, they have often reached similar conclusions. Their experiences, descriptions, anecdotes, vocabulary, the order of methods and

---

[6] *Ibid.*, 248.   [7] *Ibid.*, 249.

precepts, different amounts or doses of certain exercises and their presentation, may differ, but that is all. Indeed, some books on equitation are written better than others, some have more humour, more drama, but basically they have the same objective and use similar methods.

L'Hotte points out the similarity of certain precepts or methods when in *Questions équestres* he discusses the position and use of the rider's heels when turning a horse, adding that his analysis is nothing new, that Frederico Grisone had already described the action of each heel when going into a turn. Only the language, that of the sixteenth century, differed.[8]

D'Aure, in the preface to his *Traité d'équitation* says that it would be futile to write another manual. 'Too many people have written ably on diverse problems so that there was little chance for me to do any better.' He then points out that he wrote his book only to present 'the teachings of the *Ecole de Versailles* at a period of transition and to strip equitation of charlatanism and certain superfluities which merely served to preserve useless difficulties in the understanding of an art which should be simplified so that it can serve all social classes and be of a general usefulness.'[9]

And Decarpentry in *Baucher et son école* says: 'Since 340 BC when Xenophon wrote the first treaty on equitation that has come down to us, until 1842 when Baucher published his *nouvelle méthode*, horsemen of all countries have used procedures to teach and guide their horses that are more or less identical.[10]

---

[8] Grisone in *Questions équestres*, p. 70.   [9] D'Aure, *Traité*, V.   [10] Decarpentry, *Baucher et son école*, 5.

6
L'Hotte's spiritual teacher: Rousselet

I have included *commandant* Rousselet because L'Hotte himself gives him considerable space in his *Souvenirs* and places him directly after Baucher and d'Aure 'as a most remarkable and renowned *écuyer* at Saumur'.[1] While L'Hotte was never Rousselet's official pupil at Saumur, he, nonetheless, spent considerable time observing him riding and teaching. L'Hotte claims that when he was at Saumur the first time, he had learned more observing and riding and practising on his own than when he was receiving actual instruction.

L'Hotte discussed Rousselet briefly at the outset of his *Souvenirs* in order to place him in relief against Delherm de Novital. Towards the end of his work he takes up Rousselet once again and gives a fuller and more detailed picture of the *écuyer*. 'For the moment', says L'Hotte, 'I want to talk about *commandant* Rousselet only because I want to place him in the context of the *écuyer en chef* and thereby point out the difficulties that de Novital's character presented.'[2]

L'Hotte acquired a great deal of information about Rousselet, his beginnings, his life, personal and professional, his precepts, because he was lucky to be able to see and use the copious notes that fell into his hands after the death of Rousselet. Some of these notes deal with the *écuyer's* early life and riding. L'Hotte quotes from them at considerable length:

In Sallagousse (Eastern Pyrénées) where I was born and where my father was a sergeant of the mounted constabulary, one of our neighbours had a little donkey. He was my first mount. I was very young at the time and either a servant or my aunt alternated in supervising me.

After a few months of practice, I was able to lead my mount passably at the walk and the racking gait [amble].

At the age of five I went to school. But Thursdays, Sundays, and holidays, I attempted all sorts of things on my mount, different positions, turning to the right, to the opposite direction, sideways. I ended up teaching the donkey to canter.

One Sunday, in a field surrounded by a ditch, I saw a horse grazing. I asked the boy who was holding him by a rope to let me ride him for the two *sous* I received on Sundays. He helped me up on the horse. I forgot the little donkey. The horse barely made a step a minute. While I was on the horse I forgot that it was time for dinner. I got soundly scolded when I returned home.

Every Sunday I sought Pierron (little Pierre). When the horse was in the ditch, I could easily get on him, but in the field I had to wait until he lowered his neck. Then I got on him at the far end of his neck and, as he raised his head, I was able to reach his back where I remained seated for hours on end.[3]

The Rousselet family then moved to a little town in the heart of Roussillon. This time Rousselet rode a mule. At fifteen he went to Avignon to enrol as a volunteer in the 22nd Light Cavalry. He now began to take lessons

---

[1] *Souvenirs*, 296–7. [2] Ibid., 48. [3] Ibid., 346–7.

in equitation. One day he noticed that the horse his comrade was riding refused to obey him and asked himself why it was that a horse sometimes refuses to obey. From that day on he would ask himself these kinds of questions.

Rousselet then moved up the ranks and joined the army in 1899 as a volunteer in a cavalry regiment while Napoleon was still First Consul. Like so many officers of the period he served in the cavalry of the First Empire of Napoleon I. He was awarded the *Légion d'Honneur*, made a *Chevalier de Saint-Louis*. He also received several red badges of courage for the wounds he had received while serving in the *grande armée*. He retired from a military career in 1814 after the collapse of the First Empire.

In 1815 began his career as a civilian *écuyer* and his appointment as *sous écuyer* at the *Ecole d'Instruction des Troupes à cheval* which had its seat in Saumur for a while. Rousselet also served as *sous écuyer* in the *manège* of the *Ecole spéciale militaire* of Saint-Cyr. When the *manège* at Saint-Cyr closed its doors, he returned to Versailles in 1824. The *Ecole de Cavalerie* at Saumur, which had shut down temporarily after the Bonapartist conspiracy, was re-organized under *général* Oudinot. Rousselet returned to Saumur as *sous écuyer*. It was only in 1832 that he was nominated *écuyer en chef*.

During his sojourn in Saumur he was referred to as *monsieur* Rousselet despite his outstanding military career in the *grande armée*. D'Aure, likewise, had retired from a promising military career in order to become part of the *Manège de Versailles*.

Rousselet belonged to that race of *écuyers* who have almost vanished, says L'Hotte. He was very wise, very patient. He was an outstanding horseman and, unlike Novital, he was always polite, soft-spoken, well-wishing, and gentle with pupils and horses alike. Usually reserved and gentle, he reacted with anger when he once saw Novital produce lacerations on the flanks of his horse with his spurs. 'It is wrong to behave like this. All he has done is change the colour of the horse. From bay-brown this unfortunate creature has become white and red. I was not aware that such a thing could happen.'[4] Rousselet and Novital, so different in character, frequently confronted each other when it came to the training and treatment of their horses.

Rousselet had received his training from the *marquis* Ducros de Chabannes, author of *Traité élémentaire d'Equitation* and *Cours élémentaire et analytique d'equitation* and pupil of d'Auvergne, founder of French military equitation, and himself a pupil at and later *commandant* of the *Ecole Militaire* in Paris.

Rousselet used his stirrups long, hardly placing his feet in the irons, the typical posture of the *écuyers* of the *Manège de Versailles*. His seat was somewhat unacademic due to the wounds he had received in the eleven campaigns in which he had participated, including one in Russia. While he was a representative of the traditions of the past, his riding style was both *manège* riding as well as cross-country.

While Rousselet never published anything, his copious notes, which fell into L'Hotte's hands after his death, express the principles he used in schooling horses and training pupils. These notes reveal a certain structure and indicate that their purpose was to serve Rousselet as a guide for the instruction of his pupils, horse and man.

His distinction was to give his horse great freedom, hardly using hand or leg aids. It seemed, says L'Hotte, that he had neither hands nor legs. And while held in obedience, the horse did not have the impression that he was being constrained or subjected to a bit. By limiting his demands, Rousselet knew how to give his horse the full play of his

---

[4] Jacques Perrier, *L' Epopée du Cadre Noir de Saumur*, Directed by *général* Pierre Durand, Paris, Charles-Lavauzelle, 1992, 23.

freedom and his instinctive and natural strength. Rousselet's goal was such that in no way did he wish to exploit the natural qualities of the individual horse. Neither did he want to give him, especially through constraint, qualities that nature had never intended to give him. His equitation was such that the preservation and welfare of the horse was of paramount importance.

L'Hotte mentions that he was one day working his young horse in the *manège* when Rousselet entered the area unexpectedly. When he saw L'Hotte unsuccessfully and endlessly turning his horse to make him walk on two tracks, Rousselet said: 'Nature did not intend the horse to turn endlessly trying to do the travers but, rather, to walk straight ahead. One must keep one's young horse in a straight line for a long time.'[5]

Rousselet's horses always showed a wonderful flowing and natural movement and were in complete harmony with the rider. He was also known to have frequently made use of a silk string in place of a bit to guide not only his own horse, but schoolhorses known to pull a rider's arms almost out of his sockets. Such a strong-willed horse was Chasseur who always carried off his riders and then ended up with them in his stall, still seated if they were lucky.

One day when Chasseur had just carried off his unfortunate rider, Rousselet removed the bridle and placed, in its stead, the silk string. He got on the horse, went to the far end of the *Carrière du Chardonnet*, turned around and, at a gallop, returned to the stables, stopping the horse with a gentle 'hola' at the very line he had traced before starting. It should be mentioned that this success lay in the fact that before getting on Chasseur he had traced the stopping line with his whip under the watchful eye of Chasseur, then caressed him at length, uttering several 'holas'. It was these 'holas' that always calmed his horses.

Rousselet had already retired when L'Hotte came to Saumur for the second time as Lieutenant-instructor. But he was fortunate to witness Rousselet riding at the head of a *reprise des écuyers*.

After Rousselet's retirement, the new commandant of the *Ecole de Cavalerie* asked his former teacher to lead the *reprise*. The following is L'Hotte's account of this event:

I still see the very worthy *commandant* Rousselet, with his fine silver hair and his smiling face, wearing a long black coat-tail, white breeches, soft leather boots, riding Arc-en-Ciel, his last horse and on whom he now rode for the last time ... The freedom he gave his horse, who seemed to be playing under him all on his own, was so wonderful that when they struck off at the canter, more than once I had the impression that the horse was going to escape from the rider and execute an inappropriate lead change. But the skilful *écuyer* always got him in hand at the right moment and kept him on the right lead, if not strictly in the most perfect position.[6]

An aquarelle by Colonel G. Margot, whose illustrations adorn many a book, shows Rousselet leading the reprise, followed by *comte* d'Aure.

The following are some of Rousselet's notes, which are really aphorisms, and which L'Hotte quotes in his *Souvenirs*.[7]

'Equitation can be set down either in a few pages or in many volumes.'

'One must make the horse enjoy being obedient.' (To which, says L'Hotte, that is precisely what the gentle *écuyer* always did. He never lost his patience.)

'Act wisely and with gentleness.'

'First of all instil confidence in the horse.'

'It is much easier to use power than knowledge.'

'Try to get the horse straight in shoulders and haunches.'

'Never ask more than he is capable of.'

'Anticipate the problems rather than fight them and, above all, correct them with

---

[5] *Souvenirs*, 67.   [6] *Ibid.*, 297.   [7] *Ibid.*, 336–46.

prudence and moderation.'

'Familiarize the rider how to jump ditches and obstacles without the use of reins.'

'Tours de force and high airs, are dangerous for the rider and, above all, for the horse, and should be treated as "a kind of juggling act".'

'True persistence is necessary in progress, but one must know how and when to limit one's demands because if one pushes one's demands too far, a horse can begin to defend himself.'

'One must not always demand, nor have the same demands with all horses.'

'The intelligence of animals is almost the opposite of the intelligence of humans who use them. Proof of this can be found among the animals in their natural habitat.'

'Despite what many pamphlets say, the use of the horse, as with the art of schooling, was better and more widely understood and more honourable in the past than it is today.'

'Although they are based on the same principles, military equitation differs from *manège* equitation in the exercises they execute.'

'Military equitation must be simple in that it involves large groups of men in the cavalry; *haute école* equitation is accessible only to the privileged few.'

'Scientific methods which posit in an absolute way, are not applicable to the horse who is subjected to so many and diverse influences, whose causes escape us most of the time and make us incapable of deducing exact correlations.'

'Do not push too far scientific knowledge; any excess is a fault.'

Rousselet, as indicated earlier, taught himself to ride when he was a very young child. There are three aphorisms which deal with self-taught instruction.

'Equitation in its simplest form, can be learned by oneself, to stay on the horse, to use him for daily purposes, for the hack, for one's health.'

'There is not only one kind of equitation. There is an easy one for those who, without an instructor, want to learn to ride; there is military equitation; *manège* equitation; and one that one can call eccentric.'[8]

'Ever since the world exists, thousands of men have distinguished themselves in horseback riding without any other concept than staying on him. It is like the man who shoots and who has never learned to shoot, or the swimmer who never learned the principles of swimming, or the many artists who taught themselves.'

As one reads these aphorisms that deal with horses and equitation, one is struck by the frequent use of words such as gentleness, confidence, limiting one's demands of the horse.

To explain why Rousselet had never written anything but simply left behind notes, L'Hotte says that his riding was too personal and too instinctive to be given form, that is, to be set down.

While almost all of his aphorisms give sound and positive advice, a few of his notes also reveal a certain criticism with respect to some former masters. Rousselet also complained about the manual then in use at the *Ecole de Cavalerie*, the *Cours d'Equitation militaire*, which, he felt, devoted too much time on instruments of domination and correction.

But, above all, one finds great praise for horsemen such as d'Auvergne, Bohan, Chabannes. He also expresses the hope that equitation will one day emerge from a sort of stupour into which it has fallen during the past fifty years.

In 1842 *général* Oudinot decided to introduce Baucher and his *nouvelle méthode* to the officers and NCOs. Like so many horsemen who had seen Baucher perform at the circus, *général* Oudinot was an admirer of Baucher. But to be absolutely certain of this action, he asked *monsieur* Rousselet, whom he

---

[8] Most likely a reference to the artificial airs.

admired and whose good judgement he greatly appreciated, to visit Baucher in Paris and attend one of his sessions. This Rousselet did.

After explaining his method and principles to Rousselet, Baucher then rode several of his horses to demonstrate these principles. Baucher then suggested that Rousselet ride Capitaine. Which he did. Unfortunately, Rousselet, the man who could handle with such delicacy and sensitivity the most stubborn and undisciplined horse, could get very little cooperation from Capitaine. When Capitaine began to rear, Rousselet dismounted, saying: 'This horse is too fine and well-trained for me.'[9]

'No', says L'Hotte, '*Capitaine* was not too well-schooled for Rousselet. But a horse so perfectly schooled for complicated work, quite understandably lost all obedience the moment the actions to which he was usually put, differed, even slightly, from the combination of aids to which he was daily subjected.'[10]

In 1842, Baucher continued to put his horses tightly between hand and leg aids, giving them little freedom to move on their own. This procedure was just the opposite of Rousselet's system which took advantage of the horse's natural inclination for forward movement and who spent a great amount of time caressing and talking to his mounts. Rousselet also disagreed with respect to what he considered over-flexion of the horse's jaw and neck.

It has been said that upon his return from Paris, Rousselet was full of praise for Baucher and his method. It may be true, says L'Hotte, that after his contact with a Baucher so enthusiastic about his method, some of it may have rubbed off.

More likely is it that the modest and kindly Rousselet never openly criticized Baucher and his *nouvelle méthode*. The notes Rousselet left behind indicate his opposition to Baucher's method which he considered too violent.

Since Rousselet was neither enthusiastic nor even convinced of the acceptability of Baucher's method at Saumur, *général* Oudinot sent Delherm de Novital to Paris to confer with Baucher. This was, of course, the last thing Oudinot should have done, in view of the negative relationship that existed between Novital and Rousselet. Novital spent almost a week with Baucher and returned to Saumur a willing captive of the *nouvelle méthode* of Baucher. Of this encounter between the two men, Perrier says: 'The two men were made to get along. They had the same severity, the same inflexibility, the same age (both were born in 1796), the same tendency to dominate the horse by whatever means, including violence.'[11]

The reaction expressed by Rousselet is understandable when one considers his gentleness with horses which was proverbial. Even the most stubborn horse tried to please him. It was said of him that he knew how to talk to horses and that instead of training them he charmed them. Rousselet was held in great affection by all who came in contact with him, colleagues and pupils. Even Novital, an enthusiastic proponent of Baucher's method, and despite their confrontations, had esteem and admiration for him. He even made an exception in Rousselet's case by having Rousselet's horse brought to his quarters every morning (all the other *écuyers* had to go to the stables for their horses).

L'Hotte tells us that very likely the arrival of 'the great novateur', to the *Ecole de Cavalerie* 'was a violent blow of the whip given to equitation at Saumur'.[12] Shortly thereafter, Rousselet asked for permission to retire. L'Hotte believes that this step was 'the consequence of his disapproval with respect to Baucher's method and the discord that

---

[9] *Souvenirs*, 349.   [10] *Ibid.*, 349.   [11] Perrier, *L'Epopée*, 30.   [12] *Souvenirs*, 350.

resulted between Baucher and the *écuyer en chef* Rousselet'.[13]

However, his request to be allowed to retire was not accepted. No doubt because he was too greatly appreciated to be allowed to leave. He finally retired in 1849 and devoted himself to gardening. When d'Aure came to Saumur as *écuyer en chef* in 1847, undoubtedly Rousselet was able to spend the last two years of his career in peace, knowing that the present *écuyer en chef* had the same attitude he did with respect to the *nouvelle méthode* of Baucher.

Rousselet, concludes L'Hotte, belongs to an equitation of the past. The equitation of the eighteenth century. He brought to equitation a talent that was very personal, linked to the tradition of the past, a combination of *manège* equitation and military equitation. He was a skilled horseman, endowed with an exceptionally gentle hand, and who seemed, as L'Hotte says, never to use either hands or legs even with horses who required a considerable amount of leg aids with other riders. But he was not an initiator. D'Aure and Baucher, on the other hand, were innovators and each one, in his own way, headed a school he could call his own. To be an initiator of a school, more than talent, experience, perseverance, and passion are necessary. What is needed is a creative genius.

---

[13] *Ibid.*, 351.

7
Questions équestres

L'Hotte begins his *Questions équestres* with some basic but rather important concepts about the teaching of equitation. Discussing this aspect of equitation, as well as equitation in general, L'Hotte says that he has been inspired by his two great masters, Baucher and d'Aure.

In this initial chapter, L'Hotte also touches upon several topics that will appear in greater detail in later chapters. While individual topics such as the straightness of the horse, his equilibrium, control of his strength, his impulsive forces, the disposition of his haunches, the horse's submissiveness, his lightness, etc. appear in specific chapters, many of these topics are touched upon once again within other chapters for they are, quite obviously, inter-related.

The teaching of equitation

L'Hotte believes that a teacher of equitation must know a great deal about equitation even if he is only teaching the basic principles of elementary equitation. Besides being knowledgeable, he must have sound judgement and determination. Above all, he must have an instinctive feeling for the equestrian art. He must know and have an understanding of basic principles, which are the foundations of the teacher's equestrian art, and which he has acquired by experience and justified by logic. The totality of these principles, when joined together, can become doctrine. He must establish definite methods by which he can regulate the use of these principles in a systematic manner. But the means used to apply these principles ought not to be invariably fixed.

The principles used by the teacher must be concise and based on carefully thought out and mature reflection. They should be in accord with a practical intelligence and sound judgement. He must point out the goals to his pupil with clarity and never follow two goals simultaneously.

He must be familiar with the language and vocabulary used in equitation. Above all, L'Hotte believes that the teacher must be sober when talking, that is, he must possess a sobriety of words. It is not for nothing that L'Hotte was known as 'the sublime silent one', for sobriety of words was also his mark. In fact, the very men L'Hotte admired were those *écuyers* who talked little, men such as Rousselet and Baucher. L'Hotte mentions the fact that in his presentation of precepts, Baucher was sober with words. He then quotes the master himself: 'When I knew little', said Baucher, 'I spoke a great deal, and my verbosity was in direct measure of the vagueness of my ideas. It is, of course, the habit of those who know little to expand... Thus I passed from spreading out my words to being concise... And so the more one knows, the less one says.'[1]

---
[1] *Souvenirs*, 102.

Other great masters such as d'Abzac and d'Aure proceeded in like manner. They knew a great deal but said little. While sobriety of words must guide the *écuyer* when dealing with his pupil, he must be quiet and calm when schooling the horse.

Equestrian art, says L'Hotte, lies primarily in practice, less in theory. However, it helps the *écuyer* if he has read a few manuals on equitation, including works written by past *écuyers*. But they are not helpful to the inexperienced pupil. Only the experienced rider can find profit in them. In other words, while knowledge, principles, and doctrines are important, sound judgement and experience are indispensable.

The instructor must be guided by sound judgement so that he is able to choose the correct precepts for a particular pupil. He must also know for what kind of discipline the horse he is schooling will be employed. It is equally important for the teacher to take into consideration the nature, characteristics, and conformation of the individual horse so that in the training of his pupil and the schooling of the horse, he can make certain modifications in order to compensate for any flaws that the horse might have. The character of the rider must also be taken into account. Every rider must also be advised about conformation, that is, the distribution of weight which is indispensable to the regularity of the horse's gaits.

Regardless of the discipline to which the horse will be put, the horse must be taught obedience. It is not in his nature to want to obey because he wishes to be agreeable to us or for his love of work. He obeys out of self-preservation and avoidance of pain which cause him to react to those who can provoke it and, if necessary, produce it.

The horse's obedience lies in his memory. It is this faculty which the horse possesses to a high degree and which makes him discern the impressions he gets from the aids and their various nuances. Thus it is the language of the aids that the horse must obey.

Movements must always be executed by means of the aids, which a horse must respect rather than fear. And he must be guided by their language and not by routine when it comes to obedience. A teacher must instil in his student the idea that he must constantly vary the order of movements and never allow the horse to take any initiative. Only if the rider is more advanced and has greater equestrian ambitions, may he give the impression that the horse is acting on his own. In general, obedience is influenced by the horse's temperament, spirit, conformation, and bloodline.

The spirit of the horse is the source from which emanates his propensity either to give his strength to the rider, or keep it to himself. This determines whether one has an outgoing and generous horse, or a disobedient and stubborn one.

The degree of his bloodline is the source of much of his energy and the suppleness of his movements. A good bloodline can offset a great deal that the horse might otherwise lack.

In his teaching, the teacher must avoid speaking of a centre of gravity, for this is not fixed and varies with each horse. Furthermore, equestrian art is not a science. One cannot be scientific with respect to horses and equitation.

Calm, forward, straight

One of L'Hotte's basic principles is: 'Calm, forward, straight'[2] which the author feels should be underscored for the benefit of each and every pupil. While L'Hotte says that the methods used to arrive at and underscore principles are not absolute, the order of the afore-mentioned principle is definitely so. For the horse to understand and respond properly to the rider's demands, he must be calm and

---

[2] Général L'Hotte, *Questions équestres*, Paris: Jean-Michel Place, 1991, 13.

confident. He must be obedient. Only when the horse is calm and confident can he give the rider his impulsive forces which the rider can then use at will. The horse's forward movement must be free and positive, for it is this very first step that will reveal a great deal to the rider, that is, how the horse responds to the simple demand of his heels and indicate his desire to move forward, how he uses his strength, and how he extends and sustains this forward movement. The horse can very well execute at the walk this sustained and flowing movement forward, for the lively gaits are not necessary in order to achieve and assess this definite forward movement. It is at the slow gaits that one can determine whether a horse gives us his impulsive forces.

Haunches: seat of impulsion and impulsive forces

The haunches are the seat of the horse's impulsive forces. They must become animated at the slightest pressure of the heels and must remain constantly active. The rider must always feel the forward flow of the horse.

However, there are instances when the goal, impulsion, has not been achieved. This is evident when the horse lingers or hesitates for even a fraction, that is, when the horse does not flow forward immediately; or, if during a transition, he hesitates or falls back into the previous gait which causes him to slow down at the last step of the gait instead of activating it. Again, impulsion is lacking when the haunches do not deviate at the lightest pressure of the heels or, when going on two tracks, the croup becomes heavy and lazy; or when he hesitates an instant when asked to straighten out; or when he does not pass instantaneously from the volte on to the haunches, or pass from the pirouette either on to the shoulders or the haunches, or when he halts a moment when going from the reinback to the forward movement. All these hesitations and momentary halts indicate that the goal has not been achieved and that the haunches have not yet become sufficiently active or diligent (a word used by La Guérinière).

The animation or diligence of the haunches affects the total activity of the horse, for everything is inter-connected. His joints would become a seat of resistance if they did not become pliant and supple and, as a result, the haunches would remain inactive.

For the horse's impulsive forces to function perfectly takes considerable schooling and can only advance progressively. Any preoccupation with impulsion must always take precedence over any demands, that is, movements that follow. Once the horse is calm and obedient, the rider must learn how to direct these impulsive forces. There must be a constant preoccupation with impulsion on the part of the rider.

Even for ordinary equitation, it is important for the rider to involve the horse's weight or mass by establishing a balance between two forces, the force which pushes forward, that is, the impulsive force, and the one which moderates or contains this forward force. This balance distributes the horse's weight on his four legs, resulting in engagement of the horse's mass, the regularity of his gaits, and accurate changes of direction.

Straightness of the horse and lightness

The movements one envisages at first are simple and few in number, especially when we are dealing with ordinary or basic equitation. Thus only few modifications in the equilibrium of the horse's mass are necessary and only a limited flexibility of the joints is required. For submission of all the horse's joints is not the goal at first. It is important for the two forces, those pushing the horse forward, and those moderating that forward flow by a contrary force, to operate. Exactness is not necessary at first. For one of the main goals at the outset is to get the horse straight, to walk on a straight line, that is, the haunches must follow the shoulders in a straight line. When the horse is straight, the haunches will function properly, as will the weight distribution of the horse. When a horse walks straight or in a straight line, there is a harmonious relationship between the forehand and the hindquarters.

The rider must position and maintain the horse in a direction that is precisely determined and, after having completed certain movements that took the horse away from this determined direction, he must be able to return to it with ease. As a matter of fact, the straighter the horse is, the less will he deviate when he is asked to execute different movements and the sooner will he return to straightness.

In a sense, says L'Hotte, walking in a straight line is less difficult in that it is obvious when a part of the horse falls out of line. This is less so when a horse is walking on a curved line as there are degrees of curvature.

L'Hotte places great emphasis on a horse moving in a straight line. For when a horse goes straight, work becomes easy, correct, even brilliant, that is, he becomes light and executes movements as though he is functioning on his own. He moves 'with the lightness of a bird'.[3]

Another advantage to having a horse move in a straight line, is that the horse is able to maintain impulsion. For if impulsion begins to falter, so does the support that must be given to those movements that determine a straight horse and whatever other movements that may be demanded. Thus no impulsion means that the foundation upon which certain movements have their support have been weakened. Any movements without impulsion become heavy, uncertain, and dragging. The horse loses his free and forward movement and lacks elasticity and dash.

However, for the horseman who wishes to carry the schooling of the horse considerably further, the goal is to make the horse rigorously straight from head to haunches.

L'Hotte is careful to make the distinction between the rider who is merely interested in ordinary equitation or military equitation, and the horseman who goes beyond it.

We have noted that the horse's straightness, impulsion, muscular strength, together with the flexibility of his joints and muscles, are elements that play an important role in the training and schooling of a horse. Work that is executed correctly, easily, even brilliantly, depends upon a horse moving in a straight line and whose haunches are vibrant. In other words, a horse who moves and holds himself as though he is functioning on his own.

Impulsion, flexibility, lightness

Two elements, that is, impulsion and the flexibility of joints and muscles are of vital importance to the proper training and schooling of a horse, regardless of the discipline to which he will be employed. There is, however, a difference with respect to the degree or extent to which it is necessary for them to be developed.

For example, if we are dealing with a race horse, the major proportion to be developed will be impulsion. Yet, flexibility of the joints and muscles is also important to the race horse in that he has to react to certain movements or actions, such as regulation of speed, wide turns, or slowing down or halting progressively.

While impulsion also plays an important role in the development of the cross-country or pleasure horse, it is flexibility and the submission of the joints that are required in greater proportions than with the race horse. Obviously the cross-country horse is used in more ways in the outdoors than the race horse. With the horse used for military purposes, the proportions are similar to those required by the cross-country horse, with perhaps impulsion and flexibility having a more equal share.

---

[3] *Questions*, 23.

But it is primarily with the *manège* horse, the horse used in *haute école* equitation, that a definite balance between impulsion and flexibility must be carefully developed. While the horse used outdoors experiences a loss of impulsion when his forward movement is restricted, this does not occur with the *haute école* horse. No matter how restricted he is in the forward movement, impulsion will be retained. Impulsion continues because it is in harmony with the flexibility and resilience of the joints and muscles. This harmony and the careful preparation of joints and muscles are to be found in the *ramener*, suppleness of the poll, jaw, and neck, and the *rassembler* which is the flexibility of the haunches and the horse's ability to engage his hocks under his mass. And, says L'Hotte, the degree of perfection of the *ramener* and the *rassembler* have a common source, an ur-position, which is the straight horse. Thus we see the vital connection between straightness, impulsion, flexibility, and the *ramener* and *rassembler*. All these connecting and connected elements lead, of course, to lightness, that touchstone of Classical equitation, which means that the horseman is now able to play, as with an instrument, with all those forces of the horse which have now been submitted to him.

When one combines impulsion with the flexibility of the joints and muscles, or, rather, when the flexibility of these joints and muscles are animated by impulsion, the result is extension, shortening, or elevation of the horse's gaits. And, as noted earlier, these two elements are required in equal proportions in the horse used for *haute école*. Now the horseman can play with the horse's strength at will. He becomes, as L'Hotte puts it, 'a docile instrument from which one can ask all the movements which his body structure permits, all the *manège* movements that the imagination of an *écuyer* can envisage'.[4]

However, the slightest tension visible or felt in certain areas of the horse, that is, in certain joints or muscles, implies that his submission is not complete. Lightness will then vanish. For lightness finds its expression in the flexibility and softness of the horse's jaw, which, in turn, brings about the flexibility of the neck. If there is resistance in the jaw, then the other areas will resist as well. Equally important is the flexibility of the horse's haunches. Thus flexibility of the horse's jaw, neck, the mobility of his mouth, the flexibility of his haunches, all bring about lightness.

And lightness, which depends upon the sound use of the horse's strength, a good distribution of his weight, equilibrium, and, last but not least, straightness of the horse, will assure harmony of movements.

To the flexibility of the horse's joints and muscles and impulsion, one must add the rider's judicious use of his aids. For lightness does not only apply to the horse's schooling. It also applies to the talent of the rider. It is then that we see the rise of lightness which is 'the perfect obedience of the horse to the slightest indications of the rider's hand and heels'.[5]

Thus the schooling of the horse and the skill of the rider have a direct effect on lightness. This is *haute école* equitation, equitation raised to its highest level and which is found 'not in movements that are more or less extraordinary, but in perfect lightness and in movements that are simple as well as complicated'.[6]

Disposition of the horse's haunches and turning

The disposition of the horse's haunches, the way they react when given a new direction, that is, turning, and the period preceding the new direction, play an important function in L'Hotte's work. They have an important function in the attainment and preservation of harmony between the forehand and the hindquarters of the horse.

---

[4] Ibid., 33. [5] Ibid., 33. [6] Ibid., 35.

If, for instance, a change of direction is undertaken by the forehand, the haunches must do so likewise, otherwise the harmony of forces will be broken and the haunches will continue to move in the previous direction, whereas the forehand will move in the new direction undertaken.

To avoid any lack of harmony between the two ends of the horse, one must dispose of the seat of impulsion, that is, the haunches, and make them deviate lightly in the direction taken by the forehand. 'The position given to the head and the neck', says L'Hotte, 'must immediately find its echo in the deviation of the haunches'.[7] For example, bending the horse's head to the right when the horse insists in going to the left, does not prevent the horse from making a half-turn to the left. But the rider who concentrates his efforts on the horse's haunches and makes them deviate to the left, will succeed in making it impossible for the horse to make that half-turn to the left and, rather, go the way the rider wishes him to go. The rider must take possession of two forces on the same side, rein and heel, in order to dominate the haunches and make then deviate in the direction he wishes.

This same system will also work in obstacle jumping if the horse tends to swerve to the left when jumping. The rider must make the horse canter on the left leg, thus enabling the rider to bring the horse to jumping over to the left. Usually it is believed that a horse, cantering on the right leg, will swerve to the left. This, says L'Hotte, is not so.

The disposition of the haunches constitutes a preparatory action to a change of direction. In fact, the haunches determine the change of direction. Thus the head and shoulders, due to the kind of joints they possess, can solicit direction, but they cannot oppose it. If there is any opposition between the two ends with respect to the direction given, it will always be the haunches who win over the head and shoulders. Never will a horse's shoulders go to the right, for example, without the haunches deflecting to the left.

In his attempt to control the horse, the rider must be able to exploit the horse's haunches correctly. Thus a change of direction depends upon the disposition of the haunches which, in turn, must be linked accurately and in proper proportions, to the position of the forehand. To this is added impulsion. The result will be movements of the most varied and executed with ease and with the mere touch or breath of the aids.

It should be noted that when resistance occurs in the forehand, the seat of this resistance lies in the haunches and results in muscular contractions which will then also occur in other areas.

When there is resistance in the forehand, the rider immediately becomes aware of this resistance. This is not always the case when the resistance is located in the haunches, for the rider is not always correctly seated. The rider often tends to confuse the effect for the cause which gives him the impression that the problem lies in the forehand, thus making him concentrate too much on the jaw and neck. Complete submission of the haunches is of paramount importance, for until this has been accomplished, they will provoke resistance to the hand.

Added to the submission of the haunches, when the rider gives a slight pressure to increase impulsion, he will feel a sort of undulation pass under his seat, similar to the undulation of a sheet of water.

L'Hotte emphasizes that it is the function of the haunches to push the shoulders forward, not the shoulders to drive the haunches. But both ends of the horse have to operate in harmony with each other. L'Hotte, like d'Aure (and Baucher), uses the example of the rudder of a boat to make his point. Indeed, if one wishes to turn a boat to the left, one has to put the rudder to the left. One can

---

[7] *Ibid.*, 39.

convince oneself of this when a horse moves on a circle. One can see that the horse's shoulders move inwards whereas the haunches move outwards. Thus the horse walking on a circle, moves in a succession of tangents rather than following precisely the curve of the line.

Disposition and activation of the horse's haunches and the problems that occur, are considerably different when we are dealing with the cross-country horse, since in this case the horse is almost exclusively directed with the hand. It has therefore become common parlance to say that the rudder of the horse resides in the neck. But even here, the cross-country horse would certainly perform better if the same technique were used as is the case with the *manège* horse who, obviously, is schooled more ambitiously.

In the final analysis, the disposition of the horse's haunches is closely linked to a straight horse. Thus, Classical equitation can be characterized in two expressions: 'Straight horse, disposition of haunches.'[8] And therein can be found equitation's crowning glory: lightness.

If one accepts the fact that *haute école* equitation implies a horse who goes straight and that all changes of direction are preceded by the disposition of the haunches, then one must condemn all diagonal movements when they are presented as having to direct the usual use of aids, in that these movements go counter to the concept of a straight horse and the disposition of the haunches.

Thus diagonal actions must only make themselves felt as one of the many ways, and used only momentarily, to submit and supple the joints and muscles, and arrive at the straight position. But, says L'Hotte, if a somewhat energetic resistance occurs, one cannot depend upon diagonal actions to subdue this resistance. What is needed, here, is the use of two forces on the same side, namely rein and heel.

Bend, curvature, inflexion of neck

In the past, some *écuyers* insisted on giving the horse when moving on a straight line, a bend on the side of the neck. This, says L'Hotte is to be condemned. For the outdoor horse, this bend, also called *le placer*,[9] was not necessary. But it was considered graceful if the horse in the *manège* was bent from the withers on, with the horse looking towards the inside of the *manège*. Giving the horse, walking straight, this position was a question of fashion. However, this is not part of nature. In nature the horse always looks in the direction he is going; it is counter nature to have the horse's head bent to the side when he is going straight.

In fact, this position was not limited to the neck. Some *écuyers* of the past actually extended the head to the entire vertebral column. From this fashion derived the total failure of the straight horse.

When the horse is straight, the positions that the different movements require are all the more sound in that they deviate less from the straight position; for the less deviation there is, the easier becomes the rapid succession of the different movements. This cannot be so when the horse's inflexion becomes part of the work. The result would inevitably be the total reversing of the position each time one changed direction or went from one movement to an opposing movement.

According to L'Hotte *écuyers* of the past did not execute movements that involved rapid and consecutive changes of positions. L'Hotte stresses the fact that the horse's forces cannot be in harmony if there exists no accord between the various parts of the body.

---

[8] Ibid., 44.
[9] *Le Placer* refers to the maintenance of a horse's equilibrium at every movement that is executed; it also implies the sound distribution of the weight of the mass on all four limbs.

Thus the horse must be straight from head to haunches and inflected only when he follows a curved line.

However, when it is a question of side-stepping, the bend has a very proper place. It makes the horse look in the direction he is moving, adds to his gracefulness, and contributes to pulling along the outside shoulder. But even there the bend must be very limited so that the action of the rein which provokes it, does not act on the haunches; for a too pronounced bend could bring a pronounced reversing to the position of counter-changes in direction and analogous movements.

Bend, turning, and use of aids

The question of bends becomes important when dealing with turning. Then the question arises, should the inside heel or the outside heel be used? L'Hotte wonders how and why general opinion for a long time attributed to the outside heel the principal role of turning. All they had to do was look at how the horse in his natural state turned. The solution to this question should occur in a careful analysis of the use of aids.

A rider is moving and he is told to turn right by using only his legs. Which leg will he use? His left leg? Obviously not, since the horse will then turn to the left. Since the action produced is in direct opposition to the sought goal, it can only constitute a determining factor and only represent a rectifying means. This is the case when the outside leg is involved in the turn. And, adds L'Hotte, when we are dealing with elementary equitation.

With respect to *haute école* equitation, the use of the outside leg to turn has no longer a rectifying role but a complimentary one, fallen to the outside heel in order to perfect the turn; it is the inside heel that initiates the turn.

Shoulders and turning

Another point of disagreement, says L'Hotte, also centres around the turn. Some want the turn to begin with the outside shoulder; others with the inside shoulder. La Broue and La Guérinière uphold the first position; Aubert[10] and many modern authors uphold the second one. The question is really a moot one, for the horsemen following either of the two positions are certainly capable of turning their horses without any difficulty.

L'Hotte sides with the position taken by La Guérinière, which is, that the turn begins with the outside shoulder. Indeed, says L'Hotte, when the horse turns, his outside shoulder crosses over the inside shoulder and thus has the more difficult role, and whose first step would be made all the more difficult by the deviation of the inside shoulder if the latter took the initiative in its displacement to the side.

While L'Hotte believes that a discussion of turning and which shoulder is first used, has little value, he does try to make his position (and that of La Guérinière) more understandable. His example is given with the horse going at a *trot écouté* (a very precise and measured trot).

The horse actually turns at both ends. If the movement begins with the outside shoulder, it is helped by the inside hock which, by engaging under the mass, pushes the haunches to the outside. But if the turn begins with the inside shoulder, the outside hock, because of its deviation, forms a sort of buttress which, far from helping the deviation of the haunches to the outside, prevents it.

Disposition of haunches and turning

The concern of the *écuyer* when turning his horse, should not be whether to begin with the outside or inside shoulder. Rather, his concern should centre around the disposition

---

[10] *Questions*, 101. Aubert is the P.A. Aubert, a well-known *écuyer* who attacked Baucher. See Nelson, *François Baucher*.

of the horse's haunches when he begins to turn. The position of the haunches alone should preoccupy the *écuyer*. It is the only language to which his aids have recourse. Furthermore, he should leave it to the horse to take upon himself the duty and the moment of disposing his points of support.

L'Hotte tells us that neither d'Aure nor Baucher 'regulated their actions on the movement of the horse's limbs'.[11] For to follow too minutely a horse's raising and putting down his limbs and to regulate one's actions on one or the other of these very fleeting movements, is being too narrow. The art of equitation should be given a larger point of view or else one follows an impractical path and aggravates difficulties that are already quite numerous.

Striking off at the canter and the correct lead

The same holds true, says L'Hotte, when one strikes off at the canter on a determined leg. L'Hotte refers to Aubert once again who says that the striking off at the canter on the right leg be determined at the very moment when the left leg is placed on the ground. Aubert calls this: 'to catch the leg at the right moment'.[12] Thus when the horse places his leg on the ground, it must be felt perfectly and immediately by the rider who must be sufficiently skilled to use his hand and his legs at that very instant, in accord with the striking off. Furthermore, the immediate obedience of the horse must also be instantaneous, without which the opportune moment, the 'moment of the leg' is lost.

L'Hotte feels that the contact the leg has with the ground is much too brief to warrant such precise demands. Rather, one should allow the horse to determine the 'moment of the leg'. 'One must wait for the horse', says L'Hotte, 'for it is he who is executing the movement.'[13]

Lead changes at a determined stride

Lead changes at every stride are also a case in point says L'Hotte. There is a definite progression to follow for this movement. And as with striking off at the canter, here, again, the instantaneous reaction on the part of the horse is questioned. A lead change is not obtained as soon as the position, which solicits it, is given. 'One must wait for the horse', repeats L'Hotte, 'for it is he who executes the movement.'[14]

If one were to ask for an instantaneous lead change from an inexperienced horse, certain problems would arise. As the horse becomes familiar with this movement, he will more readily adopt the position which provokes it and undertake its execution more rapidly.

Thus when the horse's obedience is assumed, to achieve a lead change at every stride, the rider has only to regulate himself to the impetus of the canter. It is this impetus which will guide one in the use of one's aids and whose effect will be felt the moment the forehand descends to the ground.

Likewise, when one is dealing with the piaffe and the passage, it is how the totality of the horse is affected when he alternately goes from one diagonal to the other, and that the successions of our actions are regulated.

Here again, the moment when a lead change at a determined stride should be asked, that moment is determined without the rider being pre-occupied with the motions of the horse's limbs. And, says L'Hotte, 'there is no unanimity among the *écuyers* concerning the combination of aids to be used in order to obtain the intervention of the interplay of the lateral bipeds which make up the lead change'.[15]

There is, however, agreement in the use of the hand which must lighten the shoulder which has to gain ground by bringing back the weight of the forehand on to the shoulder that remains behind; consequently, the

---

[11] *Questions*, 103.   [12] *Ibid.*, 104.   [13] *Ibid.*, 105.   [14] *Ibid.*, 105.   [15] *Ibid.*, 107.

weight is placed on the right shoulder if it is a question of going from the right canter to the left canter. This is achieved by opening the right rein if the neck is stiff. If the neck is flexible, this is achieved by bending the neck to the left and sweeping the rein back on to the right shoulder.

If perfection is desired, as it should be in Classical equitation, displacing the weight must be reduced to the minimum needed, which is done by means of a light lateral movement of the hand and without modifying the direction of the neck. Any changes of direction transmitted to this area will affect the straight position of the horse which, in turn, will affect the haunches.

Lead changes and use of heel

Where disagreement exists, is in the use of one's heels. Some underscore the use of the outside heel, the so-called opposing heel; others the inside heel, the so-called direct heel. In the opinion of L'Hotte, both methods, correctly used, will achieve the desired result.

L'Hotte gives two different ways of how the lead change can be obtained. When the horse is cantering on the right leg, the lead is obtained by using the opposing or right heel, whose function is to deviate the haunches to the left which, in turn, pushes the left hock forward, making the horse traverse, which he does naturally when cantering on the left leg.

The same lead change can be obtained by using the direct, that is, left heel when its function is to bring the left hock to the centre of the mass.

The first method is used when the horse's response to the aids is not complete and is satisfactory for cross-country equitation.

The second method is used in Classical equitation and requires more delicacy and gives one the advantage of maintaining a straight horse and the means of obtaining lead changes at three and two strides and at every stride 'a tempo'. For the straight horse averts traversing as well as side inflexions; and all weight displacements are reduced to what is absolutely necessary. Thus there is no change of position to go from the canter on one lead to the canter on the other. And modifying the position which each lead change requires, becomes somewhat less sensitive, so that when one lead change has been obtained, another can be asked right away.

The ease with which one can obtain successive lead changes depends entirely upon how perfect are single lead changes. The difficulty lies in that while the-more-or-less is easy, perfection is not. In short, the use of the heels to obtain lead changes is applicable to striking off at the canter and must be obtained imperceptibly by the rider. Only then is one dealing with Classical equitation.

It is equally important in Classical equitation for the rider, when executing successive lead changes, not to twist the upper part of his body; neither should he move from one buttock to the other. Both these flaws would only disrupt the harmony which must be maintained with one's horse. Elegance would also disappear. When the rider is in harmony with his horse, he can then accompany his horse as he passes successively from one lead to the other.

Successive lead changes can be obtained in two ways:

First, by doing a complete programme or lesson which includes moving in a circle and on two tracks, first at every three strides, then two, then at every stride 'a tempo'.

Secondly, by combining these different lead changes into a single progamme and alternating them by maintaining the canter on the same lead.

This method of enhancing the programme of the canter by adding to it successive lead changes, brings about variety to one's work, avoids monotony, and prevents the horse from falling into a routine. He must never be allowed to execute lead changes of his own accord. It is the rider who gives the command, even if he lets himself be swayed by the horse's movement. The rider should seek interesting and fruitful ways to perfect the combination of forces, the distribution of weight appropriate for each movement, that is, the position for each movement.

The rider must also acquire a feel for the horse's contractions so that he can promptly eliminate any resistances that will oppose the soundness of the position; rather, he should be able to provoke those forces which will assure correction. The skilful *écuyer* should, after two or three strides, sense through his seat, rather than see with his eyes, that the horse has struck off at the wrong lead. He should be aware of the position from which the wrong lead could occur and rectify the situation before provoking the strike off. Better still, the judicious *écuyer* with equestrian tact, should not even allow the false position to occur by combatting the contractions that produce it.

Thus hard work and exceptional talent are the ingredients needed for a horseman to develop a certain finesse or equestrian tact which can give the horseman this sense, known as 'the sense of contractions'.[16]

Weight distribution and the horse's neck

While L'Hotte has discussed weight distribution in connection with other aspects of equitation, he now brings up this topic in greater detail. And from discussing weight distribution, he naturally falls into a discussion of the rising trot where weight distribution plays an important role.

When schooling a horse, it is important to understand what action is exerted by the horse's neck and the changes of attitude this entails on the distribution of the horse's weight from his shoulders to his haunches.

To this effect, an experiment was conducted by means of two scales of identical size with mobile boards; upon the one scale rested the forelegs of the horse, upon the other his hindlegs. Thirty-two horses of various conformations formed part of the experiment.

With the horse's head placed at 45 degrees on the vertical, and somewhat lowered, it became obvious that the weight supported by the shoulders was greater than the weight supported by the haunches. The difference was one ninth of the horse's total weight.

Depending whether the head was raised and back or lowered and *ramené* towards the chest, about 10 kg were carried from shoulder to haunches or from haunches to shoulders.

The experiment indicated that a long and light neck weighs more heavily on the shoulders than a short thick neck. It was noted that these changes of position brought about weight displacements.

It would have been interesting, says L'Hotte, to have made these experiments with race horses when their necks are totally extended and thus be able to determine their weight distribution and what modifications would occur.

Experiments were also conducted taking the rider's weight into account and how the horse's weight was then distributed. It was noted that the horse carries on his shoulders two-thirds of the rider's weight when his upper body is held upright; one-half of the rider's weight when he bends his body slightly backwards; five-sixths when he stands on the stirrup irons.

Thus there is a transfer of weight that is considerable, either towards the shoulders or towards the haunches. The position of the neck plays a part in this weight transfer, that is, by means of its extension or its elevation.

The rider himself can, with his own weight distribution, contribute to the modification of the horse's equilibrium and either lengthen, shorten, or regulate his gaits.

L'Hotte condemns those riders who seek a marked elevation of their horse's neck even though their horse has a naturally low neck. Not only does this action of their hand bring

---

[16] *Ibid.*, 111.

about a faulty displacement of the horse's weight, it also affects impulsion. If a certain position is imposed upon the horse which is contrary to his natural conformation, the constant play of the rider's hand to keep the neck raised, will restrict the horse and make him lose the freedom of his gaits. Furthermore, all harmony of movement will be lost, for his back and loins will be overloaded.

Quite obviously, riders would like their horse to be provided with an ideal neck elevation. But a rider should be content with what he has and be able to compensate for certain flaws by making the necessary concessions.

The rising trot and weight distribution

It has already been frequently noted in the chapter dealing with his life that L'Hotte made frequent attempts to introduce the rising trot to the cavalry. In *Question équestres* L'Hotte now uses le *trot enlevé* in his discussion of the horse's and the rider's weight distribution.

The rider's weight can be considerably distributed when he makes use of the rising trot, which can affect the horse's gaits, lengthen and shorten them, or regularize them. L'Hotte spends considerable time discussing the rising trot, its method, its advantages, and how the diagonals work in accord with the rider and the horse. He does so because it should not be forgotten that the rising trot was still a debated question with the French cavalry when he wrote *Questions équestres*. In *Souvenirs* L'Hotte tells us how he attempted to convince high ranking officers of the benefits of the rising trot, often having his men demonstrate it in their presence.

'The rising trot', explains L'Hotte, 'involves displacement of the upper part of the rider's body, and while kept within certain limits, nonetheless, exerts no less a marked action on the horse, so that the diagonal with which the rider moves in concert, covers more terrain than the other diagonal. Every rider who has practised the rising trot with some attention, must have convinced himself of this.'[17] L'Hotte also explains how the rider's displacements of his upper body affect the horse. For example, if the rider is trotting on the right diagonal and the upper part of his body goes forward and weight is placed on the stirrups, the relaxation ensuing on the left diagonal pushes forward the right diagonal, allowing it to gain terrain.

Body displacement also affects the horse's haunches when the rider returns to the saddle and when his weight is closest to the saddle. Depending upon the diagonal with which the rider has his horse trotting and gaining terrain, it also makes the haunches deviate either to the right or to the left.

While this affects all horses, it is especially appreciable with horses who are rigorously straight. For example, one single hack, at the trot, on the same diagonal, will suffice to have some bearing on the horse's straightness. When the horse is then ridden in the manège the next day, this will be obvious. It is therefore important that the rider alternate the diagonal so that the straight position of the horse is not affected, for it could affect the regularity of the horse's gaits. Furthermore, adds L'Hotte, when a horse has a somewhat marked deviation with respect to the straight position, it is easier to execute the rising trot with the diagonal on the side where the horse traverses, as it is more difficult to do so with the opposite diagonal. A number of riders have the tendency always to trot on the same diagonal and have difficulty going from one to the other.

The rising trot benefits the rider as well as the horse. It is easier on the rider, for he has to sustain only one out of two reactions. In fact, even the second one is deadened. With the rising trot has been eliminated what was formerly called 'the ailment of the horse-

---

[17] Ibid., 122–3.

man',[18] an ailment caused by the continuous bouncings the horseman experienced, and the rubbing and heating of the seat, often aggravated by the material with which the saddles were covered.

Perhaps even more than did the rider, it was the horse who benefited from the rising trot. He no longer received blows on his spinal cord at each stride. The trot now becomes more flowing and more extended with the rising trot. With a more extended trot, the rider can straighten a horse who traverses, regularize his gaits, and obtain the canter on the lead the horse heretofore refused to take.

Position of rider and the imperceptibility of aids

Throughout *Questions équestres* L'Hotte has stressed the importance of the rider's position in Classical equitation and stated that any displacement of his seat is proscribed. He also insists that his aids should be imperceptible.

The rider, says L'Hotte, should be one with his horse – in harmony – and should let the horse execute the movements. It is especially important that the rider be in harmony with his horse during changes of direction. He should neither precede nor follow the horse when he changes direction. He must accompany him. The rider who practises Classical equitation must understand that these nuances will result in a greater harmony between him and his horse.

Regardless of the movement, whether on one or on two tracks, the rider's body, especially at lead changes, must never be accentuated. The rider's seat must be almost welded to his saddle and, thus, to his horse. Movements of hands and legs must be imperceptible. No spectator must ever be aware of the use of his aids.

In other words, the rider must never bring attention to himself. It is the horse who executes the movement, who is the showpiece. The rider must merely harmonize with the showpiece.

However, when a horse tries to resist, the rider should not attempt to remain in accord with the horse as he shifts his weight. Rather, the rider must move his upper body in the opposite direction. Not so much to fight the horse's resistance, which would be futile, but for the purpose of remaining in the saddle and coping with the horse's bucking or rearing.

The horse makes use of his neck in many and varied ways. Sometimes he uses it in accordance with the movement; at others, it acts neutrally, and still others, it gives him a contrary position. This is quite evident when a horse turns. Sometimes his neck is bent in the direction opposite to the turn; sometimes to serve as a counter-weight to an inclination or tilt of the mass that is too pronounced. In this instance, the horse is using his neck the way an acrobat uses his balancer to re-establish his balance. When a horse falls on his side or is constrained, he will always throw his neck to the side opposite to where his body is lying. For this reason, it is recommended that, should a horse fall, the rider, if he can, throw himself on the side where the head is situated.

It is of primary importance that the horse's neck be maintained in obedience. The degree of submission is, of course, dependent upon the uses to which the horse is put. Yet a horse, when executing a difficult movement, or when he must jump an obstacle, must be given total freedom of his neck. His instinct alone guides him in a difficult endeavour.

When inexperienced riders are involved in obstacle jumping, instead of lowering their hands, they usually raise them. What often happens is that the horse falls on his hocks rather than lands on his shoulders. When a horse jumps an obstacle, the moment he passes over the obstacle, his head extends rather than is raised and his ears are hidden

---

[18] *Ibid.*, 128.

by the withers. The horse, moveover, seems to be looking beyond the obstacle and showing concern about getting his hocks over the obstacle rather than his knees. Thus the rider, when approaching an obstacle, must follow three words: seated, legs close to horse, hands low.

As stated earlier, the means used to acquire a straight horse are multiple. One such method was the use of the inside or direct rein. Or by pressure of the rein of opposition or outside rein on the neck. In each instance it was the use of a single rein. Use of a second rein makes more definite, complements, completes, or limits the action of the first rein.

Function of heels

In *haute école* the function of the heels is not limited to pushing the horse forward. That is satisfactory when one is dealing with elementary equitation. In *haute école*, the combination of heels, each one having a different function is of paramount importance. For example, one heel puts pressure on the sides of the horse, the other prevents the deviation of the haunches. The heel that puts pressure solicits the raising of the hock on the same side, then provokes its engagement under the mass. As the pressure increases, inflexion of the body occurs on the side where the pressure exists. This pressure must be put in one area, and backwards, according to need, and without being displaced. It is precisely this backward action made by the opposing heel that is used to deviate the haunches.

Thus the opposing use of the heel serves to obtain the straight position of the horse. As schooling progresses, the use of heels becomes more definite, they regulate themselves, and are exploited.

The piaffe, for example, is determined and acquires its rhythm from the alternate pressure of each heel, in that it regulates the raising and maintenance of the hock, and provokes, at the same time and on the same side, inflexion of the body. Likewise does the dancer place her hand on her side – the very side where her body has to bend.

Striking off at the canter, lead changes, with the horse kept rigorously straight, are obtained by means of the direct heel bringing the hock under the mass on the same side.

It is the inside heel that pushes the horse forward on two tracks. Engagement of the inside hock, under the centre, brings about the same engagement of the outside hock, due to the crossing over of the latter over the former.

When one executes the shoulder in, the outside heel must first bring the corresponding hock under the horse's mass. The crossing over of the inside hock over the outside one makes the horse bend under him the inside hock which is one of the goals envisaged.

When turning, it is the inside heel, by acting backwards, that gives the disposition of the haunches. Thereafter, the one or the other heel gives a slight pressure in one place, so that the horse feels its effect during the movement.

Thus it is the inside heel that acts, if it is inflexion that is wanted. The outside heel makes itself felt if it is necessary to draw out the outside hock which has a longer way to go and which all too often remains behind.

The same holds true for the pirouette.

L'Hotte here gives credit to Frederico Grisone,[19] who had already stated in the sixteenth century what he, L'Hotte, is saying in the nineteenth about the action of the heels. Grisone, says L'Hotte, ascribed to each heel the same function when turning that he has done. The only difference lies in the language used.

A combination of both aids, that is, heels and hand, should only be applied if it

---

[19] Frederico Grisone author of *Gli Ordini di Cavalcare*, *Questions équestres*, 70.

becomes necessary to straighten a horse who has abandoned the straight position when crossing over or during inflexion.

When a horse gets out of the straight line, his haunches are brought back by the heel on the side where the haunches deviated. The rein on the same side supports the heel. For example, if it is the left haunch that deviates, it is the left heel that presses backwards with the rein on the same side serving as rein of opposition.

However, when a horse bends, it is straightened out with the heel and the rein on the opposite side of the bend. If the inflexion occurs on the left, it is the right heel that acts on that spot and the right rein inflects the neck on the right, following the inflexion of the body that the heel has provoked.

The horse's resistances

L'Hotte uses the word 'resistances' to mean both the resistance of joints and disobedience or revolt of the horse. If a horse resists or is in revolt, he does so by means of either his neck and/or his haunches.

The neck can more easily be overcome, and since the forward movement is important, it is actually the haunches that should concern the rider.

A stubborn or disobedient horse who revolts, starts out by retaining his impulsive forces. He refuses to give them to the rider. Or, if he does use them, it is to rid himself of his rider.

The function of the rider is to channel the direction of these impulsive forces. To push the horse forward in a direct and positive way will have a positive result. As long as he goes forward he can neither buck nor rear. If he tries to bound forward, those bounds will be eased in that they will occur as he goes forward and not in place.

When the rider's legs are used to push him forward, the horse will lean against them and his defences will explode when he will feel the spurs, for the stubborn and disobedient horse will cling to the legs rather than flee them. Of course, the skilful and strong rider, whose posture is exemplary, will be able to cope with the situation. He will force the horse to respond to the constraints of his legs, especially if he makes use of the energetic and repetitious attacks of his spurs, attacks which will only cease when the horse becomes obedient.

Use of rigid reins

But there is another way of coping with a recalcitrant horse, for it is better not to have to engage in a battle. This method makes use of the rigid reins.

The rigid reins are composed of two strong steel blades covered with leather and attached to the front part of the ring of the cheek piece, where the curbchain is attached. These reins resemble ordinary snaffle reins and are supple only in the area where they rest on the withers. The rigid part must be long enough so that the rider can hold the ends when the head and neck are extended.[20]

The rider abandons the curb bit rein and shapes it into a circle so as not to disturb the horse's extended neck. He then makes a quick release knot so that, should the need arrive, he can quickly gather it up again.

The rider then picks up the rigid reins and activates them. Bearing directly on the curb chain, the horse is forced to extend his head and neck, and to give in to the action that pushes him forward.

These reins should be used with moderation at first, for they engage the horse quite naturally into the forward movement. Used energetically with stubborn horses, these reins can acquire a power that can become irresistible to the rider.

With stubborn horses, the curb chain should be tightened a little more than usual

---

[20] See also Jean Froissard, *Equitation*, No. Hollywood: Wilshire Book Co., 1978, 51.

so that the action involved can function completely.

The rigid reins can also help the rider if his horse refuses to turn. If it is to the right that the horse refuses to turn, then the rider must push the left rein forwards and the right rein backwards towards him. This gives the bit a twist, forcing the horse's head to the right. The rider then immediately follows the direction of the head, making a forward motion on both reins, thereby engaging the horse.

This technique is to be applied to horses who refuse to go forward, who throw themselves into a violent circle, who buck, rear in place, or go backwards. It must not be forgotten that the rigid reins are only for temporary use. While they are in use, the rider must also use his leg aids. Eventually the use of the rigid reins is progressively decreased and it is hoped that leg aids will make the horse go forward. It is also important that the hand should in no way impede the goal pursued by the legs, that is, the forward movement.

The rigid reins give the rider a means that is both gentle and powerful. Far from provoking resistances, these reins eliminate them, in that they do not directly interfere with the impulsive forces which the horse refuses to give. The haunches do not take the initiative; they merely have to follow the weight which has been put into action and which carries them along. The haunches feel less burdened, for the weight is carried over towards the shoulders which is beneficial.

The submission of the horse will be all the more facilitated if the source of his resistances can be found in certain imperfections affecting his hindquarters.

In short, the rigid reins take hold of the neck and paralyse the resources that the horse could use to defend himself.

L'Hotte used these reins with success on very young and undisciplined horses who had never been mounted. When he was *écuyer en chef*, he always had a pair of rigid reins available in the whip-carriers in case of need. It was Baucher who had introduced L'Hotte to these reins in 1854. Baucher had first become acquainted with them in Italy.[21]

While many of the equestrian questions L'Hotte raises in his book deal with Classical equitation, elementary equitation, as a first step to Classical equitation or to the schooling of horse and rider for outdoor equitation, also plays an important role. L'Hotte also discusses race horse equitation, military equitation, and circus equitation.

Almost all of the practices which aim at the submission of a horse have their point of departure in the animal's instincts. 'Nature', says L'Hotte, 'is the most important teacher. Its book is the most accurate, the wisest, and the most useful one can consult.'[22] And the horse becomes more obedient as these instincts are channelled and as he becomes more familiar with certain practices.

Thus the horse learns to go forward by a light pressure of the rider's heels. The postillion of the past taught the horse to go forward by jerking the bridle, as his heavy boots made it impossible for him to use either his legs or his spurs. He could, however, easily guide his horse to the left or the right by means of a simple cord affixed to the left side of the bit. To turn to the left he pulled on the cord; to the right, he vibrated the cord, or later, when the horse was more experienced, he simply undulated the cord.

Race horse equitation

To exploit the race horse, it is necessary to have a firm pressure with the hand. This is just the opposite that L'Hotte recommended when discussing Classical equitation, where

---

[21] It is interesting that L'Hotte was introduced to the use of rigid or side reins by Baucher who, in turn, was introduced to them by Italian *écuyers* during his sojourn in Milan.
[22] *Questions*, 93.

lightness was the goal. In connection with the race horse, what is sought is the more or less energetic tension of the joints and muscles of the forehand, which will provoke the tension of the other joints and bring about a very keen and sharp movement. However, while a firm pressure or tension of the hand is needed, this does not mean immobilization. The arms must exert on the reins a traction to which the race horse will instinctively give the appropriate tension of head and neck. The arms yield progressively and follow the extended neck and stop there where the head ought to be set. If need be, the arms must return to the traction if the horse does not hold the contact of his own accord. In other words, the horse must seek the hand of his own accord in order to regulate the extent of the extension of his neck of his own accord.

L'Hotte deals with what is known as *le rouler*, the circular race track of the hippodrome, when the track is short and fast and where the extension of the head and neck is extreme and when the horse's weight contributes to the final supreme effort.

The hands must follow the forehand with its extended and lowered neck and shoulders. It is at this moment of extension and lowering that the horse gains more territory with each stride.

Spurs may be used, but they should be used adroitly. To solicit engagement of the hocks, spurs must be used only when the hocks reach the limit of their extension and when they leave the ground. They will be ineffective if they are used, that is, felt by the horse at the moment when the hocks are in action. For if used then, instead of producing greater speed, they lessen it and bring about a relaxation of joints and muscles.

Regarding the position the rider must take when racing on the flat, Frederick Archer is a good example. Archer acquired a reputation racing in the hippodrome. He used his stirrup leathers long, his thighs were low, and he hardly left the saddle.

In general, the opposite position is taken with obstacle jumping and the steeple chase. One of the best steeple chase jockeys, Lamplugh, however, took the position similar to that of Archer. He did so because he did not want to disturb his horse when jumping and thus did not change his position. He also said that a rider should sit correctly on his horse in case of a fall.

American jockeys wear their stirrup leathers short. Their thighs are horizontally placed, their calves grip the horse's shoulders, their torso lies on the horse's neck, their arms are extended, their buttocks are in the air. This is to assure a good distribution of weight and is an attempt at lightening the weight that inconveniences the horse.

In their use of the whip instead of spurs, L'Hotte feels that this may have a modifying effect on the jockey's balance which may well affect the neck of the horse in that the use of a whip requires more skill than spurs and much movement, even if it is not actually used on the horse. L'Hotte mentioned this problem to M. de Baracé, a man with experience at the hippodrome, who told him: 'If I were given three horses of the same class, mounted by three men with little experience, I would be able to determine the one I wanted to win. All I would have to do is remove his whip and his spurs.'[23]

A jockey has to learn how to use a whip with both hands, for even if he accidentally hits another jockey or his horse, he is disqualified. Obviously the use of a whip requires more skill than the use of spurs. All riders, says L'Hotte, should learn how to use a whip and be able to use it with both hands.

Nature is a good teacher

L'Hotte then discusses the problem that arises when horses continually turn around in the

---

[23] Ibid., 83–4.

same direction during a race and what can happen to their hocks. In the *rouler*, the horse always turns to the right and thus it is the inside hock that carries the weight and becomes the most sensitive and, ultimately, unsound. When the hocks of 189 thoroughbred horses were studied, only 24 did not show any signs of unsoundness. L'Hotte believes that 'instinct ... often makes clear what we have to do or not do, how not to interfere with the horse, and how to help him use what nature has given him'.[24]

The same holds true with respect to the horse's neck, for when on his own, he adapts it in such a way to enable him to cope with whatever obstacles he has to face, climbing or descending steep obstacles, etc. We thus have to learn from nature how to adapt our arms.

When a horse has over-extended himself and becomes exhausted, but still has to go on, his neck extends and is lowered so that his weight, carried to the forehand, can thus compensate. No restraint of the hand should be used at the time. One can say that, generally speaking, weight takes on a greater share at the moment when the horse's strength begins to fail.

Arab Bedouins, when their horses tire, remove their bridle so that they can fully extend their necks and yet be able to continue responding to the demands put upon them.

But, warns L'Hotte, this total abandonment of the reins should not be done to horses who are used to having contact with the hand and which thereby gives them a certain kind of equilibrium. For, if the hand ceases to have an effect, their equilibrium can be shattered and, when fatigued, they can easily fall upon their knees.

Military equitation

L'Hotte was, above all, a military man and, as such, it is not surprising that he would also write about military equitation. At Saumur and at Saint-Cyr, he taught equitation to officers, NCOs, and men from the ranks, who would eventually be assigned to various regiments, squadrons, etc.

'Military equitation', says L'Hotte, 'has occupied too large a spot in my life for me not to devote a few special pages to it.'[25] His discussion incorporates the 'Regulations of 1876' which deal with instruction and exercises for the French cavalry, bringing together the schooling of troop horses and instruction for men from the ranks.

At the very outset L'Hotte tells us that military equitation is usually geared to men who are not usually very learned. Thus their instruction must be such that it can be understood by all the men from the ranks. It encompasses an instruction that includes the essentials necessary to enable men to perform well and safely and has to be kept to a minimum. These essentials will include making the horse straight, move in a straight line, execute turns that tie into straight lines, perform circles, etc. For this reason, stakes were used to mark out squares, sides, lengths, widths of the area in which to perform these exercises.

The rider has less difficulty following a straight line than a curved one and usually knows instinctively when he has fallen out of it and can remedy the situation. A horse, on the other hand, does not, of his own accord, know when he is not following a straight line. Thus it is up to the rider to bring him back to the line when he deviates. This very fact, that is, when the horse is brought back to the line, already imposes a certain degree of submission on the horse. The horse also has difficulty turning. Instead of taking two tight turns, he will take a single, wide one. It is the rider who will have to teach him how to turn correctly. When the horse goes from one end of the square to the other, he is seldom in a straight line and never turns correctly when

---

[24] Ibid., 86. [25] Ibid., 152.

returning back to the other side. Thus part of the rider's training is to school the horse by 'straightening him progressively and eliminating this arc in the bend'.[26]

When the horse maintains the straight line and the turns are executed with regularity at the three gaits, one can say that the rider has sufficient command of his aids and that the horse is sufficiently schooled for the kind of service expected of him.

L'Hotte is somewhat critical of instructors who do not devote themselves totally and who do not pay careful attention to the quality of the work of their pupils. They often fail to see that riders let their horses do what they want when going on a straight line or when turning. Then everyone loses, including the horse. In fact, says L'Hotte, the simpler the instruction and the exercises are, the more attention must be paid by the instructors and the more rigorously must the pupils apply themselves.

In general, says L'Hotte, when the four sides of the square are executed in a straight line and the corners are taken tightly, it becomes evident that the horses have become obedient, that the riders have been given a sound instruction, and that the instructors are vigilant.

L'Hotte recommends working riders and horses frequently outdoors. Not only is this healthy for both horse and rider, but instruction will be served all the better. It will do wonders to routine and monotony. Obstacle jumping should also be introduced. Since skill will be somewhat limited and sporadic in that we are dealing with men from the ranks, it is advisable for the rider to give complete freedom to the horse's head rather than restrict it.

When L'Hotte was with the 18th Dragoons, he made certain changes with respect to procedures in obstacle jumping. What made the new procedures easier was that the horses were not held back; rather their instincts were allowed to guide them.

In his presentation of the different disciplines in equitation, Classical, cross-country, and military, it becomes clear that the basic training for the rider and the horse is similar. All pupils have to be taught how to make the horse go forward, go in a circle, use their aids, make the horse straight, etc. Thus when he analyses the different kinds of equitation, certain differences depend upon the use of the aids, how they are combined, and, above all, their imperceptibility. L'Hotte makes it clear that for a horse to be used for pleasure riding or cross-country, or military purposes, the schooling of the horse is to be kept at a minimum. That impulsion is important, while the flexibility of joints and muscles is less so. When the horse is destined for Classical equitation, his schooling becomes considerably more involved and impulsion and the flexibility and submission of his joints and muscles are to be distributed equally.

Circus equitation and Classical equitation
In his discussion of circus equitation, L'Hotte spends as much time, if not more, on Classical equitation in his attempt at comparing the two.

While the differences between outdoor or cross-country, and military equitation on the one hand, and Classical equitation, on the other, are apparent, when it comes to circus equitation certain problems begin to arise. 'Equitation as practised in the circus and referred to as "haute école", is, in essence, in direct opposition to academic or high equitation',[27] says L'Hotte.

In the nineteenth century, especially when it was moved under a roof and gained in prestige, *haute école* began to be practised in the circus. For the uninitiated, says L'Hotte, *haute école* practised in the circus began to be confused with Classical equitation. L'Hotte's main thrust in his chapter on circus

[26] Ibid., 155. [27] Ibid., 171.

equitation, is to point out the differences between the two.

The function of circus equitation, says L'Hotte, is to titillate the crowd. In circus equitation the rider makes a point of showing how great and spectacular the effort is in making the horse execute certain movements. The greater and the more spectacular the effort and the movements are, the more will the spectators be thrilled and applaud. Even greater will be the success with the public, if the horse, after initially showing some reluctance to execute the movement, will eventually comply. This is especially so if the horse has to perform a movement that is not a natural one for the horse to execute. The spectator will also thrill when the rider performs a feat that is tricky, even dangerous.

Classical equitation on the other hand, says L'Hotte, demands that the rider's position and movements be calm, effortless, and regular. The rider must indicate that what he is doing is effortless, at least, it must appear to be effortless. His aids must be imperceptible, discreet. The horse must respond immediately and effortlessly. Contrary to the circus rider, the Classical rider must efface himself, must become one with the horse. Everything must be done in harmony between horse and rider. Both must give the impression that everything they do is simple. Furthermore, the horse must give the impression that he is acting on his own.

It is only in simple and pure movements that the nobility of the horse, his gracefulness, his pride, can come to the fore. And Classical equitation tries to underscore these traits of the horse.[28] 'It is nature that [Classical equitation] takes as her guide, and not the extraordinary, the eccentric.'[29]

In its simplicity and effortlessness, Classical equitation finds fertile ground when exploiting extension, elevation, and the direction of multiple movements that are natural and pure. It is the movements and gaits that are natural to the horse that should be exploited. Those that go contrary to nature should be eliminated. On the other hand, it is movements that deviate from nature that are underscored and exploited in the circus.

There was a time in the past 'when equitation was noble and beautiful',[30] and when *manèges* included the artificial airs (on the ground and above ground) in their repertoire. These airs, says L'Hotte, were actually perfecting the regular and natural airs. In the past, the ideal horse, 'had to be powerful in the haunches and generous in the mouth'.[31] Unfortunately, many wise and elegant words have disappeared from present-day equestrian vocabulary.

L'Hotte considers many movements practised in the circus as 'outside of nature'. These include the 'jambette'[32] and the Spanish walk, which, according to L'Hotte 'have no activity in the haunches, but only in the forehand'. In fact, continues L'Hotte, 'they actually hinder the advance of true dressage (schooling) rather than support it and thus are in opposition to the general and unified action of the joints, especially the diligence of the haunches, which lightness and the harmony of the gaits imperiously

---

[28] Classicism coincides with the Age of Louis XIV, the Age of Absolutism. The general terms describing this age are fixed grandeur, dignity, authority, conformity, etiquette, decorum, unity, order, harmony, balance.

Ethically and morally speaking, the age believed in fixed values, rooted in the idea of a grand design. This, in turn, is based on the notion of a mechanistic view of the universe, where all is regulated by certain ascertainable laws. The seventeenth century believed in the idea of universality, that is, the universality of laws as well as of human nature.

It believed in a reasonable, logical, consistent, geometrical, and mathematical world.

[29] *Questions*, 173.
[30] Ibid., 174.
[31] Ibid., 175.
[32] Ibid., 176. *Jambette* is a movement preparatory to the Spanish walk which involves an intensive raising of the horse's forelimbs.

insist upon."³³ On the other hand, the artificial airs of the past contributed to combatting the inertia of the haunches.

The judicious horseman knows that the *rassembler* must come after the *ramener*. For engaging the hocks prematurely under the mass would leave the hands without the necessary opposition to resistances occurring in the forehand.

In the circus side reins or fixed reins, attached to a surcingle, are often employed to obtain the *ramener*. The *ramener*, it is believed, can be obtained when the head is held in the vertical position or close to it. This position may help in assuring a certain submission of the horse's head, or make the horse appreciate the effect of the bit, or regulate the use of the horse's strength, but that is all. Resistances to the hand can still occur.

With respect to Classical equitation, the position of the head does not determine the *ramener*. It is to be found in the submission and flexibility of the jaw which is the first joint which receives the effect of the hand. When the jaw is flexible and soft, it will affect the flexibility of the neck as well as the other joints. If the jaw resists and refuses to be flexible, there is no lightness there, or anywhere else, for that matter. For resistances sustain each other. Thus the *ramener* is less a direction or a position of the head; rather it is a general state of the submission of the horse's joints and muscles.

Circus equitation seeks merely the movement itself. It does not necessarily seek lightness.

L'Hotte pays tribute to riders of *haute école* in the circus. He feels that many are competent, but that their function and aims are different from those who practise pure Classical riding. This was the case with Baucher. His work in the circus forced him to train horses and perform in a certain way. Some people, says L'Hotte, even wanted to link Baucher's work before the public with his work as an instructor and writer. There was a considerable difference between the two Bauchers, insists L'Hotte. The private Baucher only exploited the natural gaits of the horse and taught his pupils how to develop and use them. It was at the circus that he executed the unnatural or extravagant airs.

Unfortunately, says L'Hotte, equestrian terminology has changed. In the past one understood *haute école* as being a superior equitation as opposed to *basse école*, elementary equitation. Thus the term eccentric or fantasy equitation would be more appropriate to designate circus equitation instead of *haute école*.

L'Hotte also makes it quite clear that dressing up in seventeenth or eighteenth-century dress does not mean the circus or circusy and does not prevent one from doing the pure movements of *haute école*. Circus means, above all, making the horse do unnatural movements as well as dressing up.

The *grand passage*, the *doux passage*, and the *piaffe*

In this chapter in which he compares Classical equitation with circus equitation, L'Hotte spends considerable time discussing the passage. Many horsemen, says L'Hotte, see in the passage, regardless of the quality of its execution, the official trademark of *haute école*. Not so, says L'Hotte. More of the circus, rather than Classical equitation. The passage, without lightness, that touchstone of Classical equitation, is not *haute école*.

In the past, the *écuyers* executed only the *doux passage* which entails a marked flexion of the limbs and the flexibility and pliancy of all the joints. This kind of passage emerges naturally and directly from the piaffe when the horse indicates the desire to move forward.

---

³³ *Questions*, 176.

There is thus a difference between the former *doux passage* and the more modern *grand passage* which is an energetic extension sustained by the limbs and tension of the joints.

The *grand passage* can be obtained in two ways:

The first way is to obtain it directly. Here it is presented as a separate air, not part of any other, such as the piaffe. It can be easily obtained with energetic horses. All one has to do is contain the trot while increasing its energy. Obtained this way, the passage has little to do with Classical equitation. Furthermore, says L'Hotte, it is executed mechanically and automatically.

The second way to obtain the *grand passage* is when one lets it flow out of the *doux passage* which, in turn, flows out of the piaffe. Now, all the degrees of extension and shortening of action are available.

L'Hotte re-introduces his discussion of Ourphaly, *général* de Novital's horse mentioned in *Souvenirs*, Ourphaly's passage was full of energy, unlike those sad-looking 'passaging' horses one often sees, whose shoulders do all the work and whose haunches follow 'à regret' (regretfully)[34] and whose hocks have lost all their springiness. With Ourphaly, due to their energetic impulsion, the haunches pushed the shoulders, raised and opened them, and gave perfect harmony to the ensemble of the movements.

Yet, Ourphaly, like so many horses, had his weakness. He was not able to give all the degrees of extension and lacked the ability to go, by degrees, from the piaffe, to the most extended and energetic passage, and back to the piaffe. His movements did not flow.

Very few horses can go through the ascending and descending gamut without ever falling into brusqueness in the movements. What these horses lack is the total flexibility of the joints when the passage is carried to its greatest extension and still retain their pliancy and flexibility. Furthermore, when the passage is shortened and enters the piaffe, the hocks, while engaging under the mass, must retain their energy and the knees must be raised and carry themselves forward as though the horse wanted to gain territory. 'That is how the *grand passage*, the *doux passage* and the piaffe are joined and when the rider can, at will, modify the nature of the movements and regulate their extension.'[35]

It is actually the *doux passage* which requires flexibility of the joints and which contributes to the schooling of the horse and to perfection, whereas the *grand passage* has detrimental effects in that it demands tension of the joints if practised prematurely, that is, before the *doux passage* has been learned.

Our former *écuyers* knew what they were doing when they first had the horse piaffe, unsaddled and unmounted, between the pillars so that he could become familiar with the air. Only later was the horse asked to do the piaffe and then the passage mounted. Rather than execute this graceless and automatic passage (graceless and automatic for both horse and rider), it would be better for the rider to do a graceful and natural trot, precise and free, which would please the real horseman (not the crowds necessarily) who has a feeling for beautiful and graceful equitation. It is up to these authentic horsemen to show the way, otherwise, as Baucher once said, 'one would be sacrificing to false gods'.[36]

The schooling of horses

In his last but one chapter, that is, the chapter where L'Hotte compares Classical equitation and circus equitation, he also discusses some aspects of the schooling of horses for different disciplines. There are, says L'Hotte, the two schools of Baucher and d'Aure. But, adds L'Hotte, there are many other methods of

---

[34] Ibid., 183.   [35] Ibid., 185.   [36] Ibid., 187.

schooling horses that preceded and followed his two masters.

In this last chapter L'Hotte discusses the meaning of dressage, that is, the schooling of horses, and asks the question whether there is a single method that is better than any other.

Basically, answers L'Hotte, almost all of them say the same thing and have a similar goal. The discipline to which the horse will be employed will differ, and the fine tuning of the horse to correspond to its use, will differ. The various steps may be undertaken in a different sequence, the vocabulary used may differ. For example, some methods will have the horse walk right away, spend more time lunging, or seek the overall submission of the horse's joints right away. Others will initially spend more time working with the horse in place and seek successively the submission of the various regions of the horse. Some will spend a great deal of time with the horse in hand, others at the pillars, and still others will use gadgets. The procedures and the form of presentation may differ. The personal taste of the master will have an effect on how and what is presented. Above all, much will depend upon what is sought, that is, the degree of submission and the discipline of the horse being schooled.

One should, however, be aware, insists L'Hotte, that whatever the method used, none is infallible. One ingredient that each and every method needs in order to succeed is 'equestrian tact', that is, 'perfect timing and good measure'.[37] Or, as L'Hotte also says: 'The value of the means depends upon the worth of the man.'[38]

What is of value for the horseman to pursue is to determine quickly when something is amiss and react to it quickly. This implies the possession of 'equestrian tact'.[39]

The schooling of the horse in the *manège* should be frequent, but of short duration. The horse should return to the stable as joyfully as when he left it. Exercises can be of greater length when conducted outdoors which is healthy for both horse and rider. Thus one should combine *manège* lessons with outside activity. Outdoor lessons subdue the horse less than in the *manège* and are important for the horse's spirit. The outdoors will develop the horse's strength, his breathing capacity, and make him resistant to fatigue. In this manner the wise words of monsieur Rousselet stand out: 'Exercise, instruction, and work', are three distinct entities, unfortunately often confounded with each other.

It is important that one be content with only a little progress each day. Progress should be graduated. If one day an unexpected progress has been made, it must not be taken for granted. Something that has been acquired one day should not be taken as a basis the next day.

Patience is important. But more important is perseverance and knowledge. Instead of saying 'patience' one should rather say 'never impatience'.[40] Patience taken at its word is only useful when one is confronted with a recurring problem.

Methods of schooling the horse have been modified throughout the ages, due to changes in the needs and tastes of society. The nature and conformation of the horse has also been modified to correspond to the needs and tastes of society.

L'Hotte ends this chapter on methods in dressage on a somewhat pessimistic note. Unlike science, he says, one cannot say that equitation has actually progressed with time. In this respect, it is like the other arts. Modified, yes, but not necessarily progressed.

---

[37] Ibid., 190. [38] Ibid., 190. [39] Ibid., 190. [40] Ibid., 192.

8
Amazones *and* écuyères *of the nineteenth century*

Anglomania penetrated France in the early nineteenth century. The Gothic novels of Horace Walpole, Anne Radcliffe, Charles Maturin, Mary Shelley, and many others, influenced a considerable number of French writers such as Balzac, Charles Nodier, Victor Hugo, at least for a while. The more natural English garden was equally of English origin. The strict geometric design of the French Classical garden was now giving way in France to the natural garden which Rousseau, already in the eighteenth century, had admired and advocated after his visit to England. The first covered circus erected in France was the work of Philip Astley, an Englishman.

Interest in certain types of sports also came from across the Channel. And this includes a certain type of horsemanship known as *l'équitation d'extérieur*, that is, exterior or outdoor riding. Very little has been said by the social historian with respect to the rise in sports and the comcomitant changes that were occurring in society in England and in France. According to Richard Holt's *Sport and Society in Modern France*, the history of sports has been primarily left to journalists who mainly recounted record-breaking feats on the part of individuals, frequently interspersed with anecdotes by and about certain great sportsmen. But the relationship between sports and society has been given very little attention. In other words, hardly any attempt has been made to show how sports move in step with certain changes that are taking place in society, changes such as democratization, the rise of leisure, and, in connection with women and sports, the place of women in society.

In France men, that is, men primarily from the aristocracy, have always practised certain kinds of physical recreation, namely, the equestrian skills and the hunt, fencing (duelling), and shooting. With the onset of Anglomania and democratization, and greater leisure time, the bourgeoisie, haute and middle, began to emulate the aristocracy in terms of social prestige and fashion. Horsemanship, the hunt, fencing, and pistol shooting soon became the thing to do for those who could afford these recreational activities. During the second half of the nineteenth century, other recreational activities began to be introduced into France, namely, football, rugby, gymnastics, and running. Soon the *petite* bourgeoisie and, to a very small degree, the newly formed class, the proletariat, began to show a modicum of interest in certain sports such as ball games. This is a considerable change in attitude on the part of the French, since the French, especially those of the middle and lower classes, were not considered to be adept enthusiasts of sports. True, traditional village games such as skittles and quoits (not to mention the spectator 'sports' such as bear baiting and animal fights) had already existed, as had pastimes such as dancing and singing. But the *petit* bourgeois and the proletarian had, heretofore, acquired very little with which to entertain themselves.

It is interesting to note that the country that made so little of sport was the country that attempted to re-introduce the Olympic Games. This is not to say that France, in general, welcomed enthusiastically the idea of sports and the Olympic Games. Rather, the man who was responsible for the reinvention of amateur international competition was a French aristocrat, Baron Pierre de Coubertin. Unfortunately, Coubertin was ignored in France, as well as elsewhere, to the extent that, according to Eugen Weber, he was not even mentioned in the pages of the *Petit Larousse* or the *Encyclopedia Britannica*. One important factor in Coubertin's failure regarding the introduction of physical education among French youth was that he was primarily concerned with the education of the elite. To make sportsmen out of young Frenchmen, where the idea of organized athletics, especially team games as they were practised in England, was still unheard of, proved difficult. The explanation Weber gives to his question why 'sporting activities and, above all, the sporting spirit that Coubertin so valued, failed to catch on in France beyond restricted circles', is interesting. 'In nineteenth-century England', explains Weber, 'the practice of sports had become a didactic method of social integration. It was deliberately used to inculcate a particular set of socially approved attitudes, first in the schools of the ruling minority, then at all accessible levels of the public. In a deferential society, not riven by profound ideological conflicts, they coloured the language and the behaviour not of particular groups but of the nation. At the most obvious level, notions derived from games, sports and athletics – sporting behavior, fair play, respect for the rules of the game – became part of the English character, as the English conceived it and as outsiders perceived it.'[1] In France, however, Weber continues, conditions rendered such developments impossible, for the venture of Coubertin 'had begun as a private, isolated, didactic initiative ...' and had 'directed his appeal to the young of the ruling elite. But in France, this elite did not exist unchallenged and admired. Social emulation had given way to political competition.' Indeed, the Revolutions of 1789 and 1848 were still being fought.

In this atmosphere of restrained physical relaxation, of special interest is the introduction of the *vélocipède* which became increasingly popular as the century entered the period of the *belle époque*. The new men of the *petite* bourgeoisie, young clerks working in banks, insurance companies, and the newly developed department shops, found a new sense of freedom in the *vélocipède* from the routine of office.

Not to be outdone, women of the aristocracy and the bourgeoisie very soon began to show a keen enthusiasm for sports, that is, for physical recreation. Fencing, shooting, tennis, swimming, gymnastics, horsemanship, as well as the *vélocipède*, became available to them.

In *Les Femmes de Sport*, published in 1885, the baron de Vaux makes the following observation:

Influenced for the past twenty-five years by English customs, the condition of woman in France has undergone important modifications. Sport, with all the changes that it has brought with it, is now an integral part of the life of our *mondaines*, that is, our sophisticates. In the past, the dance and, by way of exception, equitation, were the only physical exercises included in the programme of feminine education. It was not even considered proper for a woman to indulge in sport ... How all that has changed today!

And, continues Vaux:

Gymnastics and everything linked to sport, in the water or on dry land, is now allowed to make an entrance in the most austere houses. Horse racing and equestrian competition have developed in

---

[1] Eugen Weber, *My France*, Cambridge, Mass.: Belknap, 1991, 223–4.

woman a taste for equitation. In the last war[2] she became accustomed to the odour of gunpowder, so much so, that she now shoots hares and rabbits... And finally, the increasing interest in the art of fencing... has given her the desire to handle the fencing foil...'[3]

And by presenting portraits of a number of women, Vaux hopes that 'the daughters of Eve will find encouragement starting from the top and take up the habit of different sports and react against the stuffy atmosphere of the drawing room. Every woman cannot ride a horse or hunt deer in Chantilly or Rambouillet, but few will not be able to allow themselves the luxury of shooting...'.[4]

And just as Coubertin believed that the practice of sports was good for one's health and moral fibre, so, too, did Vaux believe in the efficacity of sports. 'No doubt' says Vaux, 'physical exercise will have the same fortifying influence on French society that it had on English society.'[5]

The *vélocipède*, not mentioned by Vaux, is perhaps of special interest with respect to the changes taking place in the life of women. With the advent of the *vélocipède* they began to assert themselves more widely. They donned bloomers and began to enjoy the freedom to travel leisurely in the countryside and the delights of solitude. The wealth of posters, sometimes done by well-known artists such as Toulouse-Lautrec, depict women riding in the countryside or in a *manège*, sometimes alone, sometimes with companions. There are even posters advertising the *vélocipède* depicting women with few or no clothes.

This sense of freedom that women felt with respect to the advent of the *vélocipède* had a similar impact on women on horseback. But since to maintain a horse required more money and leisure, riding on horseback was limited to the aristocracy and the *haute bourgeoisie*. These women of the upper classes could likewise express their freedom by travelling leisurely or at breakneck speed, either in solitude or in the company of others.

Throughout the ages riding on horseback was, with a few exceptions, namely, the *grandes dames*, strictly a mode of transportation for women. In the Middle Ages women travelled widely on horseback on routine business or going on pilgrimages. Some even went into battle on horseback as did Joan of Arc. Before her Mathilda, the Countess of Tuscany, fought on horseback on the side of Pope Gregory VII against the German Emperor. In fiction the *Tristan* by Thomas portrays Iseut riding with her brother Caherdin and Tristan exhibiting considerable skill as a horsewoman when her horse rears. In the *Tristan* by Béroul Iseut rides 'comme un valet' – astride.

During the sixteenth century the best known horsewomen were Catherine de Médicis and Diane de Poitiers. Diane de Poitiers, an ardent huntress, rode astride. She was known to ride for three hours before dawn, and, upon her return, have a bath and return to her bed with her current royal lover. However, riding cross-saddle was considered until World War I, not only a dangerous and daring feat, but not respectable. It is rumoured that it was Catherine de Médicis who invented the side-saddle to show off her legs. On the other hand, it might very well be that she discovered that the side-saddle was safer than sitting sideways on a kind of step or bench as women did, which limited them to the walk, and yet more acceptable than sitting astride. Thus she had the pommel of a man's saddle moved a few inches left of the centreline and hooked her right knee around it so as to hold her leg in a more secure and comfortable grip. This way she did not have to sit sideways and her shoulders were pretty

---

[2] The 'last war' refers to the Franco-Prussian War of 1870.
[3] Vaux, *Les Femmes de Sport*, Paris: Marpon & Flammarion, 1885, 1–3.
[4] Ibid., 3.
[5] Ibid., 3–4.

22 A very young Marie-Antoinette astride her fiery black horse. Painted by Louis-August Brun. (Courtesy of the Musée National du Château de Versailles)

much in line with the horse's shoulders. In the seventeenth century, Madeleine de Maupin gained renown as both a horsewomen and a duelist. Usually disguised as a man, she rode astride. She then became a nineteenth-century heroine in Théophile Gautier's novel Mademoiselle de Maupin.

It was only in the nineteenth century that women began to be recognized for their equestrian skills. It was also in the nineteenth century that the terms *amazone* and *écuyère* began to be used. Ernest Molier, owner of a circus in Paris, operated primarily for his friends who were not only spectators, but also performers, distinguishes between the two terms in his book *L'Equitation et le cheval*. The term *amazone* refers to 'the woman who rides for the pleasure of sport and does outdoor equitation, that is, who rides in the Bois de Boulogne, or rides to hounds'; on the other

23 How an *amazone* should dismount. (Photo in E. Molier's *L'Equitation et le Cheval*)

hand, continues Molier, an *écuyère* 'is a woman who specializes in *haute école*'.⁶ At the end of his book, after having devoted many pages and photographs to numerous *écuyères*, Molier says: 'Man has not alone had the privilege of making a name for himself in *haute école*. Woman has also provided to *savante* equitation artists whose reputation and memory have remained with us vivid and alive.'⁷

The nineteenth century continued the use of the side-saddle and the wide skirt, but the riders made a trimmer figure by using fewer petticoats under their riding habits. Although some *amazones* and *écuyères* did ride astride, to break with tradition and not ride side-

⁶ Ernest Molier, *L'Equitation et le cheval*, Paris: Pierre Lafitte, 1911, 287. ⁷ Molier, 396.

24 A plate which appears in the book by J.G. Prizeluis, *Etwas für Liebhaberrinnen der Reiterey* (Something for those women who like riding). Leipzig, Weidmann, 1777. Note the astride seat which Prizeluis favoured for women. Most likely this is a portrait of Princess Helena Charlotte to whom the work is dedicated.

saddle, was still considered unacceptable. Quite obviously, the skirt was an impractical garb for riding astride, but wearing breeches, or a man's attire, as Joan of Arc learned to her dismay,[8] was a serious taboo, hindering women in sports until well into this century.

Anglomania had an impact on a new type of horsemanship. Emanating from Albion's shores was a new way of riding which expressed itself primarily in outdoor or exterior riding and with it the rising trot. Also introduced were shorter stirrups, gentler bits such as the snaffle or the pelham, the thoroughbred and, of course, the accompanying hound. This new style of riding began to replace *manège* riding (Classical or *savante* riding) to a large extent in France, at least among amateur riders.

Riding as an art form, that is, Classical or *savante*, with its high and low airs, had existed in Europe during the Renaissance, first in Italy, then in France. Antoine de Pluvinel, *écuyer en chef* to Louis XIII, received much of his apprenticeship in Italy under Giovanni Battista Pignatelli, disciple of Frederico Grisone, author of *Gli Ordini di Cavalcare* and

---

[8] See Marina Warner, *Joan of Arc*, Harmondsworth, England: Penguin, 1983.

25 Mlle Yola de Nyss of the *cirque Molier* giving the typical salute of the *écuyère*
(Photo in E. Molier's *L'Equitation*)

promoter of Xenophon's *On Horsemanship*. The Duke of Newcastle, who later became tutor and adviser to the exiled Charles II, had to go to Italy to learn Classical horsemanship, as manège type of riding was not practised in England.

The aim of Classical equitation is, according to Decarpentry, 'to restore to the mounted horse the gracefulness of attitudes and movement which he possessed when he was free... Equestrian art thus is akin to choreographic art, and the high school to Classical dancing.'[9] Or, to quote François Baucher who once said to Lamartine: 'You see, *haute école*, is the poetic side of equitation.'[10]

As men such as Rousselet and L'Hotte have pointed out, Classical equitation was,

---

[9] Decarpentry, *Academic Equitation*, London: J. A. Allen, 1987, 3.   [10] Baucher to Lamartine, Vaux, *L'Equitation savante*, 20.

26 Mlle Blanche Allarty of the *cirque* Molier doing the *cabriole* on d'Artagnan.
(Photo in E. Molier's L'Equitation)

unfortunately, becoming a thing of the past in the nineteenth century, gradually being replaced by exterior riding. Ironically, it was primarily in the circus that Classical riding was beginning to exert itself and in a sense, preserve itself. But the former *Versaillais*, the Classical purists, refused to consider what was being practised in the circus as Classical equitation. Only the uninitiated, these purists believed, were under the impression that what was being practised in the circus was haute école equitation. L'Hotte, himself, while not condemning circus-style *haute école*, discussed the differences between the two towards the end of *Questions équestres*.

Indeed, with the closing of the doors of the *Ecole de Versailles*, many of the men who had been schooled in Classical or *savante* riding, moved to Paris to teach the dandies and the *amazones* a new and different way of riding, namely exterior riding. D'Aure, trained, as we have seen, in Classical and *savante* riding at Versailles, where he was already known as a *casse-cou* rider, had already begun to abandon the Classical or *manège* style of riding and adapt and adopt newer ways to meet the new demands that the various changes in society were bringing about. Once settled in Paris he began to teach the young dandies and *amazones* the newer ways of riding.

Thus the demise of the *Ecole de Versailles* and *manège* equitation, together with exterior equitation now the rage, the transformation developing in the circus with the introduction of *haute école* equitation, all these factors had an impact on the controversy in equitation, that is, the Baucher/d'Aure controversy, that occurred during the early 1840s, which centred primarily around the two opposing methods of equitation, *manège* or *haute école* equitation as practised by François Baucher in the circus and exterior equitation as practised by the aristocrat d'Aure. People from all walks of life (including writers and artists such as Alexandre Dumas, Théophile Gautier, Eugène Sue, Eugène Delacroix, and Jules Janin) took sides in this controversy, beginning with the *Dauphin*, the duc d'Orléans (a *Bauchériste*) and his brother, the *duc* de Nemours (a *d'Auriste*), members of the aristocracy, the bourgeoisie, and the *menu peuple*. Thus a conflict between two opposing methods of equitation became a conflict of a social and political nature.

As noted earlier, while in the past riding as an art form had been the exclusive prerogative of men, with the nineteenth century, women began to consider riding as an art form. Women of the aristocracy and the *haute* bourgeoisie alike, began to frequent the Bois de Boulogne and the Bois de Saint Germain to reveal their equestrian skills as well as to show off their charms and the beauty and elegance of their mounts. They also frequented the fashionable *manèges* run by d'Aure, Jules Pellier, P.-A. Aubert, F. Musany, and many others. A wealth of paintings portray women on horseback, singly or accompanied by other women, children, or men; or else they are working in a *manège*. The best-known equestrian painter in France was Alfred de Dreux. Paintings also portray women in *manèges* doing *haute école*. In England the best-known painter of horses and equestrian activities was George Stubbs. Thus the nineteenth century also became, artistically, the age of the horse.

The charms and skills of many of these women, dressed correctly *en amazone*, mounted on an English thoroughbred, have been described in the works of the *baron* d'Estreillis and the *baron* de Vaux.

While almost all are horsewomen, they are equally adept practitioners of other sports such as swimming, fencing, falconry on horseback, archery, and pistol shooting.

The *duchesse* de Chartres, whose father was the Prince de Joinville and a sailor, took swimming as her 'favourite sport'. Fencing and the other arms were favoured by the *comtesse* R. de Salles. She had been taught by her father, a general in the cavalry. Archery, a sport popular in Britain and at the court of Napoleon III was practised by the *vicomtesse* de Gilly as well as the Empress Eugénie. In England the Royal Guard of Archers of Queen Victoria sponsored in July 1878 a contest of archery. The *vicomtesse* participated and won first prize.

While the writer Catulle Mendès accepts equitation as a sport for women, he becomes rather ironic in his preface to Vaux's *Femmes de Sport*. In his discussion of women indulging in sports, especially the more violent ones, Mendès says that woman, once this frail creature who needed protection, now no longer needs the protection of men, be they husband or a 'less legitimate' companion. And, bemoans Mendès, 'Alas, men forlorn and sad, now rendered useless.'[11]

It is no accident that horsemanship is the sport par excellence among the upper classes, having been an activity practised by them many centuries ago. The duchesse de

---

[11] Vaux, *Les Femmes de sport* IV.

27 Photo of Sarah Bernhardt in the *Bois de Boulogne* by the fashionable father and son photographers Jean Louis Delton. (Appears in *Chevaux et equipages*, Paris, 1878)

Chartres was as outstanding a horsewoman as she was an outstanding swimmer. Vaux allocates to her the title of 'a passionate *écuyère*'. Then there is the Polish aristocrat, the *baronne* Rothwiller, who spent almost all the hours of the day on horseback. She was a friend of the *écuyère* Elisa Petzold, who frequently accompanied the *baronne* on her *randonnées* and gallops in the Bois, where she went every morning, regardless of the weather, leaving No. 3, rue Colisée, 'doing equestrian scales and playing pieces of virtuosity along the bridle paths of the Bois'.[12] Another horsewoman of foreign extraction was the *duchesse* de Fitz-James, whose father was a Swedish minister in Paris and who spent almost all of her childhood in Paris and married a Frenchman. Not only was she a horsewoman 'of unrivalled skill', but she also experimented in horsebreeding and new methods in the preparation of different kinds of food for horses. She is also the author of *Principes élémentaires d'équitation*. Madame Bishoffsheim, North-American by birth, could also be seen, come rain or come shine, riding in the Bois 'dressed correctly in tightfitting *amazone* attire'.[13] She always rode horses over sixteen hands, loved speed. In fact, says Vaux, she was good at all sports. The *duchesse* de Camposelice was another accomplished horsewoman, 'performing equitation of the French School'[14] when she performed *haute école* in the *manège* her husband had built for her in the Avenue Kléber. She also enjoyed riding cross-country, the rougher the terrain the better, and made her horse jump very high obstacles. Then there is the *baronne* Laure Alphonse de Rothchild of the English branch, who grew up in England where she rode a pony in Hyde Park. The *baronne* de Rothchild was a fanatic who rode in the *Allée des Poteaux* in the morning and Longchamps in the afternoon escorted by 'a brilliant squadron of horsemen'.[15]

Books dealing with women and equestrian matters already appeared in 1817 with Jules Pellier's *La Selle et le costume de l'amazone*. That same year also saw the appearance of L. de Pons d'Hostrum's *L'Ecuyer des dames ou lettre sur l'équitation*. In 1842 P.-A. Aubert published *Equitation des dames*. In 1852 appeared A. Roger's *Le Livre d'équitation des dames*. In 1861 Victor Franconi's *La Cavalière* was published. That same year appeared, in French, Stirling-Clarke's *Le Cheval et l'amazone* and her *Guide d'équitation pour les dames*. In 1888 *L'Amazone au manège – à la promenade* by F. Musany appeared.

In his introduction, Musany gives interesting and amusing advice 'To his charming female readers': 'In a huge English book, *The book of the horse*, which, nonetheless, contains many interesting things, I found this passage: "The majority of *amazones* ride abominably so that . . ." Well, although we are dealing here with *amazones* living across the Channel, my French pen ceases to write and refuses to translate the very uncavalier-like expressions that end the sentence.'[16] Musany then discusses the awkward relationships which exist between teachers of equitation, especially if they are gentlemen, and their female pupils 'who fear ruffling the feelings of a delightful novice not used to being contradicted when she is told that she does not understand or does not follow the rules required which would make of her a veritable *horsewoman*. Thus a professor who is rigidly sincere runs the risk of being impertinent if he is a paid professor, or boring, if he is an ardent admirer.'[17] It is obvious that Musany has had similar experiences and urges the girl or woman to accept criticism. This kind of caution certainly does not exist in a manual

---

[12] Ibid., 40.
[13] Ibid., 141.
[14] Ibid., 155.
[15] Ibid., 127,

[16] F. Musany, L'Amazone – *au manège* – *à la Promenade*, Paris: J. Rothschild, 1888, 1.
[17] Musany, 1–2.

28 A *manège* in Paris. An *amazone* doing the Spanish walk. (Painted by Edmond Grandjean)

29 An *amazone* riding in the park with her spaniels. (Painted by Alfred de Dreux)

teaching boys or men how to ride. Towards the end of his introduction, he points out that perhaps some of the pupils might not only wish to go on long *promenades*, but might also want to experience 'all the varied and profound pleasures which equitation can provide when cultivated as an art form, and which can be found in the *manège* where they will discover all the subtleties of equitation and where they can spend delightful hours dealing with all the difficulties and identifying more and more with their mount'.[18] Musany is, of course, referring to *haute école*.

The circus, especially, offered women opportunities to exhibit their equestrian skills by practising *haute école* equitation with the high as well as the low airs, for it was in the circus that Classical riding was primarily practised and being preserved. The names of Caroline Loyo, Pauline Cuzent, Anna Fillis, Diane Dupont, Adèle Drouin, Elisa Petzold, Fanny Ghyga, Mathilde d'Embrun, and many others come to mind. The first two had at one time been the pupils of François Baucher. Diane Dupont was coached and her horse schooled by *général* Faverot de Kerbrech, one of Baucher's favourite and most important pupils and disciples.

Indeed we now witness not only the era of the *amazones* but, more importantly, the era of the *écuyères*. 'Only a few years ago', says Vaux, '*haute école* was the exclusive privilege of the *écuyer*; he alone had the ability and the knowledge to make a horse execute all the known *manège* airs: the *rassembler*, equilibrium, the necessary tact in the use of one's aids, and development of the artificial airs was the prerogative of the strong sex. Recently, woman (always curious) made her appearance; and she took her role seriously and under the supervision and direction of professors of equitation, she succeeded in making use of the horse as often and as well as can any man.'[19]

Vaux goes even one better by saying that the horsewoman has greater obstacles to surmount, in that, due to the type of saddle she has to use, she cannot use both her legs and both her hands, the right leg being hooked into a horn situated slightly left of the pommel and her right hand having to hold a *cravache*. Referring to the *écuyère* in general, he says that 'when she has the desire, the sensibility, a woman often shows herself in this instance superior to a man, even if this displeases the ego of men'.[20] Indeed, when one watches the Olympic Games today, one notes that not only do women use the same saddle as men and sit astride, but that horsemanship is one of the few sports wherein women compete with men and wherein they excel. This is due to the fact that such traits as lightness, elegance, finesse, tact, are indispensable, while strength, force, violence are to be shunned.

With Caroline Loyo and Pauline Cuzent, says Vaux, '. . . begins without fear of being contradicted, the era of the *écuyères*'.[21] Indeed, Caroline Loyo was, as Vaux tells us, 'the first *écuyère* of *haute école* seen in the circus'.[22] It was around the early 1830s that Loyo began to perform Classical equitation at the *Cirque Olympique* on a horse of Arab origin named Mamouth. Loyo had left the house where she had grown up when she was barely sixteen and, according to Jules Janin, an aficionado and critic of the circus, writing in the *Journal des Débats* 'her only fortune being her two large black eyes and a big horse, black her eyes and her horse'.[23] Not only does La Loyo, 'the diva of the *cravache*', delight everyone with her charm, her good looks, her svelte and supple body, her elegance. Above all, she is also admired for her horsemanship.

---

[18] *Ibid.*, 4.
[19] Vaux, *Ecuyers et écuyères*, Paris: Rothschild, 1893, 154.
[20] *Ibid.*, 141.
[21] *Ibid.*, 121.
[22] *Ibid.*, 107. Women had already been vaulting on horseback in the circus before La Loyo began performing *haute école*.
[23] *Ibid.*, 109.

30 *L'Ecuyère* Kipler riding with her spaniel in the park.
(Painted by Alfred de Dreux. Featured on the cover of *L'Express Paris*, June 1988)

31 Pauline Cuzent, François Baucher's favourite pupil.
(Portrait in Baron de Vaux' *Ecuyers et Ecuyères*)

Soon she is given top billing with one of her former teachers, François Baucher (Jules-Charles Pellier had been her first teacher), that is, as the most important star she was given the last performance. So that she and Baucher should not enter into competition with each other, each one was given top billing on alternate days. La Loyo left France for several years, performing in circuses in Germany and England. She was especially acclaimed in England 'where her performances became the rendez-vous of all the gentry',[24] which pleased the French anglophiles no end.

The story is told by Vaux, that one evening in London, it was raining hard and La Loyo was without a carriage that evening to take her home. When Lord — saw her predicament, he took her by the arm and escorted her to the carriage of the Duke of — one of the most important lords of the kingdom, while Earl — covered her with his coat to protect her from the rain.[25]

After her tour in England and the Continent, La Loyo returned to France and continued performing *haute école*.

When Caroline Loyo left the circus, she was followed by Pauline Cuzent another of François Baucher's pupils. The name Cuzent has remained legendary in the annals of *haute école* performed in the circus. She was considered the ideal type of *écuyère* in the nineteenth century. She was born in 1815 and began performing in 1835 on Baucher's famous horse, Buridan. Since she was the pupil of Baucher, the disciples of Baucher naturally considered her to be the only woman who truly and brilliantly exhibited the principles of Baucher's *nouvelle méthode*. As a pupil of Baucher, she had learned to flex her horse's jaw and neck, as well as his haunches, so that he could become light, balanced, and easy to ride. Her performances at the *Cirque des Champs-Elysées* and those of her horses, did, indeed, exhibit all the qualities associated with French Classical and *savante* riding: lightness, balance, and the achievement of an harmonious whole, that is, harmony between the forehand and hindquarters. She knew well how to push her horse forward, even when these movements were performed in particularly tight conditions. Her piaffes and her passages were executed with an innate finesse and regularity, a kind of floating harmony due to the ease, simplicity and regularity with which she and her horse worked, allowing no gimmicks to mar her performance. This was precisely in the idiom of true French Classical equitation.

In connection with the performance of Cuzent one is reminded of L'Hotte's comparison between the Baucher who performed at the circus exhibiting some extravagances, and Baucher the teacher who taught his pupils only movements in keeping with Classical equitation. Thus Pauline Cuzent was able to execute in the circus the purest of movements.

Anna Fillis is another one of those *écuyères* born with a natural charm and grace and an innate elegance and brilliance. Never was there a movement or a position that was excessive. For that reason she was considered the most outstanding *écuyère* of the period. Like Cuzent who preceded her by several years, she was considered one of the best interpreters of the French Classical school. This is all the more interesting since her father was James Fillis, famous circus *écuyer* who, though English by birth, lived and practised *haute école* in France. He was also the author of a well-known book, still read today, *Breaking and Riding*. It was Fillis who had trained his daughter.

Anna Fillis began to perform at the age of fifteen, first at the *Cirque d'Hiver*, then at the *Cirque des Champs-Elysées* on her two horses, Mac-Gregor and Negro. She was, as Vaux writes, the only *écuyère* who made her 'entrée in the circus through the main door, that is, without going through the regular path which

---

[24] *Ibid.*, 111. [25] *Ibid.*, 111.

the other school pupils usually had to take'.[26] Vaux describes her as having a natural elegance and an instinctive charm. She never executed movements that were exaggerated or extreme. She demonstrated what the French call 'la litotte', a Classical literary trait that can also be used in Classical riding, namely, that by saying or doing less, one is actually stating more. 'And it is for that reason', says Vaux, 'that I do not hesitate to consider her as the first *écuyère* of our times...' She is 'one of the most elegant interpreters of the French school... it is impossible to find a talent that can compare with hers. She is a transcendent individualist who arrived, through work and study, to such a degree of perfection that equitation is for her not a science but an art.'[27] Later, with her mother to serve as chaperone, and her three horses, Anne Fillis left for Italy where she performed successfully for two years, continually perfecting her performance. She also worked in Vienna in the famous Renz circus and in Germany where, with her famous horse Gant, she could 'canter backwards', as well as execute brilliant piaffes and passages. When her mother, unable to support the harsh German climate, became ill, she returned to Paris. The Germans regretted this departure, for she had become the idol of the true amateurs and purists of equitation.

A short while ago I mentioned that, according to Vaux, Anna Fillis had perfected equitation to such a degree that it had become for her not a science but an art. Indeed, when lightness, fluidity, effortless movements, imperceptible aids, and harmony between horse and rider exist, equitation becomes a veritable art. And equitation as an art is doubly difficult in that two talents are in question, that of the rider and that of the horse. Whereas in ballet, the dancer has only to dominate her legs, the painter his hands, the rider must take into account not only his or her own movements but the movements of the horse, a living creature, with a temperament, moods, and resistances. The rider must communicate with and simultaneously dominate the horse, but never with force or violence. Movements executed with little or no effort on the part of the rider as on the part of the horse is what makes the difference between an *artiste* and a competent rider. Those who watched Anna Fillis and her horses (Gant, Redouté, and Pretty-Boy) perform, whether it was 'cantering backwards', 'the Spanish walk', or 'executing flying changes in one or two tempi', were witnessing horses who were achieving the ultimate of their capabilities. Their cadence, harmony, fluidity, and lightness were perfect, leaving nothing to be desired. It is precisely these very traits, namely lightness, fluidity, balance, harmony, the body of the horse barely appearing to move, which French *écuyers* have stressed throughout the ages and of which French horsemen have been and are still so proud. *Général* L'Hotte in his *Questions équestres* defined lightness as follows: 'It is lightness that gives to *savante* equitation, to *haute équitation*, its veritable stamp...'[28] And, one might add, it was Anna Fillis who exemplified so well this French Classical horsemanship.

In addition to elegance, an innate ability, equestrian tact, or, as L'Hotte puts it 'perfect timing and good measure' and a well-trained horse, an additional quality is sometimes indispensable to the horseman or horsewoman, namely, an affinity that exists between a horse and rider. It is a very special rapport and which usually happens to a rider perhaps once in a life-time. It has often happened that a horse may be heavy, have poor conformation, but, ridden by a certain individual, can become an astounding creature, acquiring miraculously a lightness, a fluidity, a balance, and a harmony that it did not possess when standing in the stall or ridden by someone else. It is precisely this

---

[26] *Ibid.*, 159. [27] *Ibid.*, 158. [28] L'Hotte, *Questions équestres*, 11.

phenomenon that occurred when L'Hotte rode Laruns in Paris in 1866, giving him all the brilliance and lightness one can give a horse. Unfortunately, later, when not mounted by L'Hotte and merely standing in the Imperial stables, Laruns so disappointed the Emperor, that he decided not to purchase him and had him sent back to the stables of the *Manège des Ecuyers* of Saumur. It is this affinity that Anna Fillis had with her horses.

A good *écuyer* or *écuyère* must never hesitate when giving a command or executing a movement. The horse must know the rider well and have total confidence in her or his commands. It is this confidence that Anna Fillis (and many other *écuyères* such as Loyo and Cuzent) gave to her horses to the point that they would go with her to the end of the world if she did not tell them to stop.

Many of the *écuyères* trained their own horses and imposed upon them certain exercises and disciplines. For it is only when one trains and exercises one's own horse that one can know and understand the qualities and defects of one's horse. It is only then that one can determine the strength and aptitude of a horse, how much one can ask of him, how to regulate the necessary exercises to eliminate certain problems and enhance certain features.

Another important *écuyère* was Diane Dupont. She, too, exhibited what is known as the French Classical School of equitation. She had first been a successful actress. She was also a horsewoman who rode for pleasure, an *amazone*. Zidler, the director of the Hippodrome, had often encountered Diane Dupont as she rode in the Bois. On one occasion he had told her that she would soon be performing for him at the Hippodrome. Indeed, the day she heard of a little mare who was for sale, her fate was sealed. She went to see the mare, found her perfect and bought her. With a horse of excellent conformation and disposition, she felt she had to take lessons so that her seat and posture could become irreproachable.

She went to James Fillis for instruction. Very soon her horsemanship became so good that Zidler offered her an engagement at the Hippodrome. She found work as an *écuyère* more amusing and rewarding than as an actress. With her horses Dollar, a horse she had bought from Elisa Petzold who was retiring, Zampa, and Froufrou, a jumper who had twice been a winner at the *Concours hippique*, she performed at the Hippodrome, in the Renz circus in Vienna, in Berlin, at Covent Garden in London, and in Brussels. Upon her return to Paris she worked at the *Cirque d'Eté* and the *Nouveau Cirque*. Similar to the performances of Anna Fillis and Pauline Cuzent, the performances of Diane Dupont and her horses were elegant, harmonious, and expressed lightness. Dollar was so light and supple, had so much *élan* or dash, he could spring into the air to do the levade, the ballotade, or the capriole with little or no effort. He was always correct and graceful, always in the idiom of the French school.

Another outstanding *écuyère* was Adèle Drouin. She was the pupil of Maxime Gaussen and de Corbie, both well-known *écuyers*. She appeared at the Hippodrome around 1866 where she worked until it burned down. The horses schooled by Gaussen were put to the *airs relevés* of the old school, the levade, ballotade, capriole, etc. airs not much practised during the nineteenth century. Drouin's seat was so outstanding that she was never 'displaced', unlike many of the *écuyers* who were not always able successfully to take the jumps of their horses when they returned to the ground and were often displaced in the saddle.

She often worked without a bridle with her horse Diane who had been trained by *général* Faverot de Kerbrech, who, when Baucher was blind and ill, published the latest principles of the master, known as *la deuxième manière*.

Like Baucher, Faverot de Kerbrech stressed lightness as an important attribute, and that 'the quest and preservation of lightness must be the constant preoccupation of the rider. By "lightness of hand" one means the quality of the horse who obeys the aids without weighing on the hand, and without the hand experiencing the sensation of a weight more or less difficult to withstand or a force that resists the action of the hand. Lightness is felt when there is no resistance to the effects of the curb or snaffle . . .'[29]

This lightness was evident when Drouin's horse performed flying lead changes, canter strike-offs intermingled with flying lead changes and instantaneous halts followed immediately by half turns executed at the reinback, or when he performed the piaffe, the passage, intermingled with various reinbacks and immediate halts. At the end of her performance she did an extended trot into the centre of the arena with a quick and brusque halt and left the arena with a fast reinback. All these movements were performed without a bridle, with a marked lightness and without any hesitation on the part of the horse.

Elisa Petzold, together with Anna Fillis and Emilie Loisset, performed *haute école* during the first half of the 1880s. While Vaux greatly admired the grand-daughter of a rich soap merchant from Toeplitz, he criticized her for making 'too many concessions to the public and making use of germanic gimmicks, such as having her horses go down on bended knee'.[30] Vaux felt that these 'germanic gimmicks' were not necessary by so fine a horsewoman who rode so beautifully, elegantly, and with ease. Cony, especially, a smallish mare, was well disciplined and light, yet powerful in her hindquarters. In fact, all her horses were naturally balanced and both she and they performed without any appreciable effort. Cony's 'lead changes at two tempi' were executed with an erect head, immobile body, never deviating from a straight line. With all this precision, she was graceful. The final accolade given her by Vaux is when he says that 'Miss Elisa belonged to the elite, she was also someone who was herself . . .'[31]

Elisa Petzold's passion for riding and desire to be an *écuyère* was of such extraordinary proportions, indeed, that it affected the whole family. For her father, when he realized that his daughter was serious about becoming an *écuyère* in the circus, bundled her off to an Ursuline convent in the hope that she would get over this passion of hers. However, a year later, when she left the convent, her passion was as persistent as ever. Her father reluctantly allowed her to take riding lessons with the famous Gustave Steinbrecht. And her career was launched.

Countess Fanny Ghyga or Ghika was born on a large plantation in Hungary. Her childhood was spent mostly on horseback, riding through the vast parental terrain. She was then married to one of the most distinguished officers in the Serbian army. But marriage soon became a prison and she wanted her freedom. She asked for a divorce which her husband would not grant. One day a transient circus showed up in the town nearby. She joined this circus, leaving her home for ever. She did *haute école* in St Petersburg, Moscow, Milan, and Vienna. It was in Vienna that Zidler, director of the Hippodrome, saw her and engaged her.

Ghyga was, according to Vaux and d'Etreillis a distinguished *écuyère*. She was also an individualist who performed mostly 'in travesti'. Like so many *écuyères* trained in the 'germanic way', she, too, was prone to what d'Etreillis called ' germanic gimmicks'. According to Vaux, she was also too audacious and too sure of herself, which, in the end, sealed her doom. She had

---

[29] Faverot de Kerbrech, *Dressage méthodique du cheval de selle*, Paris: Jean-Michel Place, 1990, 6.

[30] Vaux, *Ecuyers et écuyères*, 147.

[31] Ibid., 148.

unfortunately acquired the habit of being too involved with the public, especially those in the second and third sections, whose idol she was. She would smile up at them, bow to them, and, in the process not pay attention to her horse who was then left to his own devices. On the last day of her engagement, she was, as usual, posing and smiling, and 'making glowing eyes' to the public, when her horse, 'who had defective hocks, no longer felt held in check, tripped, making a very brusque movement, just at the moment when the rider made an affected movement with her hip'.[32] Fanny Ghyga, taken by surprise by this movement, was unseated and, unfortunately, could not remove her foot out of the stirrup iron. She was dragged around the arena, bloody and unconscious. When she revived, she could not put her foot on the ground. She was taken to Beaujour hospital where Dr Lefort, who examined her leg, decided that it was not broken. But two days later, her leg was terribly swollen. Gangrene had set in. She died, dressed as she had been during her last performance. Her dog Turc, a mastiff, who served as her bodyguard and accompanied her to the circus and waited faithfully for her to end her performance, that night waited for her in vain. He continued to wait for a number of nights. Someone noticed him, tried to feed him, but he would not eat. He only emitted now and then a terrible howl. The circus people tried to keep him. He left a few days later and never returned. It is hoped that he died quickly on the tomb of his mistress.

While a controversy between two so-called different methods in equitation raged in France during the first half of the nineteenth century, namely the controversy between Baucher and d'Aure, a second controversy also occurred within the *haute école* idiom as performed in the circus. This new controversy centred around the equitation as performed by the riders and the training of horses. This becomes evident when one reads the works of d'Etreillis and Vaux. It should be pointed out that these books were written after the defeat of France during the Franco-Prussian war of 1870. In their discussion of the various *écuyères* who practised *haute école* in the nineteenth century, some had been trained in France by such *écuyers* as Franconi, Baucher, Pellier, Gaussen, Fillis, and many other famous horsemen such as Faverot de Kerbrech, whose aim and trademark was lightness and brilliance. Other *écuyères*, however, had been trained by *écuyers* in the 'germanic way', men such as Gustave Steinbrecht, Seeger, Plinzner, and others. These *écuyères* and their horses were criticized because they exhibited what d'Etreillis calls 'equestrian automatism' which he felt these riders and their horses were exhibiting, that is, their horses were reacting mechanically and with brusqueness and the riders were also stiff and mechanical. Vaux is especially critical when it comes to what he calls 'these germanic gimmicks', gimmicks such as making the horse go down on his knees, perform acrobatic stunts such as jumping over a table on which were placed lighted candles, or a rider picking up a scarf from the ground with her teeth, off her horse, etc.[33] In other words, it was only the purest movements that a rider and horse executed that were admired by the aficionados.[34]

It should, however, be clarified that when the term 'germanic gimmicks' are mentioned and condemned, they are not necessarily gimmicks limited to the *écuyers* or *écuyères* and their horses trained by *écuyers* from across the Rhine or the Danube. Rather, these so-called gimmicks are symptomatic of the circus

---

[32] Ibid., 143.
[33] Similarly to what the Spanish Riding School does when it performs in the US and introduces such gimmicks as making a horse jump through a flaming hoop, comedy acts, etc.
[34] One should add that this controversy between Germanic and Romanic Classical dressage still exists today.

itself. *Général* Decarpentry describes accurately the differences between *haute école* as practised by the purists and *haute école* as practised in the circus. 'It is, however, of no concern to the circus rider if a few connoisseurs, enlightened by their equestrian education, are saddened by the perversion of their art as displayed in his presentations... The circus rider must arouse the enthusiasm of the philistines by his stunts, acrobatics and airs of bravura. Extravagance of movements, sometimes even frenzy, are necessary to enchant the audience, rather than purity of style. While Baucher had real talent, he was forced, as General L'Hotte put it, "to sacrifice to false gods".'[35] Or, as Baucher, himself, used to say bitterly that 'For ten *sous* I must show off like a circus actor.' It was precisely purity of style that d'Etreillis and Vaux admired in some of the *écuyères* and which they found lacking in others. And it was performing *haute école* in the circus which contributed to the Baucher/d'Aure controversy, as well as to the decision made by the French army, first to engage Baucher to teach the officers of Saumur, Lunéville, and Paris how to train their mounts by using his *nouvelle méthode*, and then to annul this engagement. And years later, while the members of the *Comité de Cavalerie* praised the work of James Fillis, it was his performances of *haute école* in the circus, and his not being a military man, which prevented him from teaching at the cavalry schools.

While the *écuyères* who have been discussed, demonstrated brilliance in the arena, they also exhibited spirited and enterprising abilities when it came to exterior riding, a trait not always to be found among circus or *manège écuyers*.

There is an amusing anecdote which is told about Caroline Loyo. One day, Caroline Loyo and two rich and famous escorts were riding on the rather dusty avenue de Saint-Cloud. The horses her escorts were riding were beautiful and expensive thoroughbreds, while Loyo rode her favourite mare, Junon, on whom she performed at the *Cirque Franconi*. Junon, ridden by Loyo, appeared full of grace and energy, and possessed strong hocks. Otherwise she was nothing compared to the horses of her escorts.

As they walked in leisurely fashion, they discussed the worth of their respective mounts. The two owners of the thoroughbreds derided somewhat Loyo's horse. A bet was made as to which horse could run the fastest. Along the way, they met two officer-pupils of the *Ecole d'Etat major* who greeted them politely. The three riders then asked the two young officer-pupils to serve as judges to a bet they had made, namely, that Loyo's horse could not beat the two thoroughbreds in a race. The loser was to provide a supper at the Moulin-Rouge. The distance was set, namely an oak tree at a particular junction. One of the cadets took up his position about 300 feet from the starting line to give the take-off signal; the other one took his position at the large oak tree and was to determine the winner.

The three contestants left at the same time. Then Loyo, bent over her horse's neck, gave a strident cry, raised her crop, but without touching Junon, who now seemed to fly. She flew past the two thoroughbreds, and arrived at the tree seven or eight lengths ahead of the other two horses. Loyo halted the horse on her hocks, made her do a perfect half-turn, go on one knee, and then laughed in the faces of her two escorts. They gracefully accepted defeat and, apparently, her mockery.[36]

This victory seems to prove that a well-schooled and energetic but ordinary *manège* horse is capable of out-performing and beating a thoroughbred in a race. A horse trained in cross-country equitation, is usually incapable of doing *manège* work. But, then, it

---

[35] Decarpentry, *Academic Equitation*, 3. [36] Vaux, *Ecuyers et écuyères*, 116–18.

is the competence of the rider who usually determines the outcome, as d'Aure and L'Hotte were able to do. And as La Loyo just did.

Another *écuyère* who rode at dare-devil speed was Camille Van Walberg. Of Dutch origin but living in France with her family, she was sent to a boarding school in England, which she abhorred. Upon her return to France she asked her father, a horseman himself who kept a good stable, to let her ride his horses. She became a dare-devil rider who could ride any horse. Often the residents of the Maison-Lafitte, when they saw her galloping past them, wondered who this child was. One day, in a hurry, just as she was approaching the train tracks, a train was approaching and the barrier was lowered. Rather than be late, she deftly turned her horse around, got into a gallop and jumped the barrier, missing the train by a hair.

Her general education considered incomplete by her family who envisioned a successful marriage for her, she was again sent to a boarding school, this time in France. Fortunately for Camille, her father lost the family fortune and went to India to remake it. This financial change permitted her to follow her vocation – horsemanship. Though she could ride well, she was aware that she was not yet a skilled horsewoman. She took lessons from the *comte* de Montigny, a former *écuyer* of both the *Ecole de Versailles* and the *Ecole de Cavalerie* of Saumur and a remarkable horseman. Camille soon became an excellent *écuyère*.

And there is Countess Ghyga, born in the middle of a large plantation in Hungary who spent most of her childhood riding cross-country and living only for her horses and riding. Petzold was also a rider who could ride any horse. While in the *manège* she rode with harmony, that is Classically, when outside in the woods or countryside, she rode enterprisingly and was the equal of, as Vaux puts it, any 'sportswoman of England'. Anna Fills was also a fervent proponent of exterior riding.

It is, of course, not possible to consider here the many *écuyères* (as it was not possible to consider the many *amazones* riding in the Bois) who enchanted and delighted the vast and socially diverse circus public throughout the nineteenth century. As Vaux and Molier have frequently stated, the nineteenth century was, indeed, the era of the *écuyères*. Their prestige was considerable. They were admired and honoured by all levels of society. The same can be said of many *écuyers*, men such as François Baucher, Jules Pellier, Laurent Franconi, and James Fillis. It was these men, but especially these women, doing *haute école* in the many circuses of the period, who gave the circus class and dignity and who kept *haute école* equitation alive. They were even admired and supported by many amateur and professional purists who went to the circus to applaud them. Baucher, for example, was greatly admired by the *duc* d'Orléans who leased a loge and, with his family, often came to see him perform; he also visited him frequently at the *manège* where Baucher taught.

The *écuyères*, especially, were admired and respected. This esteem and prestige they were given, differed markedly from how society usually treated ballet dancers, performers at the *variétés*, actresses, and even opera singers. Many of the *écuyères* came from the aristocracy, women such as Mathilde d'Embrun, Countess Fanny Ghyga, the *baroness* von Rhaden; some came from the bourgeoisie like Elisa Petzold, daughter of a rich soap manufacturer. Some were the daughters or wives of great *écuyers* like Anna Fillis or great circus families like Cuzent. Molière's wife, Arletti, also performed in the circus. Some even managed to make good marriages. Emilie Loisset, trained by Caroline Loyo, was engaged to a Prussian officer, Prince Hazfeldt. Unfortunately the marriage came to naught when the horse Emilie was riding fell on top of her and crushed her. Her sister, Clotilde, also an *écuyère*, was engaged to another Prussian officer, Prince Reuss. The girls came from the famous Dutch family of circus performers headed by Antoine Loisset. Caroline Loyo married into this family. Loyo, as we have seen, was herself held in great esteem when she toured England.

Why was so much honour, esteem, and prestige given to these *écuyères* of the nineteenth century and not to other female performers? Perhaps this discrepancy can be explained by the fact that since horsemanship was and always had been the prerogative of the upper classes, that is, the men and women of the aristocracy and the *haute* bourgeoisie, who admired those skills, it is understandable that they would admire and respect the *écuyères* who exhibited these very skills. Men and women of these social classes enjoyed being entertained by performers of the ballet, the theatre, the opera, but could not identify with them, as they could with the *écuyères*. In fact, we know from accounts and novels, that they were often scorned by the women who went to see them and used by their husbands and sons. But the skill of the *écuyères* could instil the admiration and respect of other horsemen and horsewomen, even if they were performing in the circus. Many of the *écuyères* were carefully chaperoned by relatives, especially when they travelled to perform in foreign countries. And if no relative was forthcoming, as with Fanny Ghyga, her mastiff Turc took that role.

9
L'Hotte's legacy

As we have seen, L'Hotte compared pure *haute école* equitation with circus haute école equitation and discussed methods in dressage in his two before last chapters of *Questions équestres* (chapters 12 and 13). He ended his chapter on the schooling of horses on a less than optimistic note when he said that equitation, like many of the other arts, has not progressed much with time. Modified, yes, but not progressed. One almost gets the impression that he believed, as did Rousselet, that equitation may have even regressed to some extent.

Indeed, says L'Hotte, methods of schooling have been modified due to changes in the needs and tastes of society; the nature and the conformation of the horse, his size, have also been modified to conform with the tastes and needs of society. Yet, L'Hotte continues, these changes have not necessarily improved the training of pupils and the schooling of horses. Whether schooled for military purposes, cross-country or pleasure riding, for the hunt, obstacle jumping, *manège* riding, the goal has always been similar if not the same. It was La Guérinière who put it most succinctly: 'By means of hard work, the aim of dressage is to make the horse light and obedient so that he is pleasant in his movements and comfortable for the rider. This is valid for the hunter, the military horse, and the school [*manège*] horse.'[1] These are requisites that all riders, regardless of discipline, hope to find when they take up equitation.

L'Hotte begins his final chapter with a presentation of the great horsemen and *écuyers* who have illuminated certain periods in history with their instruction, their written works, and their precepts. The vast equestrian truths, says L'Hotte, have come to the fore at all periods. They belong to all schools.

There are a number of connecting ideas – a golden thread – between the precepts developed and transmitted by the true masters of equitation. If these truths have not always been disseminated, it is either because prejudices have prevented their dissemination, or they have simply been omitted because they have escaped the attention of horsemen and *écuyers*.

Almost all horsemen and *écuyers* endowed with the spirit of observation, together with knowledge and considerable experience, have been able to come up with ideas, methods, precepts, and principles similar to those made by many of their predecessors. After all, the horse, that is, his psychic and physical nature, has not changed much. Neither has man, physically, psychologically, and emotionally changed much since medieval times. But the knowledge required to school the horse presents and has always presented an endless task and a constant search.

---

[1] La Guérinière, François Robichon de, *Ecole de cavalerie*, Vol. I, Paris, La Compagnie, MDCCLXIX, 113. Also the recent English translation London: J. A. Allen, 1994, 79.

L'Hotte further states that if equitation has not followed a progressive path, at least 'the history of equitation teaches us that great artists have stood out and illuminated the field at certain given periods'.[2] To this category of great teachers who have appeared at different times, L'Hotte mentions La Broue, Pluvinel, Duplessis, La Guérinière, Nestier, Lubersac, d'Auvergne, Chabannes, d'Abzac, Baucher, and d'Aure. Each one, in his own way, says L'Hotte, has contributed to the greatness of French equitation.

An important question which L'Hotte raised in his last chapter is why some of the great *écuyers* have not produced great pupils. When L'Hotte raises and tries to explain the question of great masters not producing great pupils and disciples, he is, perhaps, also attempting to explain and, even justify, his own lacuna.

L'Hotte gives a rather lengthy explanation to this question in the hope of 'doing justice to the men who have been involved in equestrian teaching and who have generally been reproached for not having produced outstanding pupils. It must be understood that by pupil we are speaking here of *écuyers* of real worth whose talent as teachers corresponds to their talent as practitioners.'[3]

The equestrian art, says L'Hotte, has always produced less outstanding men than have the other arts. The equestrian art is a complex art and involves three special requirements that the other arts do not have.

First, there is the practitioner himself.

To become a somewhat complete horseman and *écuyer*, the practitioner must possess qualities that are seldom incorporated in one individual. These qualities include a man's physical make-up which has to be specific and well defined. The sculptor or painter is free from such requirements.

The horseman must be both energetic and calm, gentle without weakness, steadfast without harshness. He must always be master of himself, be able to act on the horse by opposing traits, such as, opposing patience to impatience, calmness to violence, energy to laziness. He must have moral courage and never be discouraged. No difficulties should make him flinch. Perseverance, a quality all artists must have, the equestrian artist must possess of it to a greater degree. He must be intelligent and understand the psychology of the horse. For he must be aware of everything. He must possess equestrian tact which will make him aware of the nature of the horse's contractions.

Equestrian tact, that is, 'l'àpropos et la mesure' (perfect timing and good measure),[4] which will develop in time, is essential to the *écuyer*, the artist-horseman, just as a sense of colour or a sense of harmony is essential to the painter or the musician.

A long period of practice and considerable experience are necessary for the rider to become an *écuyer*. To gain experience is more important in the case of the artist-horseman than it is for other artists. For example, says L'Hotte, d'Aure's *Traité d'Equitation* of 1834 and his *Cours d'Equitation* of 1853 are appropriate examples with respect to the importance of experience. Comparing these two works of d'Aure, L'Hotte believes that one can clearly see how the time that elapsed between the two works produced a marked distinction between the earlier pupil and the later master, revealing greater equestrian knowledge and talent as a horseman during the later period of his life.

The second requirement is the horse.

The horse, says L'Hotte, adds to the equestrian art an additional and complex dimension. First, the horseman must be

---

[2] *Questions équestres*, 197.
[3] Ibid., 199.
[4] I have translated *mesure* as 'measure', that is, 'beat'. Taken together with *l'à-propos*, which I translated as 'perfect timing', 'measure' seems more appropriate. It should also be noted that in seventeenth and eighteenth-century France the term *mesure* also meant 'moderation' which I also considered, but discarded.

familiar with the horse, have studied him in order to know how to submit him to his will and direct his movements.

If one considers the horse as raw material just as the sculptor considers marble or clay as raw material, then the problems of the rider differ considerably. The sculptor usually finds the raw material the same. It may vary in its consistency, but it does not have a will or a disposition of its own. The raw material of the rider varies considerably, not merely between different horses, but in the same horse from day to day. His moral behaviour can change from one day to the next so that his physical or mental condition will force the rider to react to these different conditions. How often does a rider have success one day, only to fail abysmally the next day, merely because the horse has changed either physically or mentally. The instrument of the musician is inert of itself and the same action will always produce the same effect. It is quite different with the horse. Life, his will, animates him and therein lie the thousand and one nuances in the way he presents himself and responds to the artist who rides him.

In a way, there can occur a deception on the part of the rider of which the musician is totally free: the loss of his instrument. If the musician loses his instrument, he can usually replace it quickly, and his artistry can continue with little or no interruption. With the rider the loss of his instrument, the horse, can have horrendous consequences. For it means that several years of work are lost and that it will take him several additional years to school and put into a fine and final condition the horse who will replace the one he has lost.

If he has a high sense of his art, the horseman, like the other artists, will be eternally in quest of the nuances of his art, and the purity of his work. 'In general, the moment an artist believes that he has achieved the summit of his art, he reveals the extent of his mediocrity. The true artist, on the other hand, who thinks he sees the end of his efforts disappearing as his talent increases, proves thereby the value and range of his sensibility, for it lets him see his goal move farther away from his reach, which, in turn, gives him more and more the sense of the nature of perfection.'[5] Likewise, the true artist-horseman, the *écuyer* who has become one with his horse, feels that perfection is never attainable. Yet his quest goes on for the unattainable perfection.

L'Hotte mentions d'Abzac and Baucher as examples of two *écuyers* who were for ever searching for perfection. D'Abzac at the age of eighty said that he was still learning something new every day, every time he got off his horse. And, says L'Hotte, there was the constant search on the part of Baucher for newer and better ways to achieve lightness. These two men, whose talents were considerable in the schooling of horses and who came close to perfection, still did not feel that they had achieved it.

L'Hotte retells how one day he had told Baucher that he was never quite satisfied with the schooling of his horses. To this Baucher replied: 'But it will always be this way. There is always something more that one wants.'[6]

In short, when one considers the means with which each artist makes use of his instrument, it becomes evident that the artist-horseman has greater difficulty coping when compared with the sculptor or musician. With the rider, all parts of his body come into play and have to be agile as well as in harmony with himself and with his horse in order to make the joints and muscles of his horse become flexible so that he can extend or shorten his movements and harmonize them.

The third problem involves the person who transmits the equestrian art, namely, the teacher.

---

[5] *Questions*, 208.   [6] *Ibid.*, 209.

These difficulties are based, first, on the lack of permanence in equestrian matters; secondly, on the difficulties the teacher has in instilling confidence in his pupil.

To grasp properly the first of these obstacles, L'Hotte resorts once again to making a comparison with painting. When the painter makes a stroke of the brush on his pupil's canvas, or a pencil mark to his drawing, the result remains constant under the eyes of his pupil, for the teacher's rectifications are permanent. They will impress themselves in the mind of his disciple and elucidate the teacher's intentions and feelings. But with respect to equitation, it is different. The work of the master and the schooled horse can only be appreciated by the pupil momentarily. The rectification made by the master of the pupil's false position or an irregular movement is only fleeting.

Furthermore, the master encounters certain difficulties in trying to convince the pupil of the validity of the principles to which he is being introduced. To do so takes time, for the means at the disposal of the *écuyer* are insufficient, primarily due to the lack of permanency in equestrian matters and the variable conditions which the horse presents. In equestrian matters, the same actions do not always produce the same results. Another difficulty that the *écuyer* encounters is that he has to make the pupil appreciate the validity of the methods and the means that he uses. He also has to deal with the doubt that often takes hold of a pupil. It has often happened that a pupil will say of the teacher: 'He does not always do what he says.'[7] An *écuyer* worthy of this name, always does what he teaches; and does better than the pupil. If facts sometimes give credence to this statement made by a pupil, it is because the pupil is not aware that a precept may have a myriad of modifications in its application and yet does not lose the import of its validity.

The sphere of action of the teacher is extensive and he has in his hands the wherewithal to make a horseman out of his pupil. But primarily a pupil for cross-country or pleasure riding. He can give his pupil the right posture, regularize his position and, then, let him be in harmony with his horse. He must show him how to use his aids with precision. By giving him clear and precise demonstrations, he can point out to him the goals he has to follow, and demonstrate for him the means that regulate indoor and outdoor exercises. Above all, he can serve as an example, enlighten him, and develop an equestrian sensibility in him by making him aspire to the impossible. The work that an *écuyer* has to accomplish when the pupil has greater equestrian ambitions contains all of the above-mentioned prerequisites, but is, of course, considerably greater and lengthier.

At a time when d'Aure and Baucher shone in all their greatness, it was certainly not the masters that were lacking. Everyone recognized in d'Aure his brilliance as a horseman. True, some, contrary to L'Hotte's personal opinion, felt that d'Aure lacked the gift of transmitting his knowledge.

'When it came to Baucher, apart from his irreproachable and sound horsemanship, no one could deny him his most remarkable talent as a teacher. For there one could perhaps discern the most striking side of this learned *écuyer*. True, Baucher was not asked to direct a training school of equitation, but his whole life was spent teaching in France and in foreign countries.'[8]

L'Hotte mentions briefly the rivalry that occurred between the schools of d'Aure and Baucher which brought forth passionate disciples and which, nonetheless, gave French equitation an unprecedented lustre. But outstanding *écuyers* are rare, adds L'Hotte, not only today, but at all times. Only d'Aure, a man of true talent, could replace d'Abzac at the *Manège de Versailles*.

If *écuyers* of merit were a rarity in France,

---

[7] Ibid., 213. [8] Ibid., 216.

they were even more of a rarity outside of France. And foreign countries were often forced to seek men outside their own countries, unable to find them inside their own. French *écuyers* were sought after to take up positions in other countries, for example, men such as d'Abzac and, before him, the Marquis de la Bigne of the *Manège de Versailles*, to name but a few. It should also be remembered that eighteenth-century France was invaded by foreigners of distinction who came to observe the various cavalry schools as well as to take instruction in them. And Henri Baucher, says L'Hotte, the son of François Baucher, became part of an English duke's stables.

Also not many works on equitation emerged from foreign countries. Everyone knows that the works of La Guérinière became the equestrian bible beyond the Rhine.

In conclusion, says L'Hotte, the rarity of outstanding écuyers and the absence of outstanding disciples and pupils, is caused by the great demands that the equestrian art makes.

I have spent a certain amount of time discussing certain questions that L'Hotte raised in his last chapter because some of them are applicable to him. But before attempting to answer some of them, I would like to bring up once again, the criticism made by Jacques Perrier.

As I pointed out earlier, L'Hotte has been accused of immodesty relating to certain facts and events about himself, especially as they pertain to the various successes he experienced in his career as a military man and as a horseman and *écuyer*. His immodesty has been compared with the modesty of Decarpentry by Jacques Perrier. But it should not be forgotten that L'Hotte's *Souvenirs* are the personal recollections of a man who has retired to the place where he was born. There is also the possibility that the retirement of a man who was still vigorous and who did not want to retire, may be the cause of some bitterness and (if immodesty there is), his immodesty. We also know that at the end of his career he had difficulties with the authorities during his last sojourn at Saumur as commandant at the *Ecole de Cavalerie*.

In his book *Academic Equitation* Decarpentry for the most part analyses and describes methods and movements in academic equitation, how these movements have been interpreted and executed by various *écuyers* of Classical equitation, and presents the reader with his own comments and judgements. Quite obviously, *Academic Equitation* is not the *mémoires* of a retired general; rather, it is the outstanding work of a very much active general.

When L'Hotte mentions the successes he has experienced throughout his life, it is not due to self-aggrandizement, but an attempt to present the events in his life as they occurred or, as a man of over seventy remembers them to have occurred. And when he says to his two nephews 'it is for you that I am writing, for you that I am retracing the memories of my childhood, my youth, my career',[9] one should take this statement for what it is. It is, as he says, a way of giving advice to his two nephews; but it is also for his own peace of mind that he is retracing his past life. There may be exaggerations with respect to events and details. Memory can become blurred with time. Above all, it is the sentiment, the feeling, the emotion of the autobiographer, rather than the facts themselves, that may have changed between the time when writing his *mémoires* and the time when the actual events occurred many years earlier. This discrepancy often happens to writers who, in their attempt to catch and recollect the past, present this past with the emotions and feelings of the present, that is, the time of the writing. This is especially true when one is writing about the experiences of one's childhood.[10] Without wanting this to happen

---

[9] *Souvenirs*, 21.   [10] Jean-Jacques Rousseau's *Confessions* is a case in point.

or being aware that this is happening, the perception and, especially, the emotions of the present may colour the past. It is difficult to recollect the emotions of the past and rid oneself completely of the emotions of the present.

In his *Souvenirs*, L'Hotte emerges as a very honest man, a man who preferred criticism and sound advice to flattery when it came to his riding and the schooling of horses. He always found that criticism was helpful and, usually, given to be helpful. L'Hotte believed that the flatterers were all too often seduced by the spectacular movements exhibited by the rider, rather than the purity of the movements. Here was a man who was ready to sacrifice ranking and promotion rather than betray Baucher's method.

When one looks at L'Hotte's *Souvenirs*, it is the many personal reflections and anecdotes which animate the book. While he was considered to be a cold and reserved individual who said little, he emerges as a lively story-teller in his old age.

L'Hotte is not always presented by other horsemen and *écuyers*, especially those of today, with glowing admiration and affection, as is usually the case with Baucher. (One detects a similar negative attitude with respect to d'Aure.) One discerns in many present-day French horsemen a feeling of betrayal when it comes to an evaluation of L'Hotte and d'Aure, betrayal for not having made an effort to keep alive *haute école* equitation at the institutions where they taught. Reference is often made to 'le fil conducteur', – the golden thread – that has been, if not broken, at least weakened or become frayed.

We have seen that L'Hotte (like d'Aure) as *écuyer en chef* and, later, as commandant of the *Ecole de Cavalerie*, never seriously tried to bring back to the *Ecole de Cavalerie* the *nouvelle méthode* of Baucher, that is, *manège* riding, or the practice of the high or artificial airs. Rather, L'Hotte followed primarily the precepts of d'Aure, reserving for himself and his personal horses, the precepts of Baucher when he was off duty. It should not be forgotten that L'Hotte, as a career officer, was bound to adhere to the principles of the French Army as they had been set down for the instructor-officers of the various French cavalry schools. He could not have done otherwise. Resignation would have been his only recourse. And this, quite obviously, he did not want to do. His love for the military and military life and duty was too deeply ingrained in him. The many examples cited by him of officers who had resigned and later regretted this (d'Aure is a case in point), occur too frequently in his *Souvenirs* not to be considered as a very personal and important point. In a way one can say that L'Hotte's strict adherence to army regulations did pay off. Whereas men like François Dutilh (Barada) and Charles-Hubert Raabe, both proponents of Baucher's method, never made it beyond the rank of captain, L'Hotte became a general.

As we have seen, it was primarily when L'Hotte became commandant of the *Ecole de Cavalerie* in 1875 that he officially proscribed practice of the artificial airs and gaits, even during the *reprises des écuyers*.

However, L'Hotte's knowledge of both types of equitation, cross-country or military and *manège* equitation, served him well. So that when he proscribed *haute école* equitation and the high airs, he could do so with authority. No one could accuse him of prohibiting *haute école* equitation out of inadequacy or ignorance, as had been said of d'Aure by his critics. The letter written to him by Faverot de Kerbrech in July 1890 is sufficient proof of L'Hotte's ability to school his horses in *haute école*, adhere to military or exterior equitation, and synthesize the two schools.

We have seen in the chapters dealing with Baucher and which form part of his *Souvenirs*, that while they are filled with praise and admiration for the master, L'Hotte, nonetheless, expressed certain reservations with respect to certain methods introduced by Baucher, namely, the suppling of the horse's jaw and neck which L'Hotte considers excessive, and the lack of impulsion which, he felt, was a characteristic of Baucher's horses.[11]

When one takes these reservations which L'Hotte expressed with respect to Baucher into consideration and juxtaposes them to his criticism of Saint-Phalle's work, one is rather surprised at the outburst that occurred when L'Hotte and Saint-Phalle met in Lunéville through the intermediary of Faverot de Kerbrech who admired the two men for their equestrian skills. For the criticisms L'Hotte made with respect to certain methods used by Baucher, are similar to those made by Saint-Phalle. And while L'Hotte's reaction to Saint-Phalle was undoubtedly due to the latter's criticism of Baucher, there is, it seems, another, perhaps more valid, explanation.

An explanation for L'Hotte's negative reaction becomes evident when one reads his *Souvenirs*. When L'Hotte was *écuyer en chef* at Saumur, he was approached by d'Aure's publisher who asked him to edit d'Aure's latest book and bring it up to date. This L'Hotte refused to do, saying that to do so would be an insult to his master. He had no right to rewrite the book. When the publisher then asked L'Hotte to write his own manual on equitation, L'Hotte again refused, indicating that this would imply that he wanted to replace d'Aure's book, currently used by the pupils at Saumur, with his own. More importantly, he believed that he was, as yet, not sufficiently experienced to write a manual about equitation and dressage. L'Hotte was then forty years of age. When one reads his *Souvenirs* one becomes aware that the terms 'experienced' and 'inexperienced' juxtaposed to the word '*écuyer*', appear so frequently that one must take them into account when attempting to explain the Saint-Phalle incident.

When Saint-Phalle wrote his *Dressage et Emploi du Cheval de Selle* in 1889, he was twenty-two years of age. In the eyes of L'Hotte, he was certainly too young and too inexperienced a horseman to write a mature and perceptive book about dressage and the use of the saddle horse. After all, what equestrian experience could so young a man have acquired? That Saint-Phalle was immature and inexperienced is also stated, albeit obliquely, during L'Hotte's outburst at the dinner table.

When one compares the number of pages L'Hotte devotes to Baucher and to d'Aure, one is aware that when he discusses and defends d'Aure he does so with greater enthusiasm. While he defends Baucher and calls him 'the greatest *écuyer* who ever lived', there seems to be missing in these chapters on Baucher the same degree of vigour he devotes to d'Aure, and, above all, one does not find the many anecdotes which are interspersed here and there and animate the chapters on d'Aure.

One should, however, not forget that when L'Hotte discusses d'Aure's precepts and riding skill, he is also discussing his own skill, as well as many of his own precepts, his own thoughts. Furthermore, L'Hotte and d'Aure belonged to the same social milieu. They had the same origins, both were Saint-Cyriens, they spoke the same language. They often went riding cross-country together or visited the Haras du Pin together. Quite obviously, there was more contact between the two. With Baucher, it was primarily a teacher-pupil relationship; indeed, a close relationship, but not a social one.

While L'Hotte was a skilled rider, some critics have said that he was a poor teacher. In a footnote to *Baucher et son école*, Decarpentry says that L'Hotte 'while endowed with great skill as a rider, was less so as an instructor'[12] and that his coldness and reserve verged on being a stubborn mutism.

---

[11] The Baucherized horse as of 1849 is described in *Souvenirs*, 111.

[12] Decarpentry, *Baucher et son école*, 39.

Furthermore, Decarpentry, quotes *général* Mennessier de la Lance, in *Maitres écuyers du Manège de Saumur* as saying: 'His cold and reserved disposition prejudiced his teaching. He did not try to please and he made few pupils... His personal work was done in private and no one could risk an indiscrete glance in the *manège*.'[13] However, Decarpentry acknowledges that the pupil of Baucher and d'Aure, that is, L'Hotte, 'while the equal of his two masters in the practice of equitation, had surpassed them by far with respect to the theory of equitation'.[14] Indeed, even Baucher once told L'Hotte that his (the latter's) horses were better trained than his own had ever been.

One of L'Hotte's pupils, Gaborit de Montjou, who became the seventeenth *écuyer en chef* at the *Manège des Ecuyers* has expressed great admiration for L'Hotte and his skill as a horseman. Under his authority, Montjou could boast of a number of outstanding *écuyers*: Saint-Phalle, Decarpentry, Detroyat, Danloux, Wattel, Lafont, who formed a group known as the *Pléiades*. While Montjou was Squadron Captain at Lunéville, he often observed L'Hotte, the *muet sublime*, who, during retirement, had become more volatile than when he had been an instructor at Saumur or Saint-Cyr. Montjou, with many other cavalry officers and horsemen, was one of the many visitors L'Hotte received at Lunéville during his retirement. *Général* Lafont, a member of this *Pléiades* while praising Montjou, also praised L'Hotte when he said: '"I consider commandant de Montjou the complete horseman of *haute école*, in the same way that *général* L'Hotte defines such a horseman as one who embodies perfection in the execution of a natural movement, rather than an artificial movement, which is often erroneously considered as being the characteristic of *haute école*, but is actually part of circus equitation."'[15]

I have frequently said that there is a golden thread running throughout the history of equitation in France, linking men and schools from the sixteenth century on to the nineteenth century and the present. Men such as Solomon de la Broue, Antoine de Pluvinel, François Robichon de La Guérinière, to name but a few, can be eminently considered as forming part of this golden thread and contributing in no small way to what has come to be known as the French Classical School of Equitation.

Taking this into consideration, it is interesting to note that Etienne Saurel in his *Histoire de l'équitation*, says that 'what is known as French doctrine and the precepts that have been applied to contemporary equitation, have been mainly taken from nineteenth century *écuyers* who were involved with and followed the teachings of the *comte* d'Aure. On the other hand', continues Saurel, 'when it comes to higher level or *haute école* equitation, it is to Baucher and his many military disciples, especially L'Hotte and Faverot de Kerbrech, from whom derive the precepts applicable to this type of equitation.'[16]

Saurel further states that to discuss the main traits of the French School one must include the history of the *Manège des Ecuyers* of the *Ecole de Cavalerie*, which contains many more illustrious names than those of the *Ecole de Cavalerie*. It is also interesting to note that while many of the *écuyers* were members of the *Cadre Noir*, the *Cadre Noir* as such, merely functioned *de facto*, or, as Jacques Perrier puts it, 'remained a myth until 21 January 1986'[17] when it was officially linked to the *Ecole Nationale d'Equitation*, thus acquiring a *de jure* entity.

I have also tried to point out that there is not only a golden thread weaving its way

---

[13] Decarpentry, *Maîtres écuyers*, 48.
[14] Ibid., 47.
[15] Perrier, *Maîtres écuyers*, 76.
[16] Etienne Saurel, *Histoire de l'équitation*, Paris, Stock, 1971, 321–2.
[17] Perrier, *L'Epopée*, 9.

from the past to the present, encompassing the names of many great *écuyers*; but there is also a crossing over between the various schools of equitation and the men who practised and taught the equestrian art in these schools.

In view of what Saurel said earlier, it seems to me that he is stating, by implication, that, as far as modern French equitation is concerned, the *Manège des Ecuyers* played a greater role in the development of French equitation than did the *Manège de Versailles*, in that, firstly, it was able to make a greater degree of synthesis of both types of riding; secondly, that it was able to do so because the *Ecole de Cavalerie* continued to prosper, while the *Ecole de Versailles* had to close its doors. To substantiate this point, Saurel refers to the 1942 edition of the *Manual d'équitation et de dressage* to be used by the officers and NCOs of the *Ecole de Cavalerie* of Saumur. This manual makes clear that the goal is to preserve the fundamental rules of Classical equitation, as well as to introduce into the rules of Classical equitation, contemporary horsemanship, that is, horsemanship of the new age. The rules to which the manual refers are, of course, the precepts set down by La Broue, Pluvinel, La Guérinière, d'Aure, Baucher, L'Hotte, Faverot de Kerbrech, and others.

Saurel also points out that the rules stated in the *Manual* of 1942 for the Officers and NCOs of the *Ecole*, while eliminating the military aspect, have become part of the *Fédération Internationale d'Equitation*. Both have identical goals, namely instilling the pupils with the past, that is, with the precepts of the French School of equitation.

Saurel also states that where *haute école* equitation is concerned, it is to Baucher that one must go. Yet, it is somewhat difficult to discern a golden thread in Baucher and discover from whom he received his early equestrian training.

Baucher tells us that as a boy living in Versailles, he watched and admired d'Abzac riding on the parade grounds. We also know that when at thirteen he joined his uncle in Milan, he spent a great deal of time watching renowned *écuyers* of the Neapolitan Riding School schooling their horses. He also tells us that he read manuals on equitation written by famous horsemen of the past, but that, containing many lacunae, they did not contribute much to his equestrian experience.

However, this so-called lacuna in Baucher's background does not actually concern L'Hotte, as it has concerned many other *écuyers*. 'If one does not know at which school he began his instruction', says L'Hotte, 'that is of little concern, for without a doubt, his genius, so totally original, proceeds only on its own, and no school could claim as its pupil the one who became the most illustrious of masters.'[18]

Yet, in an oblique way, there is a golden thread linking Baucher to the past. While in Milan, Baucher frequently observed *écuyers* such as Frederico Mazuchelli. It should be remembered that Mazuchelli was in the tradition of such *écuyers* as Frederico Grisone, Cesare Fiaschi, Giovanni Battista Pignatelli, and others. It was Pignatelli who instructed La Broue, Pluvinel, the Duke of Newcastle, and other noblemen in the equestrian art. While Pluvinel and La Broue discarded some of the less gentle methods used by the members of the Neapolitan Riding School in the schooling of their horses and eliminated the use of some of the harsher bits, they did retain many of the principles and methods they had learned from them. It is perhaps in this way, that is, linking him to the Neapolitan Riding School, that one can speak of a golden thread linking Baucher to French Classical equitation of the past. As far as linking him to the future, we know that Baucher produced a vast number of pupils

---

[18] Souvenirs, 231–2.

and disciples, men such as Faverot de Kerbrech, L'Hotte, Charles-Hubert Raabe (who was also influenced by Rousselet), the *barons* de Vaux and d'Etreillis (both also the pupils of d'Aure), Louis Joseph Rul, and others.[19]

There is also a golden thread linking the *écuyères* performing *haute école* in the circus to horsemen and *écuyers* such as Baucher, Pellier, Gaussen, Faverot de Kerbrech, the *comte* de Montigny, and others who trained many of these *écuyères* and schooled some of their horses or taught them to school their horses.

Ecuyères such as Loyo, Cuzent, Fillis, Dupont, Drouin, and Petzold, they, too, were in search of lightness and purity of movement to be found, as L'Hotte put it, 'in the action of the rider and how the horse reacts to those forces that are alone useful to the movement that is envisaged . . .'[20] All sought harmony between horse and rider. If some of these *écuyères* went beyond purity and simplicity of movement, as advocated by the purists, and indulged in certain 'gimmicks' to the detriment of lightness and purity, it was due to the circumstances under which they operated: the circus and the crowds who wanted to be titillated.

As one surveys the extensive and rich history of the French school of equitation, one cannot but become aware that the quest for lightness was foremost in the minds of French horsemen and *écuyers*. Methods, sequence, styles, even vocabulary, may differ but the goals were the same: a horse who responded immediately to the imperceptible aids of the rider, a horse who was light on the forehand and/or on the haunches, achieved, in varying degrees, by means of the flexibility, submission and play of joints and muscles, a horse who could flow forward freely and energetically, without constraints. But lightness is also a requirement on the part of the rider. A quote from Nuno Oliveira's[21] *Reflections on Equestrian Art* summarizes succinctly the meaning of equestrian art. And, while summarizing equestrian art, it is equally applicable to other equestrian disciplines.

Equestrian art is the perfect understanding between the rider and his horse. This harmony allows the horse to work without any contraction in his joints or his muscles, permitting him to carry out all movements with mental and physical enjoyment as well as with suppleness and rhythm. The horse is then a partner, rather than a slave who is enforced to obey a rigid master by constraint.

To practise equestrian art is to establish a conversation on a higher level with the horse; a dialogue of courtesy and finesse. The rider obtains the collaboration of the horse by the slightest hint of a demand, and the spectator can then see the sublime beauty of this communion. He will be touched by the grace and the form, and captivated as if he were hearing the most grandiose music . . .'[22]

Oliveira ends this introduction with the following advice, advice also given by L'Hotte:

The apex of perfection in equestrian art is not an

---

[19] Whether the term 'pupils' is correct, is difficult to say. All these horsemen came to Baucher as competent horsemen. Both L'Hotte and Faverot de Kerbrech were already skilled horsemen. Faverot de Kerbrech received his early training from his father, a skilled horseman. When l'Hotte became the pupil of Baucher and d'Aure, he, too, was already a skilled horseman. While d'Aure and Baucher gave him his equestrian polish, his early master, Dupuis, who gave him his fundamentals, should not be forgotten. Dupuis, as has already been mentioned, learned the equestrian art from the Marquis de Marialva, the *grand écuyer* to the Portuguese Court who, as Perrier says, most likely taught L'Hotte in the tradition of La Guérinière.

[20] *Souvenirs*, 126.

[21] Michel Henriquet says that Nuno Oliveira was a synthesizer of some of Baucher's precepts (for example, work in hand) and the *Manège de Versailles*. See interview in *Dressage and C.T.* See also Jean-Claude Racinet 'Was Oliveira a Baucherist?', *Dressage and C.T.*, no. 103. April 1995.

[22] Nuno Oliveira, *Reflections on Equestrian Art*, London: J. A. Allen, 1988, 17–18.

exhibition of a great deal of different airs and movements by the same horse, but rather the conservation of the horse's enjoyment, suppleness and finesse during the performance, which calls for comparison with the finest ballet, or the performance of an orchestra, or seeing a play by Racine, so moving is the sight of perfectly harmonized movements.[23]

---

[23] Oliveira, 21.

QUESTIONS ÉQUESTRES
by
Général L'Hotte

translated by Hilda Nelson

To my nephews

ARTHUR L'HOTTE
Captain of the 18th Dragoons

HENRI DE CONIGLIANO
Lieutenant of the 1st Cuirassiers

Lunéville, 28 October 1895

Somewhere in his *Souvenirs, général* L'Hotte says that seldom did he get off his horse without immediately jotting down reflections suggested to him during 'his conversations with his best companion'. The numerous exercise books which he filled with fine and tight writing during his long life contain the result of sixty years of practice and study. The first of these note books contains the notes that the adolescent of fourteen had written down after each lesson with *commandant* Dupuis.[1] This first entry already reveals his passion for horses. The last entry ends October 1894 and includes the observations the old *écuyer*, already in his seventies, continued to record after having ridden his last horses, Glorieux, Domfront, and Insensé, in the solitude of his little *manège* in Lunéville. Whole copy books are devoted to the teachings of d'Aure and Baucher.

From this accumulation of precious material, *général* L'Hotte was able to extract elements for a work on equitation of considerable value. Eliminating from this work everything that he considered superfluous, he reduced the material and shaped it into the little book we are presenting today to the public. These two hundred pages contain the very essence that make up the doctrine of this famous *écuyer*.

In a few enlightening formulae, he defines the principles of his art. In three words, he indicates the goals to be pursued. And without losing himself in the presentation of the means by which these goals can be attained, means which, as he puts it, 'vary *ad infinitum*', he limits himself to delineating some very clear directions.

From this body of principles, of goals to be followed, and the execution of procedures, a simple and clear method emerges, avoiding all complications and based upon common sense and equestrian tact.

To these teachings, *général* L'Hotte adds general considerations pertaining to the art which gave him so much joy during his lifetime. Some of the pages which summarize the thoughts that occupied his mind so frequently, constitute a veritable philosophy of equitation. For example, the chapter where, after having made an outstanding comparison between equitation and the other arts, he explains why, in every age, *écuyers* of merit were few and hard to find, and why they produced few pupils of merit.

Academic or *savante* equitation makes up a large part of this body of 'equestrian questions', but the other disciplines have not been forgotten, and the chapter pertaining to military equitation, despite its brevity, is rich in its presentation of useful exercises. At a time when two years of service are being introduced, making the role of the cavalry officer difficult to pursue, it is useful to realize how extremely simple were the procedures of instruction recommended by the author with

---

[1] *Un Officier de cavalerie, Souvenirs du général* L'Hotte, Plon-Nourrit, Paris, 1905.

respect to the Regulation of 1876.

In the course of his work, *général* L'Hotte discusses the different methods of dressage, that is, the schooling of horses. With an impartiality that is calm and composed and with the perfect equity which always characterized him, he condemned none.

Those who expected to find in this work a collection of infallible 'recipes' which will make all horses marvels of lightness and all horsemen accomplished *écuyers*, may perhaps be disappointed. It is appropriate at this time to remember the anecdote told by Gaspard Saunier and retold by *général* L'Hotte in his *Souvenirs*:

I remember when one of France's important lords brought his son to M. Duplessis who was the head of all the famous *écuyers* I have mentioned. I remember, I say, that this lord said to him as he approached him: 'I am not bringing you my son so that you can make of him an *écuyer*; I only want you to teach him how to harmonize his legs and his hands so that he will know how to make his horse do what he wants him to do.' M. Duplessis answered him, in my presence, who had the honour of being one of his disciples at the time: 'My Lord, for some sixty years now I have been trying to learn what you are asking me to do and for which you are honouring me; you are asking me precisely to do what has been my life's ambition to learn.'

Général L'Hotte is well acquainted with many horsemen, even professional ones, who resemble the 'Lord' of whom Gaspard Saunier speaks. But he always succeeded in rising above this tendency. And we cannot conclude this short introduction without quoting the words of the author of *Questions équestres* as he ends his analysis of the different methods of dressage:

No method, no matter how logical and well ordered it is, can give results that are infallible, for every equestrian action, in order to obtain the effect that is anticipated, requires what no work is able to give: *perfect timing and good measure*, that is, *equestrian tact*. Furthermore, one can also say: 'The value of the means depends upon the worth of the man.'

This preface appeared in the 1906 edition of *Questions équestres* and was written by the anonymous editor, H. N.

Chapter 1

Teaching. – Principles; doctrines; means; method. – Variety in the application of the procedures of instruction. – Speak little, but to the point. – Each art has its own language. – Disagreement between the equestrian and scientific languages. – Art cannot be learned from books. – Goals to be followed: calm, forward, straight. – Characteristics of lightness.

Inspired by my two illustrious teachers, Baucher and d'Aure, together with my own learning and understanding which is based on considerable experience and which today has become my share, I am thus approaching some equestrian questions.

In equitation one must know a great deal in order to teach even the most basic equestrian elements. To this knowledge, the *écuyer* must include intelligence, will, and, perhaps above all, a certain feeling for his art, useful not only to direct him in his teaching, but also in his own personal practice.

In the course of his teaching, he must distinguish between:

Principles, the foundation of his art, established through experience and justified by logic (reasoning);

Doctrine, which finds its expression in theories which flow from the body of principles brought together;

The *Means*, that is, the procedures of execution;

The *Method*, which links the means to the precepts, and regulates the order of their use.

The means, upon which the application of principles depends, cannot be invariably fixed, whether one is dealing with the rider or with the horse. When one is dealing with the means, the conformation of the horse, the temperament of the rider, and the natural disposition of each horse, frequently require temperaments or modifications that only the knowledge and experience of the master can understand. By means of his sound judgement, which must always guide him in his personal practice as in his teaching, the teacher must know how to choose among the many precepts, which ones can be applied to the pupil he is teaching or correspond to the disciplines to which the horse being schooled is destined.

Whatever his use, the point of departure is the same: the obedience of the horse. Obviously, the obedience of the horse lies not in his desire to be pleasant to us, even less in doing his duty. It lies merely in the instinct of preservation which makes him want to avoid pain, thus making him respond to whatever warning is given by those agents which can either provoke pain or, if need be, inflict it, in order to obtain obedience. Our means of domination have no other basis.

Domination of the horse lies in his memory, this faculty to remember, which the horse possesses to a remarkable degree, and which makes him understand, by means of our aids, the varied nuances that their language imparts. In principle, it is this language that the horse must obey, the language of the aids, and not of routine, unless we are dealing with basic dressage (schooling), applicable to a horse whose future is to be obeyed by all kinds of hands.

Routine is the result of many repetitions of movements, always executed in the same sequence, so that, having acquired a habit, the horse executes these movements on his own, and sometimes even against the will of his rider. To avoid this – and this is absolutely necessary if dressage (schooling) has a somewhat higher goal – one must constantly vary the sequence of movements and never allow the horse to take the initiative.

Any execution of movements must be done by means of the aids, and the horse must respect them, rather than fear them. To repeat, it is the language of the aids and not of routine that the horse must obey. On the other hand, regardless of the goal of dressage, this obedience is influenced by his spirit, his disposition, his bloodline, and his conformation.

From the horse's spirit and disposition emanates his predisposition to give us his forces or, on the contrary, to retain them. Thus one either has an outgoing and generous horse, or a stubborn and recalcitrant one. His temperament allows him, in varied ways, to appreciate the touch of those agents which will guide him. Here, the ticklish horse has a singular reaction.

The degree of his bloodline, which determines his energy and the elasticity of his actions, emerges from his origins which place him close to those superior breeds such as the Arabian or the English thoroughbred. Without exaggerating, one can say that with respect to the horse destined for the saddle, the nobility of his bloodline can offset almost everything he lacks, and nothing can replace it. Only those so endowed are made of steel; the others, that is, the ordinary horses, are only made of iron.

Every true rider must possess the necessary knowledge to enable him to judge a horse's conformation, the distribution of his weight; this sound distribution is indispensable to the regularity of his gaits and the ease with which he can be guided.

In that the saddle horse is not large, lightness is one of the primary conditions he must fulfil and, in principle, his mobility is in an inverse ratio to his weight.

It is no different with respect to the rider. One does not find Herculean types, fighters, men with athletic constitutions in the ranks of gymnasts. Their weight makes this impossible, and they have the upper hand due to their muscular power, despite its development.

The heavy horse by losing his mobility, also loses his individuality and, unless he is endowed with certain high qualities, under a saddle all heavy horses resemble each other. Light horses, however, retain their individuality even when they are not endowed with great qualities. The heavy saddle horse, however, has a use: as a mount for a heavy rider. And all things being equal, the excess weight of the rider, compared to the weight of the horse, makes it easier for him to carry his rider.

Equestrian doctrines, like the practical means to which they relate, do not necessarily have to be brief in their presentation. But this is not the case with respect to principles which form their essence. Rather, all principles must be expressed in a few words which have no synonyms. Or else the principle has not found its true formula.

The *écuyer* can achieve this brevity only with the help of mature reflections, which takes time, and to which one must add perseverance and practical intelligence. It is there, that is, in perseverance and practical intelligence, and not in speculation, that the *écuyer* must find his inspiration. From this source alone he can develop principles which are truly useful in the use of the horse, and give them permanence and total devotion.

Sobriety of words must guide the *écuyer*, be it when instructing the rider or schooling the horse. He must point out goals with clarity and never pursue two goals simultaneously. And that is how the great masters proceeded, the d'Abzac, the d'Aure, the Baucher. And because they knew a great deal, and precisely because of that, I say, they said little; but when they spoke, they spoke judiciously.

Therein lies the difficulty; only therein can be found the talent of the true master. The true master also knows how to find expressions that present an image. Perhaps they are not always perfect in the eyes of the purist; but no matter, for, when images are startling they are far better than the use of the most correct language; expressions that give an image can be better understood by the rider.

Every art has its own language and has only rarely borrowed from scientific languages. When it comes to the use of language, the equestrian art has sometimes even found itself in disagreement with the language to which science is devoted. For example, the term 'force' in equitation only applies to muscular action and never to the weight of the mass, whereas in mathematics weight also represents force.

In my opinion, when the distribution of weight and its translations also involve proofs or conclusions, the *écuyer* must avoid speaking of the centre of gravity. First, because here the point that gravity occupies is not fixed as it is with an inanimate body, for its position varies constantly with a live animal. Secondly, because equestrian conclusions must not rest on the point of a needle, for art expects to be treated in a vaster way, more practical, more understandable to one and all.

Interfering with the centre of gravity when dealing with equestrian questions could also open the way to mathematical conclusions. And these mathematical conclusions, in that they are positive and absolute, cannot be applied to equitation; for nature will never divulge to us all her secrets and the horse will always reserve for us new facts and surprises, which emerge from life itself.

Neither can equestrian language present any uniformity as is the case with scientific language, the latter being based on reason and logic, whereas the former is profoundly dependent upon the personal feeling of the *écuyer*. Thus equitation, especially with respect to its synthetic parts, is presented in terms of expressions, and becomes part of the *écuyer* – of an *écuyer* with experience and knowledge, of course – no matter to what school he belongs and regardless of the worth of the masters who taught him.

The beginning instructor usually starts out being very verbose. He is inclined to impart everything he knows. He also tries to be scientific where it is not applicable, a trait often used to hide a lack of practical knowledge. Only when conciseness and simplicity can find a place in the language of the *écuyer*, will he be able to extract the essence of his increased knowledge.

Books dealing with equitation are only useful to the rider already familiar with the practical aspects of horsemanship. Equestrian art cannot be learned from books, which instruct only those who are already knowledgeable.

As to equestrian theories of a more or less learned nature, it is up to the *écuyer* to acquaint himself with them. They are useful for a complete understanding of the practice of his art, perfecting his teaching, as well as familiarizing him with all those discussions that pertain to his art and his teaching. One can, however, say that in general academic theories, no matter what they are, cannot be present in the mind of the practitioner at the very moment when he is fully engaged with his mount.

To guide a rider in his practice in an ongoing way, he needs other simpler directions. These he will find in the succession of goals to be pursued, because they are simple to envisage and few in number and can thus always remain present in his mind. These goals can be expressed in three words: *calm, forward, straight*; and instead of *straight*, I will say: *direction*. The order in which these three goals are to be followed, are invariable and absolute, and one must seek the one that follows only after having achieved the preceding one. So that the horse can appreciate our actions and respond correctly, he must, above all, be calm and confident. Every one surely knows from his own experience that any work undertaken with an irritated, impatient, and worried horse, preoccupied with his surroundings or afraid of his rider, can only be unpleasant.

For the horse to be calm and confident, he must give us his impulsive forces so that we can make use of them. A free and positive movement forward is the first test; it characterizes the goal offered to the rider who wishes to subject his horse to only a few demands. The result will be positive when, at the first use of the heels, the horse responds by extending his action, with his forces flowing and keeping the forward movement, without the movements achieving an appreciable elevation.

It is in this manner that the horse can be put positively and freely into the forward movement, even when he is walking. The lively gaits would not give this result, if the trot, instead of being free and deliberate, would gain in elevation rather than in extension, and if at the canter, the horse, instead of extending, would fall back on himself. It is how the gait, whether slow or fast, presents itself; it is not in the lively gaits themselves that one can determine whether the horse is giving one his impulsive forces in such a way that will satisfy the demands of ordinary equitation.

However, for the horseman who has higher aspirations, the goal will be attained only when the horse executes every movement and in all situations, and shows the desire to go forward. This is how it must be, even for the jumper at the pillars, and without his pulling on the ropes that contain him.

As long as a horse lingers on his legs even for an instant when one wants him to go forward and move in a flowing and imperceptible manner; as long as during a transition from a lively gait to the walk, he falls back and slows down into the previous gait instead of activating it immediately when taken; as long as the haunches do not deviate under the slightest pressure of one of the heels, or, when moving on two tracks, the croup becomes heavy and lazy and the horse hesitates for a moment to move straight forward; as long as he remains in the volte and does not go instantaneously from the volte on to the haunches, from the pirouettes either on the shoulders or on to the haunches, into a straight walk; as long as he lingers momentarily from a reinback to a forward movement, and is not bearing straight and forward, without this being demanded, at that very moment when the actions determine the reinback, then at no time has the goal been completely achieved. The haunches, this seat of the impulsive forces which must become animated, which must vibrate at the slightest touch of the heels, have not become sufficiently active, or *diligent*, to use an expression of La Guérinière.

In the course of work, the active play of the haunches must be continuous. At no time must the haunches be inert, lazy, with the horse's strength remaining fixed within them. The rider must always feel their strength flow forward, or disposed to doing so, if another direction is indicated.

The activity or diligence of the haunches affects the totality of the horse and provokes animation. It is there that everything hangs together; and its joints and muscular force would be unable to remain inactive without becoming a source of resistance, having thus become alive and active at the first use of the aids.

When the activity of the haunches has responded fully, the horse, by its very reaction and in all circumstances, will seem to be saying: 'I want to go forward.' The perfect functioning of the impulsive forces can only be achieved at great length; but what is important in the long run, is that preoccupation with impulsion is of greater importance than the demands which follow.

Now that the horse has become calm and has put his forces at the disposal of the rider, it becomes a matter of channelling them. Two methods present themselves, depending upon whether the horseman is more or less skilled. If the horseman is not very skilled, this can be achieved by a repetition of changes of direction (rein changes) as well as movements in general which will make the horse bend to his demands. This method must also be used by riders who have limited goals in the schooling (dressage) of their horses.

It follows that there is no need to make use of procedures that have perfection as a goal. What is important here is to act upon the mass by establishing a balance between the forces that push forward and those that contain or moderate. Depending upon the conformation of the horse, his weight will be sent to the very spot which will determine its good distribution.

Regularity of gaits will flow from this good distribution of weight, and changes of direction will be obtained by engaging the mass in the direction indicated, for it has only to cede in its totality. The movements one has in mind, in that they are simple and few in number, require only few modifications with respect to the equilibrium of the mass and thus a limited flexibility of the joints and muscles.

It would thus be superfluous to linger on exercises dealing with procedures that have the complete submission of all the horse's joints and muscular force. The goal will have been achieved when, without any marked effort on the part of the rider, the forces that determine the sought-for movement, that is, the forward movement, will win over the opposing forces. A rigorously exact position is not the goal here. With this goal in mind, it is a question of walking in a straight line; but it is not too important if the neck or the haunches do not follow exactly the straight line, as long as the horse, as a whole, does not deviate. But when we are dealing with an *écuyer* whose goals in dressage are more complex then that is another matter. His aim must be a rigorously straight horse, straight from head to haunches. And his work must depend upon this goal.

In principle, the domination of the horse will be complete when the rider can position and then maintain the different parts of the horse in an exactly determined direction and then, after all the movements that have required the horse to deviate, take up again, without difficulty, this straight position. The straight line which extends from head to haunches has been chosen for a certain direction, not only because it corresponds to the natural movement of the horse and serves as a link to the various movements; the straight line presents a base that is even more assured, in that it does not allow even a degree of deviation, as does the curved line; it is one and indivisible, and determined most absolutely.

Furthermore, when the horse is straight, the hindlegs follow exactly in the steps of the forelegs. From this follows that the haunches and shoulders function in a such a way that they assure the accuracy of their reciprocal play.

The two haunches thus function equally and the distribution of the horse's weight is regular. Their movements are easy, the forces that emanate from the two ends of the horse, from their combined play, experience no contradictions, and function towards a common goal: direct forward movement, and to which the horse has agreed, or, if one prefers, been fine tuned, aligned, harmonized. These different expressions all have the same meaning.

However, if, when walking straight, the haunches deviate from the straight line as they follow the shoulders, one will see, at the same time, the following disintegrate: the harmonious relationship that existed between the forces of the forehand and the forces of the hindquarters; the precise distribution of weight; the ease with which one can take different directions; and how the haunches, in their opposition to the shoulders, will form a buttress. The result will be that the horse, like a string instrument, will have lost his chord.

In the course of work, the positions demanding the different movements, will be all the more correct, in that they will deviate less from the straight position. The less the deviation is apparent, the more perfect will be the execution, and the easier will the quick succession of the most varied movements become, even contrary movements. It is then that to the spectator the horse will appear to move with the lightness of a bird.

For the *écuyer*, work done accurately, with ease, and brilliantly, depends upon a horse who is straight and whose haunches are vibrant, and whose constant ambition eventually results in: *A horse who moves and handles himself as though acting on his own.* This kind of perfection in execution – and one cannot state this too often – depends upon the regularity of the energy of impulsion.

If impulsion begins to weaken, there is also a weakening in whatever support is needed for the procedures that require a straight horse and the positions that command the different movements. For not only has the base upon which these procedures depend, been afflicted; moreover, the execution which follows suffers the consequences brought about by the weakening of impulsion. The movement forward then loses its positive and free action and becomes uncertain, questionable, and dragging. All movements have lost their elasticity, their dash. All execution becomes soft and sluggish.

Generally speaking, the lack of impulsion affects all the actions of the horse. For he then loses all the means of behaviour, whatever they are, and will soon not even know how to cope with exercises. All can be summarized in only two words: no impulsion, no horse. It should be noted, that seeking the straight position, which includes the straightening of all false inflexions and bends which can occur between the head and the haunches, and which, for that very reason, dries up the principal sources of resistances which the joints and muscles can present.

But *lightness*, whose characteristic lies in *the elastic and springy flexibility* of all joints and muscles, can only be acquired after all resistances have completely disappeared, that is, with the disappearance of all inopportune contractions. Assuming that this has been achieved, one must be convinced that lightness, this touchstone of Classical or *savante* equitation, can be maintained in the course of work only with the help of harmony, which the rider must establish in the play of forces, and which are dependent upon him.

Some explanation is needed here; but first I must enlarge the question.

Chapter 2

Definition of equestrian art. – On what does the submission of the horse rest. – Combination of impulsion and the flexibility of joints and muscles in the race horse, the cross-country horse, the military horse, and the *haute école* horse – the *ramener*, the *rassembler*. – Their position is to be found in the *ur*-position: *the straight horse*.

Seen from a general perspective, equitation is the art of co-ordinating the muscular forces of the horse. This definition finds its justification in the following considerations: *force* – that is, muscular action – and the *weight* of the horse are the two elements to be exploited in order to control him, with the exception of that part that makes up the temperament of the horse. It is thus necessary that force and weight are in accord and have the same goal. But, since weight or mass is in itself inert, its transfers are subordinated to force, that is, the sound use of force will produce a sound distribution of weight. Thus I am able to justify my definition of equestrian art. And in order to complete this demonstration, I will add that one is able to master force or, if one wishes, muscular power, the moment one has managed to combine closely impulsion with the elastic flexibility of all joints and muscles.

If one reviews the different purposes that the saddle horse has, one becomes aware that, for all these uses, his submission rests upon the flexibility of his joints – let us say upon his springs, for they are veritable living joints and muscles – obtained jointly with impulsion which is the very essence of movement.

Regardless of the use to which the horse will be employed, the combination of these two elements is indispensable to his submission, for they give one the means to direct him. However, the proportions of these two elements differ, based on the use to which the horse will be put.

When one is dealing with the race horse, impulsion dominates considerably and must be carried to its highest point, whereas the flexibility of joints and muscles should be such to allow it to regulate the horse's pace, make a large turn, obtain a halt by slowing down gradually.

With a cross-country horse, impulsion still plays a greater role, but its proportions are less; however, the flexibility of joints and muscles must be slightly greater than with the race horse, for the cross-country horse has more varied requirements.

The horse used for military purposes, has proportions similar to those of the cross-country horse, with impulsion being raised to a degree higher, due to the more diverse and pressing requirements.

When we come to the *haute école* horse, there must be a definite balance between impulsion and the flexibility of joints and muscles; neither the one nor the other must dominate.

It should be noted that if we hold back only slightly the forward thrust of the cross-country horse, the military horse, or the race horse, impulsion will cease to function; its disappearance is due to the imperfect flexibility of the joints and muscles. Whereas when one deals with an *haute école* horse, no matter how restricted his movements are, the impulsive forces retain their action and their play never ceases because they are completely in accord with the flexibility of the joints and muscles which, in this instance, must be perfect.

Perfectly functioning joints and muscles can only be acquired after the muscles, or, if one wishes, the cords that make them move, have been disciplined and shaped, making them agree in their combined action. This accord or harmony depends upon two essential applications and the order which regulates their pursuit:

(1) The *ramener*, characterized by its sustained position and elasticity, involving the forehand in its different parts to assure a sound functioning;

(2) The *rassembler*, characterized by the flexibility of the haunches which includes the engagement of the hocks under the mass; the different degrees of engagement in proportion to the nature of the movement sought.

But everything depends, ties in, and is connected with the horse. And so it is with the *ramener* and the *rassembler*, whose perfection depends upon a common source, an *ur*-source (an original or common source), which is *the straight horse*, which I have already discussed and which I will discuss again.

Chapter 3

> Classical or *savante* equitation. – A definition of *lightness*. – Lightness is the characteristic of Classical or *savante* equitation, regardless of whether the movements are simple or complex. – Force and weight of the horse are two elements to be exploited in order to control him. – What the straight position signifies.

This said, what follows will deal especially with Classical or *savante* equitation, that is, with the most demanding and most delicate requirements to which a horse is put.

When one combines impulsion with the flexibility of joints and muscles, as well as elasticity and springiness, extension of gaits are obtained as easily as are their shortening or their elevation. The rider has the ability to play, in a sense, with the forces of the horse whose inflexions and bends are put at his disposal. The horse then becomes a docile instrument and one can ask of him all the movements of which his structure is capable and all the *manège* airs that the imagination of the *écuyer* can fashion.

If submission of the horse is characterized by the flexibility of his joints and muscles which impulsion animates, on the other hand, maintenance of this flexibility during one's work is proof of the sound use of the aids employed by the rider and of their total accord with the horse's structure. When we say that the schooled horse must possess flexibility of joints and muscles, we are, of course, dealing with Classical or *savante* equitation; and it is from the accuracy of the actions of the rider that what is known as *lightness* emanates, that is, the perfect obedience of the horse at the slightest indications of the hand or the heels of the rider.

In that lightness also characterizes the condition of the horse who is perfectly schooled and the soundness of the means employed in order to guide him, it follows that the expression 'lightness' applies to the schooling of the horse as well as the talent of the rider. It is its criterion. Should the horse resist in some area, perhaps because his submission is not complete, then the resistance will manifest itself through a tension in certain joints and muscles, which will bring about a change in lightness.

Likewise, not only a lack of harmony between the rider and the horse will occur, bringing about a resistance in the horse; rather, harmony will not be assured if the rider is not able to awaken and maintain this play of forces in keeping with each movement. From this it follows that lightness – perfect lightness, of course – finds its formula when the rider *puts into play those forces and how the horse makes use of those very forces useful to the movement envisaged*. All other manifestations of strength will produce a resistance which, as a consequence, will alter lightness. The better the horse has been schooled and the more skilled the rider, the more complete will lightness be.

From now on, it becomes evident that if *haute école* is the result of the best schooled and the best ridden horse, if it represents the application of the most elevated art, it cannot lend its name to movements, no matter how brilliantly performed, as soon as they are executed without the quality of lightness. The stamp of *haute école*, of Classical or *savante*, of artistic, high equitation, regardless of how one names it, finds its expression not in movements that are more or less extraordinary, but in perfect lightness; regardless of whether the movements are simple or complex. Above all, lightness finds its expression in the submission of the jaw which is the first area (joint) receiving the effect of the hand, thus its submission becomes evident when it responds with elasticity and springiness to the action that solicits its play. The mobility of the jaw does not only mean submission; the flexibility of this area goes farther, provoking the flexibility of the neck, then all the other joints, due to the inter-relationship that exists instinctively between all the muscular contractions. Due to this very inter-relationship, resistances sustain each other; thus if resistance of the jaw should occur, there would be a similar occurrence in the other areas, and *vice versa*.

From these considerations emerges a very special important fact, namely, that the submission of the jaw is a sign of lightness. This gentle and soft giving of the jaw, which should express itself only as a light murmur, must occur at the first summons of the hand and during the course of work; it must stop as soon as it is no longer provoked. To return to the image, I say that the horse who has become light, must be neither silent nor talkative.

The sound use of the horse's forces, which is a sign of lightness, will bring about a sound distribution of weight, as well as balance, which will result in harmonious movements. The horse's straight position, expressed by a harmony between the antagonistic forces, followed by the exact distribution of weight, assures the harmony of movements when the horse moves in a straight line. It is important to preserve this straightness in the course of the many different changes of direction which occur in the course of one's work.

These changes should operate in such a way that they do not affect lightness, this criterion for the correct use of force.

Chapter 4

Disposition of haunches. – The horse Amerah. *– A straight horse, and the disposition of haunches: that is the alpha and omega of Classical or* savante *equitation. Cross-country equitation – and the disposition of haunches. – An important seat of resistances lies in the haunches. – The straight horse balancing between the heels. – The rudder of the horse lies in the haunches rather than in the forehand. –* Turning. *– Use of the two ends of the horse. – How the horse moves on a circle. – Two ways of using the forehand to turn.*

The importance of the *disposition of the haunches* and their reaction to a new direction and the preceding one, is presented here. If a change in direction is only undertaken by the forehand, the harmony of forces is broken and the haunches continue to move in the previous direction, whereas the forehand takes a new direction. The haunches then form a sort of buttress and impede the change of direction; no matter how light the horse was when moving forward in a straight line, a more or less marked resistance will occur at the moment when the change of direction begins.

To avoid such a lack of harmony between the horse's two ends, one must take command of the seat from which impulsion originates, and make the haunches deviate slightly in the area that corresponds to the new direction taken. The position given to the head and neck will immediately agree with the deviation of the haunches. It is in this manner that the harmony of forces, obtained when the horse moved straight forward, will continue to be maintained during the many diverse changes of direction, whether moving on one or two tracks, or executing pirouettes. It is all the more important to consider first the haunches and make sure that they are not displaced to the side as easily and as quickly as are the head and neck. One must understand that the disposition of the haunches constitutes the action preparatory to a change of direction and that the change of direction occurs with the head taking precedence.

Calling up an image, I say that this preliminary disposition of the haunches is the stroke of the tiller, preceding and determining the change of direction of the boat. And, similar to the stroke of the tiller, the disposition of the haunches determines the change of direction; in fact, it demands it, whereas the position given to the head and the neck can merely solicit it.

Indeed, one controls and guides the horse by acting on both ends; but certain facts, occurring every day, prove that it is the haunches, rather than the forehand, which determines direction. This can be logically understood. The forehand, that is, the head and neck, by virtue of the type of joints they have, while able to take certain positions independent of the rest of the body, can only solicit the direction given to the shoulders, but cannot determine it. On the other hand, it is different with the haunches, in that there is a close connection to the trunk so that their disposition obviously determines the direction of the shoulders.

And so, if there is any opposition between the direction given by the forehand and that of the haunches, it is always the haunches which win out. For example, a horse wants to return to the stable and makes a half turn to the left. The rider will be unable to oppose this turn if he opens the right rein which bends the horse's head and neck to the right. The horse will succeed in making his half turn to the left if the haunches, resisting, push him in this direction in their refusal to deviate to the left.

Another example: A man on foot leads a horse who wants to escape. The man pulls with all his strength on the curb reins which he holds in both hands. The horse gives him completely his head and neck which bend heavily to the left. But he flees nonetheless to the right because it is in that direction that the haunches push, for they are inflected to the left. Everyone dealing with horses has seen this many times. Thus the rider has to preoccupy himself with the exploitation of the haunches if he wants to have the necessary power to control the horse.

Putting all reasoning aside, one particular fact of which I became aware in Saumur, convinced me of the power that derives from the disposition of the haunches and the importance one should give it for the ease of all movements.

I happened to be in one of the *manèges*, the *manège* Kellermann, when a *reprise* of officers was about to be staged. The horses were, as usual, standing in a row in the centre line, waiting for their riders. At the far end of the row was a horse called *Amerah* who stood out because of his small size and his playfulness. Like all the other horses participating in the *reprise*, he was a stallion, with a long mane, and of Navarine breed. Standing opposite him was his groom who held him by the end of the rope tied to the caveçon. Left to his own devices, the little horse set out to canter. Then, always facing the groom, he began to execute a series of counter-changes of hand with an ease and a lightness that was astonishing, never ceasing to canter.

Quite astonished, I followed this activity closely, and noticed that a deviation of the haunches towards the outside always preceded and facilitated markedly each return movement. I questioned the groom who told me that this playfulness was typical on the part of the little horse. I profited from this observation, realizing that instinct had suggested this to him.

All changes in direction must include very markedly the disposition of the haunches. When linked correctly to the position given by the forehand, all with the correct proportions, and with impulsion also correct, then the most varied movements can easily follow, the horse appearing to obey at a mere touch or breath of the aids. This is how it should be with respect to Classical or *savante* equitation and wherein Baucher was without a rival. Two expressions suffice to characterize this: *A straight horse, disposition of haunches.*

This is the alpha and omega of Classical or *savante* equitation, whose crowning glory is lightness. Its importance lies in the disposition of the haunches which must also be a part of cross-country equitation. Cross-country equitation, it is true, does not lay claim to controlling the strength of the horse which characterizes Classical or *savante* equitation, whose trait is the purity of harmony. But one must still dominate the forces of the horse to the extent that this is necessary for his ordinary use.

This domination will find its main obstacles in the haunches, the seat of the most common and most energetic resistances that a horse can present. His instinct seems to tell him that his power lies where his impulsive forces reside, and he does not willingly give them to us.

Thus, when one asks for the deviation of the horse's haunches, he is inclined to withdraw them from us, at least in part, by making his shoulders participate in the movement which, in turn, makes the displacement to the side decrease the submission we wish to impose upon the haunches. One must vigorously oppose this tendency, otherwise one may never properly dominate the haunches or completely isolate them. When a deviation is requested, the shoulders must remain exactly in the direction they were initially going if the horse is moving, or remain in place if the horse is at a halt.

In the latter instance, one must not seek the immobility of the shoulders; the opposite is true, especially if we are dealing with Classical or *savante* equitation. For lightness, which must never be lost from sight, requires the playing of all joints and muscles and its perfection never allowing them to remain inactive.

How often do resistances of the forehand depend upon a lack of submission of the haunches. The reason for this is that there is a solidarity that manifests itself between all the muscular contractions, thus causing the resistances to support each other. Due to the mode of rapport between rider and horse, any resistance of the forehand is immediately felt by the rider; his hand indicates this to him as soon as the resistance manifests itself. But he does not always have in his seat the necessary feeling to tell him that there is a resistance emanating from the haunches.

The impression the rider gets from his hand often fools him and makes him take effect for cause, thus making him concentrate his efforts on the jaw and the neck. He should, rather, question the horse's haunches, ask them to become active, to deviate to the right or to the left, separating themselves with lightness. He will then see how often resistances perceived by the hand, had their source in the inertia of the haunches.

The haunches will cease to provoke resistances to the hand only after they have submitted completely, which can be determined by how they separate themselves, that is, when they deviate promptly and with springiness to the light pressure of one of the legs. Only then is the rider able to put the horse straight and balanced between his heels.

When this point has been reached, if the rider provokes a light increase in impulsion and does not allow the mass to cede, he will feel a sort of undulation, as though a sheet of water were passing under his seat. That is where the rider finds his goal if he decides to pursue Classical or *savante* equitation. It is not for nothing – and I believe I am giving proof of this – that I am giving such a lengthy role to the haunches and their control of the horse's forces.

When one examines carefully the construction of the shoulders, one can see that they are constructed in a way so that they can react to the haunches and to the impulsion that emanates from them. Indeed, the shoulders have certain qualities and imperfections which are part of their nature; but often they function and extend poorly because the haunches do not push them correctly. By forcing somewhat this image, one could say that the shoulders and haunches are similar to the arms of a windmill and the force that puts them into action.

When the hocks drag and function poorly, it is wrong to say, as is often done, that 'The hocks are not following the shoulders.' More accurate would be to state the opposite, that 'The hocks do not push the shoulders.' For it is not up to the shoulders to pull the haunches, but, rather, it is up to the haunches to push the shoulders forward.

Now the cross-country horse is guided almost solely by the hands and the rider is disposed to using them rather than the legs. Thus it has become a common statement to say that the rudder of the horse lies in the neck. This may be true when one is dealing with an obedient horse and when only ordinary equitation is involved. But, as already stated earlier, it is quite different when one is dealing with the kind of equitation which places greater demands and expects harmony between the forehand and the hindquarters, especially if the horse refuses to be obedient. In this instance, while the rider is able to direct the horse's neck as he intends, he is not really in control at guiding a recalcitrant horse in the direction he refuses to go.

For example, one should remember what I said earlier about the horse who, wanting to return to the stable, tried to do so by making a half-turn to the left. Bending the horse's head to the right does not prevent the horse from making a half turn to the left. But the rider who concentrates his efforts on the horse's haunches and makes them deviate to the left, thus forming a kind of buttress, will make it impossible for the horse to turn to the left. The rider has then made use of two forces on the same side, the right rein and heel, to dominate the haunches and thus make them deviate. It is only when the rider has inclined the haunches towards the left, that is, after having assured the proper direction by preparing himself against the half turn, can the move forward be solicited.

Every time there is another defence on the part of the horse, the same succession of procedures must be taken up. A similar situation exists in obstacle jumping, when the rider should strike off at a canter on the left leg, if his horse, going over an obstacle, is inclined to swerve to the left. For then the rider can more easily bring his mount to cross over towards the left and thus better prevent him from moving obliquely in that direction, that is, to the left. This is contrary to the general belief that the horse, cantering on the right leg, will move obliquely less easily to the left. But the results indicated by the disposition of the haunches favour this way of proceeding. Experience attests to that.

Likewise, it is also important to prevent the horse from increasing his impulsion, which would occur due to his desire to dominate us and shy away from an obstacle he does not want to approach.

Concern with the disposition of the haunches ought to be considerably less when we are performing outdoors than when we are practising Classical or *savante* equitation. Yet its importance is too great for the rider not to pay some attention to every need of the horse, regardless of its use.

D'Aure made frequent use of the disposition of the haunches and with great skill helped himself with a timely rein of opposition, both in the *manège* as well as in cross-country equitation. The rudder of the horse resides thus in his hindquarters rather than in the forehand. But one would be going against the nature of the horse if one were not to utilize both ends simultaneously. To convince oneself of this, one has only to examine the horse when left to himself, see how he turns and makes use of his instinct. A horse has just escaped from the hands of the man who was leading him, and, animated, he falls into a cadenced trot, energetically sustained. The eye of the spectator can easily follow the methods the horse uses to make his turns. Unless, of course, fear will make him fall brusquely back on to himself. Otherwise, his shoulders will never move to the right without his haunches deviating to the left. And as long as the horse turns, it will be so.

One can convince oneself of this by examining the imprints on the ground left by the horse's feet who has been put to trot in a circle on the lunge. They indicate that the shoulders cross inwards, whereas the haunches cross outwards. This crossing or overlapping is all the more appreciable if the trot is positive and the circle in which the horse turns does not have too large a diameter.

The horse moves instinctively on a circle, taking a succession of tangents; he does not move on the curve of the line he follows. It follows that with schooling, one can make the mounted horse bend, but only to a certain degree, for if the joints of the neck give the region the degree of inflexion that the rider appreciates, the same does not hold true with respect to the loin or back, especially not with the dorsal stem, whose joints accept only limited play.

With respect to cross-country equitation, although the rider directs the horse with the aid of the hands, the haunches are nonetheless asked to participate when turning. One cannot act on one of the two ends of the horse without directing the other end. It follows that when the hand determines the displacement of the shoulders to the right, this also provokes the deviation of the haunches to the left. This reaction always occurs, regardless of how the head and neck are utilized in the turning. They can be used in two ways.

To turn to the right, the head can be directed to the right and take along the neck, then the shoulders, in the direction of the turn. Or else, the head can be turned to the left, then pressed back on to the neck which deviates to the left while bending and carrying its weight to the right so that the shoulders are carried along in this direction.

In either case, the haunches, based on the reaction they have, contribute to directing the horse towards the right. In the first case, this is done by deviating to the left, a natural result due to the displacement to the right of the other end of the horse. In the second case, it is by bending to the left. This inflexion is provoked by the bend of the neck which instinctively tends to extend itself along the whole vertebral stem.

The actions of the rider, responding to these two different uses of the forehand regarding turns, are: in the first instance, opening of the inside rein, that is, the direct rein; in the second instance, pressure against the neck on the part of the outside rein, that is, the rein of opposition.

The first instance is the simplest and most natural one, the one that the horse can easily understand and whose effect is the most obvious. The second instance can only be effective if the neck is sufficiently flexible.

When asked to turn to the right and the neck does not bend to the right, then, on the contrary, the turn to the left would be provoked. Indeed, the pressure of a rein does not indicate an opening rein, yet its effect is so. Thus when asked to make a turn to the right, the pressure of the left rein on the neck makes the shoulders bear to the right. But this pressure is also accompanied by a backwards action, corresponding to the use of the rein of opposition, frequently used to control a resistance of the haunches, sometimes so light to make use of them by seconding the action of the heel on the same side.

If it is the effect, caused by the traction of the rein, that predominates, which often occurs when the neck does not bend, the haunches then will bear to the right and the horse will face towards the left. This is what happens to the young horse who has not become familiar with the bridle and when the rider, wanting to lead him only with the left hand, places his hand to the right. Depending upon the way his neck responds to this action, he will be inclined to turn either to the right or to the left. If one does not want this to happen, one must then have recourse to those methods of dressage which will make the horse obedient to the left hand, then allow the passage of time, so important a factor in the schooling of the horse, and whose goal is ordinary equitation.

Chapter 5

Inflexion to the left of the vertebral column; its causes; its consequences. – Work required in obtaining the straight position. – Consequences of an unconquered resistance. – Combination of aids necessary for having a straight horse. – Reins. – Heels. – Use of each heel.

A bend or inflexion of the vertebral column just mentioned with respect to turning, does not only manifest itself when provoked by the rider. It exists, one could say, *a priori*, to varying degrees, in all horses. This bend usually appears to the left. The reasons for this are the following.

A foal, lying in its mother's womb, is usually bent to the left, its head touching its shoulder on that side. Then comes the daily work of the rider. The horse is always inclined to look at the man who comes towards him. And it is from the left that the rider approaches the horse in order to feed him, groom him, saddle and bridle him. It is also on the left that he is asked to make a half turn when leaving the stable, since he will be ridden or led by hand that way. I have also noticed that most horses seem to prefer to lie down on the right side and this decubitus agrees with the bend to the left.

In Austria and Germany, when they are led by hand on walks, many horses are provided on the right with a false fixed rein attached to the surcingle so that the bend of the neck to the left is prevented. Some have stipulated that to combat this bend all that is needed is to have the mane fall to the right. This is their explanation: To see the movements of the rider, the horse turns both to the right and to the left, but is incited to turn his head more to the right than to the left due to the fact that his mane, lying to the right, prevents him from seeing properly.

The idea of the real importance of where the mane falls, was strongly defended by M. de Sainte-Reine, a horseman of great worth, whom I know well. I remember how his love for horses made him pick up nails and sharp points along the road, fearing that a horse's hoof could be hurt.

To solve the problem of inflexion to the left of the neck, there is the common belief – and how often have I heard this – that by bending the neck to the right one is suppling that side. But the opposite is true, it is the retraction of the muscles on the left that then disappear. Generally speaking, when one flexes a joint, it is not the muscles determining the flexion that one is suppling, but, rather, those that are located on the other side, for it is those that must give, must relax.

An inflexion to the left, so frequent with horses, has a tendency to make the haunches push the shoulders to the right. Thus, as long as this false position remains, perfect harmony of movements cannot occur, for it will be impossible to establish an exact relationship between the forehand and the hindquarters to assure this harmony. And the *écuyer* will have to face continuous source of resistances.

High equitation expects that this source be eliminated. Work is arduous and long and requires all the talent of the *écuyer*. This is what the famous d'Auvergne once said: 'The horseman, by means of all the art's perfection, spends his whole life correcting this imperfection.' Baucher could not have said it better.

Indeed, the rigorous straight position can be obtained only through perseverance and intelligence, which consists in pursuing resistances in all their manifestations, so that they can be fought and destroyed. Should a resistance not be completely vanquished and destroyed, and should the rider go on to other things, he would certainly encounter this resistance in the course of his work whenever it could manifest itself. But art is not ungrateful and the struggle against resistances should be of continuous interest to the *écuyer* who has a real feeling for his art. If the work is laborious, the goal offered him is too rich in happy results not to try to achieve it. The straightness of the horse is of such importance that it constitutes – I have said this and am saying it again – the basis of Classical or *savante* equitation. And the straight position is the touchstone to lightness.

The practical means that lead to this straight position, in that they are directed by the resistances that oppose it, vary, as do the resistances themselves. They thus call upon all the combinations that the upper and lower aids call for. I will give an outline of this: The two reins, by acting together, can serve as opening, pressure, or traction reins. When I discussed turning, which the hands asked, I indicated how, on the one hand, the forehand was affected, and how, on the other hand, the hindquarters were affected, which were brought about by these different actions which I executed using a single rein. But, if needed, the other rein converges to either strengthen, complete, or limit the action whose results I already developed. In this manner the actions of the two reins are combined. One must add to this the support given by the more or less energetic, but absolutely immobile, wrists, when one is localizing the effects of the hand on the forehand.

I have not yet said anything about the effects that the combined action of both heels can have. I will now give some of the details. When I say: 'heels', it is obvious – and I have said so elsewhere – that I mean legs. Spurs also have considerable value.

I have already dealt at length with the role of the haunches in the exploitation of the horse's forces. This role is too important not to draw attention, in a special way, to the aids that are called into play and which control the hindquarters, namely, the heels. Their function is not merely to push the horse forward, to bring the croup either to the right or to the left. Those functions are simply effects and are quite adequate when dealing with ordinary equitation.

High equitation requires other uses from the heels. These I wish to introduce. They demand attaining the straight position and the execution of different movements. The combined action of the two heels give the following results when one heel presses the sides, the other one opposes the deviation of the haunches.

The heel that acts by pressure and which is the first one I mentioned and upon which the desired effects must concentrate, actually solicits the raising of the hock on the same side, then provokes its engagement under the horse's mass. And, by means of its increasing energy, this pressure determines the body's inflexion and, ultimately, the bend on the side upon which it is exerted.

The heel called upon to produce these effects, must put pressure only in one place, whereas the opposing heel, which merely acts as needed, exerts its pressure backwards, but without having to displace itself. This latter action must also be used when one wishes to deviate the haunches. Executed properly, the spectator should never be able to see it.

The consequences that the pressure of a heel has, and which I have just mentioned, are, of course, applied to high equitation and not to elementary equitation. But they can, nonetheless, find their source in the instinct of the horse. Indeed, this action of the heel, first of all, brings about the play of the hock which is close to the point where the pressure occurs. If the action increases, the horse responds to it by inflexion, as he would in the stall when his body does not cede to the pressure applied on his sides by the hand. The inflexion of the body, which is increased by a more pronounced pressure, brings about a bend.

These effects, based on instinct, and which serve to obtain the straight position, become more definite, more regular, and are then exploited as dressage (schooling) progresses.

Thus the piaffe is determined and gets its rhythm from the alternate pressure made by each heel that regulates the raising and the support of the corresponding hock, at the same time provoking a certain bend of the body on the same side. In a sense this is similar to the effect that is produced when a dancer, for support, places her hand on her flank on the side where her body is to bend.

Striking off at the canter and lead changes are obtained with the horse maintained rigorously straight by means of the direct heel and drawing the hock on the same side under the mass. Likewise, the inside heel pushes the horse forward when he moves on two tracks. Engagement of the inside hock under the centre brings about the same engagement of the outside hock due to the crossing of the latter over the former.

A similar reason must guide us in the use of our heels when we practise the shoulder in. So that the crossing of the inside hock over the outside one, makes the horse bend under him the inside hock, which is one of the goals of this lesson, the outside heel must first have brought the corresponding hock under the mass.

With respect to turning, in that the inside heel has set the disposition of the haunches by acting backwards, it is up to the one or the other heel, by pressing on the area, to make its effect felt in the course of the movement and in accordance with the position of the horse. If inflexion is what is wanted, then it is the inside heel that acts; the outside heel must make itself felt, if it is the outside hock that is to be brought into play; for the outside hock has more distance to travel and often remains behind. The same holds true for the pirouette.

There is really nothing new in what I have said here. Frederico Grisone, living in the sixteenth century, when it came to turning, attributes to each heel the same function that I have just indicated. Only he expressed himself in other terms, using the language of the period. With respect to a combination of upper and lower aids, I apply them only when straightening a horse who has left the straight position by crossing or bending. Combatting these two false positions requires a combination of contrary aids, the one resulting from inflexion being the most frequent, but it is also the longest one, and the most difficult to eradicate.

When the horse traverses, the haunches are brought back on to the line that the shoulders follow; this is accomplished by using the heel on the side where the haunches deviate and is seconded by the rein on the same side. Thus should the horse traverse to the left, the left heel presses backwards and the left rein reacts to the haunches, functioning like a rein of opposition. When the horse bends, he is straightened by the heel and the rein on the opposite side of the bend. Consequently, if the bend is to the left, the right heel acts in place, the right rein bends the neck to the right, following the bend of the body that the heel provokes.

I will now cease discussing the use of the combined upper and lower aids. Their applications will be found elsewhere.

Chapter 6

Equestrian practices based on instinct. – The race horse. – The *rouler*. – The moment when the spurs must be felt. – The fixed position of the rider. – Position of Frederick Archer, of American jockeys, and Lamplugh. – Inconveniences of the crop. – Opinion of M. de Baracé. – Importance for every rider to use both hands. – Unsoundness in the hindlegs of thoroughbreds. – The horse's instinct can enlighten us. – The roles of force and weight in movement. – Why troop (military) horses come down on their knees when abandoned by the rider's hand. – The importance of getting horses used to going up and down inclines. – The hunters of the *comte* d'Aure. – Nature is the primary master.

One should note that almost all practices to which the horse is put, as well as the effects of heels which I have discussed, find their point of departure in the instinct of the horse. His obedience increases as he becomes more familiar with certain practices.

That is how the horse goes forward at the slightest pressure of the legs, after having first been subjected to kicks with the heels. When kicks are used, the creature can only answer by fleeing out of rebellion; and, by virtue of his very nature, this is the first reaction that the horse instinctively expresses; unless, of course, the disposition of the horse shows stubbornness.

The postilions of the past, due to their heavy boots, were unable to use spurs or even their legs; instead they jerked the bridle. This had an instinctive effect on the horse, making him extend his head and neck, which moved him forward. This made people say that the bridle was the spur of the postilion. One can still see peasants employing this same procedure to make their horses go forward. I will also say that with a simple cord, attached to the left side of the bit of the foremost horse, the carriage driver can make him turn either to the left or to the right; to the left by pulling on the cord; to the right by giving sharp jerks to the cord, and, later, by merely waving it. He does this because the instinct of the horse makes him turn his neck where the traction occurs, making him throw his head to the side opposite to the one where the jerking movement is felt.

If from one extreme to the other, one goes from the work horse to the race horse, in order to channel him, one can see methods used that are based on the instinct of the horse.

The first condition that the race horse must fulfil is a fixed (set) contact with the hand. To bring about this contact, the rider must move his hands in a way that is diametrically opposed to the one I indicated when we were dealing with Classical or *savante* equitation, and where I proposed lightness as a goal. For when we are dealing with the race horse, far from having lightness as a goal, the procedures to be used must be a more or less energetic tension of the joints and muscles of the forehand; this will bring about a tension of the other joints and muscles, as well as a very keen movement, which will produce a firm support that is indispensable to the development of all the means at the disposal of the horse.

However, to bring about a tension of the neck, the hands, while fixed, must not be immobilized, as they are when attempting to conquer resistances. Far from that. The arms, acting as resilient joints and muscles, must exert traction on the curb reins; the horse will oppose this tension instinctively with his head and neck. The arms, then yielding progressively, will follow the neck as it extends, stopping at the point where the head should be set; they should then return to exerting traction if the horse does not, of his own accord, hold the contact.

One must make use of the horse's instincts and bring him to seek the hand of his own accord as well as make it possible for him to regulate the different degrees of extension of the neck. I will discuss this point when I deal with racing.

I will now turn to the *rouler* which aims at an extreme extension of head and neck; extension is so great that weight must give all it can to execute the supreme effort. The *rouler* has to be well regulated. It cannot function if the arms move in a disorderly manner and act on floating reins, which greatly agitates the horse, disunites him, and brings disorder to the horse's actions. Unfortunately, one sees this all too often with riders who are not familiar with competition in the hippodrome and who lose all their *sang-froid* (self-possession) when they approach the winning post. So that the *rouler* can be effective, it must function in accord with the actual movement of the gallop; this is how this accord works.

The hands, initially placed low and fixed, must then be raised slightly. This is the first sign the horse receives. Then, at the moment when his shoulders leave the ground, the wrists, with a slightly circular movement, increase the tension of the reins and thus, due to the increased action of the arms, bring about an instinctive movement of opposition on the part of the horse, making him extend his head and neck. The hands now follow the extended forehand which must be complete when the shoulders are lowered, which will enable them to cover more ground with each stride.

The *rouler* demands from the rider not only knowledge regarding the horse's movements, but also considerable practice in the field to arrive at a sound performance. He must also maintain his *sang-froid*. Executed poorly and at the wrong moment, the *rouler* can be disastrous.

Equally important is that the spurs, always having an instinctive effect, act in harmony with the movement of the gallop. In that the spurs solicit engagement of the hocks under the mass, if their effect is felt at the moment the hocks produce their effort, far from bringing about an increase in power, they decrease it, by stopping in its course the relaxation of the joints and muscles. The spurs must act precisely at that instant when the hocks have reached the limits of their extension and leave the ground. It is then that the spurs bring back the hocks under the mass and make them cover more terrain.

The moment the spurs must make themselves felt can be easily grasped, for they come close to the sides of the horse, at the moment indicated earlier, in that they were naturally provoked by the very impetus of the gallop. The accord of hands and heels with the succession of actions at the gallop assures a union between the haunches that push and the shoulders that receive. If at the same time the rider is able to give rigidity to his position and maintain the movements which the action of his hands and heels make in this tight circle, no difficulties will arise with respect to the horse's regularity of action, which must always occur. Loss of energy will thus be avoided.

One will thus see come together all the resources that the rider can bring forth, which lie in the strength and the weight of the horse. These resources will result in the goal pursued, which is a sustained speed, whose sense of pace and movement is so very important, and will give the degree of its capability. Then the horse will, at the same time, appear to slide like a shadow.

The position that the rider must take cannot depend upon rigid requirements, at least as far as racing on the flat is concerned. To become convinced of this, one can mention the position taken by Frederick Archer and American jockeys, and that of Sloan. Frederick Archer who, for ten years, had a reputation that no one could surpass, used his stirrups long, his thighs slung low, and he seldom raised himself from the saddle.

American jockeys, who are very popular today, based upon their success, use their stirrups short. Their thighs are placed horizontally, their calves grip the shoulders of the horse, their body lies on his neck, arms are stretched forward, buttocks in the air. Indeed, they form a sort of V and remind one rather of a monkey clinging on to a horse. Immobilizing themselves in this bent fashion, the American jockey assures himself a solid posture by distributing his weight. Regardless of the position taken by the jockey, this is an important point. For any displacement of weight disturbs the horse in the use of his strength. But this position taken by the American jockey, no matter how grotesque it is, can be taken only in races on the flat, and only with horses who are well prepared, who exert themselves voluntarily, asking only to be exploited to the fullness of their capabilities.

The position taken in obstacle jumping is the opposite of the position taken by American jockeys. When approaching an obstacle, Lamplugh, in order not to disturb the movement of the horse, never modified his position. His skill and his familiarity with this type of course, allowed him to do so. He used to say that the rider, in general, ought to be seated properly in case of a fall.

It would seem that blows from the crop to whip the horse forward, rather than pricks from the spurs, and in accordance with the instinctive disposition of the horse, would be preferable. But in that the crop removes one hand from the reins, the point of support could be modified and the neck less securely supported. Generally speaking, the actions relating to the hands could be lessened and rendered less efficient. Large movements of the arms, if they become necessary, would no longer allow the rider to act in close proximity and could interfere with the rigidity of his position. Furthermore, because he has to distance himself from the sides he has to hit and the violence he has to use, the crop, to be useful, requires more skill and better timing, than do the spurs. A single strike with the crop could suffice to break off the relaxation of the joints and muscles, if it is applied at the moment when the hocks are at the peak of their effort.

If the intervention of the crop is considered indispensable, to obtain the same effect, it would seem that to simply menace the horse with it would suffice; this could be expressed by propellers or windmills, and would allow the rider to act in closer proximity. Since this has primarily a psychological effect, the menace alone does not require the same timing as does the blow.

One day when I was talking to M. de Baracé whom I have already mentioned,[1] and who has had much experience pertaining to the hippodrome, I brought up the difficulties that the correct use of spurs and, especially, the crop required. He replied: 'If I were given three horses of the same class, ridden by gentlemen with little experience, I

---

[1] *Un Officier de cavalerie* – *Souvenirs du général L'Hotte*, Plon-Nourrit, Paris, 1906.

would be able to determine which one I wanted to win. All I had to do is take away his crop and his spurs.' But with some horses the crop is absolutely necessary. Then one has to overlook the inconveniences and problems that its use offers.

The rider sufficiently skilled and experienced to ride horses of this type, must be sufficiently skilled to use the crop with either the right or the left hand. For should a horse approach him on the right, he should be able to use the crop with his left hand, as he would be disqualified were he to hit another horse or his rider. Every horseman should be able to acquire the skill to be able to use the crop with either the right or the left hand. He will surely see its value in the course of his practice. The same holds true when lungeing. The horseman should be able to hold the lungeing whip in the hand close to the horse, regardless of the direction he is going.

To school jumpers at the pillars, it is especially advantageous for the *écuyer* to be able to hold the lungeing whip in either hand with equal skill. I will mention here a detail I noticed with respect to English thoroughbreds and which may be caused by the practices at the hippodrome.

In October 1879, the *Ecole de Saumur* owned 189 English thoroughbreds. After a careful examination of their legs, it was established that certain details of unsoundness afflicted them. This indicates that the bog spavin, when found in only one hock, is found almost twice as often in the right hock than in the left hock; whereas exactly the opposite is true with the spavin. Its cause is to be sought. Could it not lie in the fact that the turns are always made to the right, tiring especially the outside region of the inside hock and the inside region of the outside hock. These areas depend upon the side on which the horses put their weight when they are leaning. Of these 189 English thoroughbreds, it was established that only 24 had sound limbs.

Thus we see how instinct manifests itself through the strong will of the horse, often telling us how not to interfere with the horse and how to help him use what nature has given him. Similarly does the horse use his neck when, allowed to act on his own, he has to deal with various obstacles, such as going up or down steep inclines. How he holds his head tells us clearly how we have to use our arms.

I will discuss now how the horse instinctively uses his neck when, allowed to use it as he wishes, he still has to go on although already exhausted. He extends his neck and lowers his neck so that his weight, brought forward, replaces the strength he has lost. It is obvious that no constraint of the hand is to disturb the position of the neck which the horse instinctively lowers. One can thus say that, generally speaking, when a horse is moving, weight acquires a larger share the moment strength fails. This is similar with the child who has not yet acquired sufficient strength or the old man who has lost it. In order to walk, both have to place their weight forward by leaning forward.

The same holds true for the person who is tired. One has only to observe a troop of infantrymen on a march and who, at the end of the march, are exhausted. When they start out, the men, knapsack on their back, walk with straight backs, knees braced. At the end of the march, the body begins to lean forward, knees are bent, and it seems as though the legs, no longer pushing the body, are dragged by it. Like the exhausted horse, the man follows his instinct. He does not have a surer guide.

It is said that when the Arab sees that his horse is exhausted, to make him continue walking, he removes the bridle as a last resort. The horse is now no longer concerned with the painful Arab bit, and by totally extending and able to loosen his neck, he is able to respond again to the extreme demands of his master. To depend thus upon the instinct of a horse may appear imprudent if one judged a fall to be imminent when a horse no longer has contact with the hand.

It is true that in the ranks of the Cavalry, horses often come down on their knees when the hand lets go – and also when the rider no longer holds them, I must add. But there is a reason for this. These horses are used to moving with a specific equilibrium which the hand gives them. But if, without any warning, the hand ceases to be effective, this equilibrium weakens by acquiring an overload on the shoulders when fatigue sets in; and falling on to their knees can be expected. The situation is, of course, quite different with the help of frequent schooling. For then the troop horses are used to moving in the various different positions that their neck takes on.

It is seldom that one can find traces of falling on the knees of horses belonging to peasants. And yet, they walk with their neck extended and low. But they are used to that. It is true that these horses are not overloaded by the weight of a rider. Sometimes, however, in the past, as opposed to those of today, the horses of Lorraine were light and often put to the lively gaits. The driver usually drove his cart, seated astride on the horse, taking the place of the bearer. And I am not aware that horses in military campaigns, whose knees showed sign of having fallen, fell any more frequently then than today.

But any traveller who has travelled on horseback in the Pyrenees has, on occasion, certainly noticed that the horse he was riding was a reformed troop horse and that his knees bore the marks of having fallen when employed in a regiment. What is the first and constant recommendation of the guide? Not to use the reins. In his free state the horse does not stumble although the paths he has to follow present difficulties of all kinds. Because, since he has left the ranks he is now on his own, given a free head and neck, free of all constraints, moving under his own instinct; he has acquired the habit of covering steep terrain. This habit is necessary so that the horse is prevented from falling, which he, himself, fears. But domestication has sometimes hindered him from acquiring the skill needed to keep him from falling, and he has not been allowed to get used to covering the kind of terrain that could bring about falls.

This is also the case with the training of the race horse who, on the terrain he covers, does not encounter either ruts, stones, or uneven ground. Lacking the training, he must be made to cover all kinds of terrain that are steep, uneven, all those difficulties that his foot has ignored. At first, especially if he is somewhat inattentive, he will frequently stumble. The hand can sometimes give him a warning. But, more often, it will not prevent him from stumbling. Little by little, through exercise and experience, he will become skilled and be able to go over, without stumbling, the worst kinds of paths.

In my study on the *comte* d'Aure, I said that when he was the *écuyer cavalcadour*, his hunters were the ones most requested and I gave the reasons for this. Walking alongside the king, giving the king the easiest path, d'Aure made his horse walk along ruts. Thus his hunters became naturally sure-footed, a skill which became the object of envy at the court.[2]

Thus with the help of his instinct which nature has given him as guide, the horse can acquire a skill that the *écuyer* with all his talent, can never give the horse. Nature is the most important teacher. Its book is the most accurate, the wisest, the most useful to consult. From the effects found in its pages, we are led to the causes that engender them. Better than the most seductive theories, the most beautiful dissertations, the book of nature enlightens us and guides us in our practice.

---

[2] *Un Officier de cavalerie – Souvenirs du général L'Hotte*, Plon-Nourrit, Paris, 1906.

Chapter 7

Some controversial points. – Diagonal movements are to be condemned. – The bend *of the neck. – When turning, inside heels or outside heels? – The rider's actions based on the motion of the horse's limbs. – One should only be preoccupied with the position and let the horse take care of the timing to dispose of his points of support. – Our actions should depend upon the position of the horse. – Lead changes. – Use of the opposing heel or the direct heel? – Striking-off at the canter. – A feeling for contractions.*

I will now approach certain controversial points.

If one accepts that the straight horse and the disposition of the haunches should precede all changes of direction and if one considers this important in the practice of high equitation, it then follows that diagonal actions should be condemned when they are used regularly as aids. This is so, due to the contrary effect these actions have on the straight horse and the disposition of the haunches. Diagonal actions should be used only as one of the many means, but only momentarily, to submit the joints and muscles and to achieve the straight position.

Should, however, a somewhat energetic resistance occur, in order to control it easily, one cannot have recourse to diagonal actions. The use of two forces, rein and heel on the same side is then necessary.

If one tried to solve the problem by using the right diagonal when the haunches or the shoulders refuse to deviate to the right, the right rein, in the first instance, the left heel, in the second instance, would give support to the resistance by supporting the opposition either from the shoulders to the haunches or from the haunches to the shoulders.

The *bend* on the side given to the neck when the horse goes straight forward and upon which the *écuyers* of the past insisted, must be condemned. This *bend* also known as *le placer*, was not used when dealing with horses employed outdoors. But it was accepted that when in the *manège* the horse lacked gracefulness if he were not bent in the direction he was moving. This bend had to emanate from the withers with the horse looking towards the inside of the *manège*. Depending upon the schools, the inflexion of the neck was more or less pronounced. From this came the *complete bend*, *the arched bend*, or the *half-bend*.

This position given to the horse who walks straight ahead, is a matter of fashion, of convention, and has nothing to do with the laws of nature, which, in fact, reject them. Is it not the way nature works, namely, to look in the direction one is moving; consequently, is it not going against nature to carry the head to the side when one moves straight ahead? The bend in the neck also indicates another result, stated by the *écuyers* who practised it. The bend was not just limited to the neck, but extended to the whole spinal column. From this derives the total failure of the straight horse.

When I discussed the straight horse and underscored its advantages, I said that in the course of one's work, the positions requiring the various movements were all the more accurate in that they deviated less from the straight position and served as their link; thus the less the deviation was felt, the easier became the rapid succession of the varied movements. This cannot be so when the horse's inflexion becomes part of the horse's regular work. What will then result is the inevitable total reversal of the position every time one changes direction or when one goes from one movement to a contrary movement, regardless of the nature of the movement.

One must, however, defend the *écuyers* of the past, for they did not execute exercises that took into account quick and successive position changes. Be that as it may, in principle, the horse cannot be completely harmonized in the use of his forces if there is no accord between the different areas disposed to follow the line. From head to haunches, the horse must be straight if he is following a straight line; bent, only if he is following a curved line.

However, when side-stepping, the bend has its place. It makes the horse look in the direction he is moving, adds to his gracefulness, and contributes to bringing in the outside shoulder, which has the most difficult task. Nonetheless, the bend must not be very pronounced so that the action of the rein provoking it does not affect the haunches and thus does not bring about a marked reversal of position in the counter-changes of direction and analogous movements.

The disposition of the haunches due to its marked action which determines the direction, could perhaps enlighten one with respect to certain questions. This also applies to the question that deals with the use of the inside heel or the outside heel when turning. One has even the right to ask oneself how this opinion, which gives the outside heel the main role, has persisted among those who, taking nature as guide, have seen how the horse, in a state of freedom, executes his turns. But without taking this into account and without lingering on the consequences that emerge from the disposition of the haunches, the question ought to be resolved from a simple analysis of the aids.

A rider is moving and asked to turn to the right using only his legs. Would he ever consider using his left leg? Certainly not. For the horse would most certainly move to the left. Thus the moment when an action produces an effect that is in direct opposition to the goal sought, it cannot constitute a determining action; it can only be a way of rectifying. This is the case with the outside leg when turning, that is, when one is dealing with elementary equitation. However, if high equitation is involved, the situation is different. The outside heel no longer has a rectifying role but, rather, a complementary one, that is, it aids and enhances the turn, but the initiative always belongs to the inside heel.

Another question that always remains unanswered, is the one that pertains to the action of the rider, whether he regulates or not the motion of the horse's limbs. There is even disagreement amongst those who belong to the first opinion. Thus some want the turn to begin with the outside shoulder; others with the inside shoulder. La Broue, La Guérinière belong to the first group; Aubert and many other modern authors to the second group. Without going any further, one can see that the question loses much of its merit, since the members of both groups knew exactly how to turn their horses. However, if one had to choose between the two opinions, it is with the position of La Guérinière that I would side.

Indeed, it is the outside shoulder which crosses over the inside shoulder when turning and bears the brunt of the action; its first step would be made more difficult by the deviation of the inside shoulder if the latter took the initiative with respect to the displacement to the side. La Guérinière and Aubert only mention the shoulders, but the haunches should also be taken into account, whose play also gives credence to La Guérinière.

To make what I am going to say more easily understood, I will put the horse into the *trot écouté* (a precise and measured or moderated trot), which is what Aubert does when he demonstrates the function of the shoulders. One must remember that the horse turns at both ends. If the movement begins with the outside shoulder, it is helped by the inside hock which is engaged under the mass and pushes the haunches to the outside. Whereas, if the turn begins with the inside shoulder, the outside hock, because of its deviation, forms a sort of buttress which, far from helping the haunches to deviate to the outside, can prevent it.

The discussion into which I have just entered is, as I see it, of no value or interest to the *écuyer*. Quite different are his concerns when he sets out to dispose of the haunches as a point of departure with respect to the position required for making a turn. The position alone should pre-occupy him. It is the only language to which his aids have recourse and he must allow his horse to take on the duty and the time to dispose of his points of support. The same holds true for every other movement, except the turn.

D'Aure, with his extensive experience, and Baucher, who attempted the most complicated movements, neither one nor the other, regulated their actions on the motion of the horse's limbs. In equitation, it is not a question of refining or following minutely the horse when he raises or puts down each of his limbs, or of regulating one's actions on one or the other of these fleeting actions. One must look at art from a wider perspective, otherwise one will follow a path filled with difficulties, already so numerous and inherent in equitation.

It is the same when striking off at the canter on a specific leg, based on which one is put down, as established by Aubert. Aubert wants the striking off at the canter on the right leg to be determined the moment the left hindleg is placed on the ground. This is what Aubert calls 'seizing the leg at the right moment'. Thus the placing down of the leg must, at the same time, be felt by the rider who must be sufficiently skilled with his hand and legs to put them, at that very moment, into play, in accord with its being raised at the canter. The obedience of the horse must be instantaneous otherwise the right moment, that is, the moment of the leg, is lost.

What demands are to be satisfied during so fleeting an instant when the leg has contact with the ground! To cope, at least in part, with these difficulties, Aubert advises abandoning any use of the hand. With cold horses, he suggests the clicking of the tongue or a light smack with the whip behind the boot which he substitutes for leg aids.

When one is dealing with Classical or *savante* equitation, there are certain movements which require a great deal of precision in determining how they are to be used. This precision can correspond to the motion of the limbs, but it is not the motion that regulates our actions. It is the position that the horse takes in general and whose leg motion is only the consequence which guides us and makes us sense when our aids must act.

This is also the case with lead changes at every stride. To achieve this one must follow a progressive pattern. In principle, a lead change is not obtained as soon as the requested position is given. The same holds true of the striking off at the canter. One must wait for the horse, for it is he who executes the movement. If one were to ask a lead change from a horse not yet familiar with this movement, one would have to force him into it by an inversion of the shoulders and the crossing of haunches, which intelligent horsemen condemn. As the horse becomes familiar with lead changes, he will more easily take on the position which provokes the movement and respond more promptly to its execution. When the horse's obedience is assured, in order to execute a lead change at a determined stride, the rider has only to regulate the impetus of the canter. It is the impetus which will guide him in the use of his aids and whose effect must be felt the moment the forehand comes down on the ground.

With respect to the piaffe and the passage, it is how the horse, in general, affects the position by moving alternately from one diagonal to the other and which regulates the succession of our actions. The moment when the lead change at a determined stride must be requested, that moment is determined without the rider having to concern himself with the motion of the horse's limbs.

What combination of aids must be used to obtain the intervention of the play of the lateral bipeds, which actually constitutes the lead change, there is no unanimity of opinion on the part of the *écuyers*. Agreement exists, however, on how the hand is used to lighten the shoulder which has to gain ground, which is, to bring back the weight of the forehand on to the shoulder which has to remain behind; that is, on to the right shoulder, if one goes from the right canter to the left canter. This can be achieved by opening the right rein if the neck is stiff; if it is supple, by flexing to the left and letting it flow back on to the left shoulder.

In Classical or *savante* equitation, perfection demands that weight displacement be reduced to the ultimate limits needed, by means of a light lateral effect of the hand and without modifying the direction of the neck; for any change in direction transmitted to this region, will affect the straight position of the horse in itself and the reaction it has on the haunches.

Where disagreement exists is in the use of the heels. Some urge the use of the outside heels, also known as *opposing* heels; others the use of the inside heels, known as the *direct heels*. If these two methods are correctly used, both can give the sought for result. Thus for the horse cantering on the right leg, the lead change will be obtained by means of the opposing heel, that is, the right heel, when employed in such a way as to make the haunches deviate to the left; this deviation pushes the left hock forward while making the horse traverse, which he does naturally when he canters on the left leg. The same lead change is obtained by means of the direct heel, that is, the left heel, when it is used – as already indicated elsewhere – in such a way as to draw the left hock under the centre of the mass.

These two methods find their use:

The first one, when the horse's obedience to the aids is not complete. On the other hand, it satisfies all the requirements dealing with cross-country equitation. Furthermore, the horse can, without any inconvenience, traverse a little in the practice of ordinary equitation.

The second one, a more refined and delicate use, offers Classical or *savante* equitation the advantage of keeping the horse straight, an invaluable advantage for this type of equitation, enabling one, without difficulty, to obtain lead changes at every three strides, two strides, and at every stride 'a tempo'.

This is understandable. The straight horse avoids any traversing and inflexions on the side. He demands that all weight displacements be reduced to what is absolutely necessary. Therefore there is no change of position in order to go from the canter on one lead to the canter on the other lead. And modifying the position which each lead change requires, becomes then somewhat less sensitive so that when one lead change has been obtained, another can be asked right away.

Obtaining successive lead changes without difficulty depends entirely to what extent the single lead change has been perfected. Here lies the difficulty and, as in everything else, if the more-or-less is easy, it is quite different when dealing with perfection or what comes close to it.

Everything I have said with respect to the hand and the heels in order to obtain lead changes is also applicable to striking off at the canter. Both must be obtained with no apparent movement on the part of the rider when we are dealing with Classical or *savante* equitation.

With respect to successive lead changes, one must avoid twisting the upper body or moving from one buttock to the other. Unfortunately, the rider is all too often inclined to make these movements which disrupt the harmony that he must maintain with his horse. These movements are disgraceful in themselves and good taste condemns them. They destroy all the elegance and charm of the air in question. If the rider remains closely linked to his horse, he only has to accompany him in the gentle rocking in which he seems to find pleasure and which makes it possible for him to canter successively from one lead to the other.

Successive lead changes can be executed in two ways:

(1) By doing a complete programme which includes moving in a circle and on two tracks, first at every three strides, then at two strides, then at every stride 'a tempo'.

(2) By combining these different lead changes into a single programme, alternating them and maintaining the canter on the same lead.

This method of enhancing the programme dealing with the canter by adding to it successive lead changes, brings about variety to the work and avoids monotony, preventing the horse from falling into routine and never allowing him, on his own, to continue lead changes which were not asked.

Instead of attempting to regulate his actions based on the motion of limbs, the *écuyer* will find a whole gamut of studies that are interesting and fertile, by applying himself to perfect the position, that is, the combination of forces and, as such, the distribution of the mass that is correct for each movement. In order to be able to destroy quickly resistances which could oppose the correct position and bring about the use of forces to assure accuracy, the *écuyer* must try to acquire the feeling of contractions. In order to put this feeling into evidence and to make its value appreciated, I will, for example, take the horse who, when asked to canter on the right lead, responds by a combination of forces, and canters on the left lead.

The rider who lacks any equestrian feeling can only know when the canter is on the determined lead by means of his eyes. The rider who can feel his horse through his seat, after two or three strides at the canter, is able to determine whether the horse took off on the left lead. The judicious horseman with sufficient equestrian tact able to appreciate the position from which the canter on the left lead emanated, will rectify it and, before provoking the strike-off, will replace it by the correct position to canter on the right lead. The *écuyer* who has a feeling for contractions will not have to rectify the false position in that he will not let it occur. He will prevent it from happening by combatting, at the very outset, the contractions brought about by the false position and replace those that bring about the correct position at the strike-off at the canter on the right lead.

The scale that I have established should suffice to indicate the speed that dressage (schooling) can take, based on the degree of talent the rider, undertaking it, possesses. One must, indeed, be gifted in an exceptional way for equitation and spend a great deal of time at it finally to acquire this very fine feeling, called the feeling for contractions. But the results that come with this feeling are too enviable not to try to acquire it. To know how to prevent mistakes rather than having to correct them, dressage can, with help, move rapidly and its execution can achieve perfection.

Chapter 8

Distribution of the horse's weight between shoulders and haunches. – Modifications which can bring about changes in the neck's position. – The rising trot; its mechanism; its advantages.

When dealing with a horse, especially for cross-country use, it is important to know what the action of the neck and the changes of its position will have on the distribution of the horse's weight between his shoulders and haunches.

The following are some experiments made by means of two scales, of the same size, with mobile boards; upon the one rested the forelegs of the horse, upon the other, his hindlegs.

Thirty-two horses of varied conformation were used in these experiments. The average weight gave the following results:

With the head at 45 degrees on the vertical, more lowered than raised, the weight supported by the shoulders is greater than the one supported by the haunches by about one-ninth of the horse's total weight. Using this position of the head and depending whether it is raised and thrown backwards or lowered and *ramené* towards the chest, about ten kilograms are carried from the shoulders to the haunches, or from the haunches to the shoulders.

These same experiments indicate that a long neck, although light, puts more weight on the shoulders than a thick, short neck, and points out that these changes of position bring about weight displacements that are considerably sensitive. Just a simple reflection is sufficient to indicate this.

No other experiments with respect to changes in neck positions than those mentioned were conducted. It would have been interesting to know what the modifications would have been with respect to weight distribution had the forehand been totally extended as, for example, with a race horse put to the utmost of his capability. With no weight information supplied, one can guess at the overload that a neck stretched out in this manner would bring to the shoulders to the benefit of the haunches.

Other experiments were conducted to determine how the weight of the rider was distributed over his mount. They indicated that the horse carries about two-thirds of the rider's weight on his shoulders when the rider holds his torso straight; one-half when the rider inclines slightly backwards; five-sixths when he stands on his stirrup irons. One can judge from this that considerable weight transfers can be obtained, either going towards the shoulders, or towards the haunches, when the position taken by the rider is combined with the horse's extension or elevation of his neck. Without going to any extremes, the rider can find, in the distribution of his own weight, the means of contributing to the modification of the horse's equilibrium (a great advantage that ought to be sought), for the purpose of either extending or shortening the horse's gaits or to regularize them. D'Aure excelled therein.

The experiments I have just mentioned, which indicate how the position of the horse's neck can influence his weight distribution, ought to suffice in pointing out the error that riders often fall into, when they are determined to ask of their horses a marked elevation of neck when, actually, nature has given them a low neck. The action of the hands that seek this elevation do not even cease when there is an inopportune displacement of weight; they go even beyond that and interfere with the impulsive forces so that there is no longer a generous forward movement. Naturally, every rider would like to have a horse with a good conformation and provided with a neck set high. But all saddle horses are not built so advantageously and the rider must be able to take advantage of the situation by making the necessary concessions.

Besides, one must be convinced of this: the rider will never be able to maintain the neck high if the horse's conformation is quite different from what I described as desirable. The horse will only for a moment be able to maintain his neck, of his own accord, in the position imposed upon him, which is contrary to his conformation. If the demands of the rider are overdone and his hands are constantly readjusting to the horse's opposition, the latter will feel constrained and lose the freedom of his gaits; his back, his hocks, overloaded, will be hampered in their play, and the harmony of the movements will be destroyed. The goal to follow here must be limited to the support and the elasticity of the neck – nothing more. If one wanted to achieve its elevation, this could be solicited, but only momentarily. The rider must then allow the neck to take the position that corresponds to the horse's conformation whose dressage he has undertaken.

To underscore the importance that the rider's body and the distribution of his weight exerts on the gaits, that is, on their extension, their shortening, their regularity, it is time to bring up the rising trot. It is well-known that with this kind of trot, the rider's torso moves alternately forwards and backwards, then returns to its original position. These displacements move in accord with the raising and putting down of the same diagonal biped. The rider receives the reaction produced by the relaxation of the biped with which he is in accord and cedes to it, by inclining lightly and progressively his torso forward. Then, supporting himself lightly on his stirrup irons, he remains, for an instant, in this position, the buttock close to, but away from, the saddle, while the relaxation of the other diagonal takes place and whose reaction is thus avoided. The buttocks are then placed again on the saddle at the moment when the diagonal, *with* which one trots, is put down again.

Before going any further, I said *with*, not *on*, as is usually said, because this latter expression can cause some confusion with the rider as he supports himself on the irons when the diagonal, in opposition to the one with which he must be in accord, makes his stride. The displacements of the torso which involves the rising trot, although kept within limits, also exerts on the horse an action that is rather sensitive, so that the diagonal, with which the rider moves in concert, covers more ground than the other one. Every rider who has practised the rising trot with some attention, has certainly been convinced of this fact.

Here is the explanation:

Let us suppose that the rider, trotting with the right diagonal, has just received the reaction produced by the relaxation of this diagonal and yields to it. When the inclination forward of the rider's torso reaches its limit, and he supports himself on the irons, that is the moment when the whole effect of the relaxation of the left diagonal occurs, which moves and pushes forward the right diagonal which is, at the moment, supportive.

The latter now gains much more ground than the weight of the rider, now totally brought towards the shoulders, solicited.

When, in turn, the right diagonal comes down, it is the moment when the rider reaches the back of the saddle and lets himself go backwards. The weight of his torso, carried closer to the haunches, annuls the effect produced by the relaxation of the right diagonal and, therefore, restricts the extent of the ground that the left diagonal covers and is, at the moment, supportive.

Aside from the influence exerted by these two transfers of opposite weights due to the displacement of the torso, it should be noted that the rider, finding himself away from the saddle at the moment when the left diagonal comes down, the relaxation of the latter continues to be favoured. Contact once again with the saddle when the right diagonal comes down, results in a chock, but no matter how light, still impedes the relaxation of this diagonal. The effect of this light chock becomes especially perceptible because of the moment when it is produced and corresponds to the departure of the relaxation.

The diagonal with which the rider trots gains more ground than does the other one, and results in the haunches being pulled to that side and, as a consequence, making them deviate to the right if the rider is in accord with the right diagonal.

The effect is appreciable with all horses, but especially with those who, through dressage, have acquired a rigorously straight position. A single hack (ride outdoors), trotting constantly with the same diagonal will suffice to affect the horse's straight position. This will be noticeable the following day when the horse is ridden in the *manège* at the beginning of the working period.

With certain horses whose straight position has been strengthened, there are some who are so affected by the displacements of the rider's torso, that, already after the first stride, the haunches deviate either to the right or to the left when the rider alternates from one diagonal to the other.

One must thus trot with both diagonals if one wishes to prevent the straight position of the horse from being affected, as well as the regularity of his movements and to equalize the work of his limbs.

Seldom is the horse who has not been developed through schooling, and who has been trotted indiscriminately with one or the other diagonal, able to trot with equal ease. A preference for one or the other diagonal finds its source in certain imperfections of the horse's structure, nature having apparently neglected one part of its work. Then, too, it may be the result of a false position acquired through habit.

With the horse who shows a marked deviation from the straight position, the rising trot is always taken as easily with the diagonal on the side where the horse traverses, as taken with difficulty with the opposite diagonal. In this case, one sees horses lose all the brilliance of their actions, expressing difficulties and confusion in their movements. There are even those who are so embarrassed that they actually change their step, so that the solicitations exerted by the rider's body, rather than opposing the traversed position, go along with it.

It is also to be noted that, either by habit or due to an irregularity in their position, a number of riders have a marked predisposition of always trotting on the same diagonal and have great difficulty going from the customary one to the other. To do so without interruption, it is sufficient to receive the two reactions which succeed each other and, instead of ceding to the first one, cede to the second one. To have no preference for a diagonal says something favourable as much for the rider as for the horse.

The advantages that derive from executing the rising trot are numerous. First of all, the rider gains greatly from it in that he has only to endure one reaction rather than two; even the second one has strangely been deadened. Also the illness, formerly known as the 'illness of horsemen', and which was quite common, has completely disappeared. This problem was caused by the heating of the seat due to the chocks and the rubbing that were experienced, increased even further by the cloth or velvet that covered almost all of the saddles at the time.

Both the horse and the rider, but, perhaps more so the horse, benefited from the rising trot in that he no longer had to receive those chocks with which his dorsal column, set in motion, had to cope at each stride. Now his gait becomes more flowing, extending of its own accord when the moment of rising is undertaken.

The rider, too, by trotting this way, finds resources with which to straighten the horse who traverses, regularize his gait, and obtain the canter on the lead the horse had refused to take. To achieve this latter result, the rider must trot with the lead which the horses cannot take and progressively lengthen the gait. When the horse arrives at the end of the trot and can no longer sustain this gait, he will be forced to take, of his own accord, the canter on the side he traverses, striking off on the lead that gains the most ground and which is the one with which the rider trots.

Chapter 9

The rider's position in Classical or savante equitation. – The rider accompanies the horse. – Any displacement of the seat is proscribed. – The aids must be secret, that is, imperceptible. – It is the horse who executes. – The position of the rider during a horse's defences. – The position of the horse's neck when in a state of freedom. – Submission of the horse's neck when mounted. – The horse's relative freedom when obstacle jumping.

When practising Classical or *savante* equitation, the rider's position must be an academic or Classical one. This position must never be altered in the course of work. During changes in direction (rein changes), in order to be in total harmony with the horse, the rider's disposition of his body must never precede that of his horse, or even follow it, but, rather, *accompany* it. This entails a certain something which the rider, practising Classical or *savante* equitation, must possess.

The same holds true for all movements, be they on one or two tracks, and, especially, for lead changes, when the rider's body must never be accentuated. Displacement of the seat is proscribed at all times; the rider must always remain welded to his horse. Movements of hands and legs must be secret and remain invisible to the eye.

Finally, everything that draws attention to his person must be avoided by the rider. It is the horse who is executing the movements, the rider must merely try to be in harmony with him.

In cases of defences, far from remaining in accord with the horse's shifting of weight, the rider must put the upper part of his body in the opposite direction, not so much to combat these defences by opposing the weight, which is totally insufficient in attempting to paralyze them; rather to stay in the saddle and resist any bucking or rearing.

The horse makes use of his neck in many different ways, whereas in a free state, he disposes of it freely. Sometimes he places his neck in accordance with the movement, at others it is placed indifferently, or else he gives it an opposite position.

In the course of the same turn, one can observe the horse giving his neck different positions, sometimes placing it quite to the side opposed to the turn; often as a counterbalance to an inclination of the mass that is too accentuated.

In this instance, the horse uses his neck as an acrobat uses his balancer to re-establish his equilibrium. This occurs also in other circumstances. If a horse accidentally falls on his side or is constrained to submit to an operation, he throws his neck with force on the side opposite where his body lies. The rider should also use as principle that, in case a fall on the side is inevitable, he should throw himself, if he can, on the side where the horse's head is located so as not to fall under him.

The freedom with which the free horse uses his neck is, of course, not possible when he is mounted. It is absolutely necessary that the neck be held in obedience and that his degree of submission corresponds to the demands of service put upon the horse.

However, when a horse is asked to make an effort requiring all the means of which he is capable and that he knows what he has to do by the very object that motivates his effort, such as an obstacle to jump, then every amount of freedom must be allowed him in the use of his neck. His instinct alone, rather than anything the rider can do, will guide him in using the different resources that nature has given him.

The freedom of his neck, so important in helping the horse get around and over obstacles, does not mean abandoning his head, which is a questionable practice on the part of riders, but also for cavalrymen, because the latter must choose between total abandonment of the head or its constraint, and their choice cannot and must not be in question. If the solidity of these riders is compromised, and if they do not want to clutch at the reins or avoid a fall, they must grab the pommel of the saddle. Under these circumstances, it is the least bothersome solution.

With respect to skilled riders, familiar with obstacle jumping, they know that they must give the horse the full freedom of his neck without, for all that, having to abandon his head.

It should be noted that when one is dealing especially with obstacle jumping, the inexperienced rider, instead of lowering his hands, always raises them. As a result, the horse sometimes falls back on his hocks instead of landing on his shoulders after having jumped over the obstacle.

One has only to see horses jumping freely to be convinced to what extent the raising of hands hinders the effort that the jump claims.

A horse who is free approaches the post. The spectator, placed behind him, follows him with his eyes and sees his ears above the line of his back. At the moment when the forehand is raised to go over the obstacle, his head and neck, far from being raised, extend rather, and the ears, hidden by the withers, disappear. The horse now wants to see beyond the obstacle and, at the same time, appears to be more worried about passing his hocks than his knees over the obstacle.

The concern the rider must exert when approaching the obstacle can be expressed in three words: *seated*, *legs close*, *hands low*.

When I say *seated*, one must not see there an exaggerated backward inclination of the body which overloads the hindquarters and lessens the effect of the relaxation of the hocks when taking off. The rider must be seated by pushing his seat under him so that with the spring of the horse, the seat is carried along as though by a sheet of water; the inclination of the body backwards is only the consequence, occurring after the relaxation of the hocks.

Chapter 10

When the horse revolts. – How to control him. – Rigid reins; their importance; their description; their use to make the horse go forward, to obtain a turn, to combat certain defences; their effect on the horse's psyche. – First application with the 1st Cuirassiers. – *Mameluck*. – *Capucin*. – Experience before *général* de Noue.

When the stubborn horse begins to rebel, makes use of his defences, attacks, he sometimes puts everything he has at his disposal. Both his neck and his haunches are then employed. The neck is the region which can most easily be controlled. But since we are, above all, dealing with the forward movement, the rider must be especially concerned with the haunches.

When the stubborn horse begins to rebel, he starts out by retaining his impulsive forces, which he refuses to impart to us. When he does use them, it is to get rid of his rider. It is therefore necessary to make him put his forces into action, and give them a direction so that they cannot be used as a means of defence.

The forward movement, if positive and bold, will bring this about. As long as he is kept in hand, he can neither buck nor rear. He cannot use his defences without falling back on himself. If he begins to leap and bound, they will be less effective and less frequent, since they will occur when he is advancing rather than when in place.

However, instead of giving in to the pressure of the legs which urge him to go forward, the stubborn horse leans against them and, if his defences do not occur at the moment, they will explode as soon as the spurs make themselves felt, for the stubborn horse, instead of fleeing, grips. Of course a vigorous rider with a good seat will be able to win out. He will make the horse respond to the pressure of his legs whose power will be multiplied a hundredfold by the repeated energetic and lively attacks of his spurs, attacks which will continue until he has obtained the horse's obedience and which will stop as soon as this has been achieved, but without the legs ceasing their pressure as promptly.

But should the preservation of the horse be the primary concern, it is better not to enter into a struggle. The rider will be able to avoid a struggle by using *rigid reins*. I will expand on this. What makes me want to expand upon this in greater detail is that although the use of mechanical means to stop recalcitrant horses are numerous, it is not the same with those kinds that are used to make a horse who refuses to go forward, do so. These kinds are not numerous and their positive use is often difficult.

Rigid reins are composed of two strong steel blades covered with leather and attached to the front part of the eyes of the cheekpiece, where the curb-chain is located.

They look like ordinary snaffle reins and are supple only where they lie on the withers. The rigid parts must be long enough so that the rider can hold the ends when the horse's head and neck are extended. To make use of them, the rider must put aside the curb reins, form a knot so that, should the occasion arise, he can quickly retake them. When put aside, they should form a ring so as not to interfere with the extension of the horse's neck.

To push the horse forward the rider takes up the rigid reins and acts on them with a forward motion. In that they have a direct bearing on the curb-chain, the horse is obliged to extend his head and neck and cede to the action that invites him – if need be, pushes him – forward.

These reins must be used with moderation at first, for their action engages the horse so naturally in the forward movement, that he usually obeys immediately. But when one is dealing with stubborn horses who resist energetically, if the reins are used with vigour, they acquire a sort of irresistible power. With these kinds of horses, the curb-chain must be tightened slightly more than usual, so that they can fully receive the intended action, and without the cheek straps of the bridle playing a part in the action.

The rigid reins can also offer the rider powerful resources to make the horse, who refuses to do so, turn. If the horse is to turn to the right and he refuses to do so, the rider pushes forward the left rein and pulls towards him the right rein which gives the bit a twist, obliging the head to move to the right. As soon as the head has reached the direction to be followed, the rider, moving the two reins in a forward movement, engages the horse.

The methods I have just described are to be used with horses who refuse to move forward, do a head with tail, that is, throw themselves forward in a brutal semi-circle, buck, rear in place or back. However, rigid reins have a lesser effect with horses who defend themselves but still go forward. In that the movement forward can be as vigorous as one wishes it to be, defences lose a considerable amount of their force and, if the neck is maintained fully extended, the raising of the croup alone will be made possible.

In that the use of rigid reins is simple and easy, only a few moments suffice for one to catch on. The rider has only to modify the usual movement of his arms which must now act forwards and no longer backwards. While the rigid reins are in use, but only used temporarily, the legs of the rider must not remain inactive. They have to act together with the action of the reins whose use is progressively diminished when the horse responds positively to the legs and the spurs alone.

This final stage, which must eventually be achieved, will occur all the more rapidly in that here the hands act directly in accordance with the goal pursued by the legs; the rider is no longer, as so often happens, opposing with his hands what his legs are supposed to accomplish.

The rigid reins provide a means of control that is simultaneously gentle and powerful. Far from provoking any defences, these reins eliminate them in that they do not directly deal with the impulsive forces that the horse refuses to give us. The haunches must not take any initiative; they have only to follow the weight, first put into play on their own, and which carry them along. They even find themselves relieved, for the transfer of the weight towards the shoulder is to their advantage.

The means commonly used to control the horse and make him understand our wishes, derive from the command we have over his forces. But one can also act directly on his mind. That is what the rigid reins do. By taking hold of the horse's neck, not only do they immobilize the resources the horse can use to defend himself, but since he can no longer use his head freely, in a way, he finds that he is also unable to act freely.

I began using the rigid reins when I was

Captain-instructor with the 1st Cuirassiers. We first tried these reins on the horse belonging to my friend, Captain Paul de Courtivron, an outstanding horseman. This horse reared in the most dangerous manner. I had experienced this, myself, one day, and I can still see my friend, pale and trembling, when he thought that the horse had fallen on top of me; he had made a half-turn on the side of the *manège* along which I was going, when he reared. After a while, the rigid reins had an effect on his defences and we were able to abandon them.

My function as Captain-instructor entailed the schooling of all the young horses. The mounts the regiment received came from the plains of Normandy and the marshlands of Rochefort and Saint-Gervais. The largest part of these horses had never been ridden prior to coming to the corps. Many had never experienced any constraints.

The first and most important difficulty one has to overcome with these horses, whose disposition is far from generous, was to get them to move boldly straight ahead, mounted by a rider. For those who were unusually recalcitrant I used the rigid reins and had considerable success. Not having at my disposal the reins I have described, I replaced them simply by sticks and strong string. Despite its ugly appearance, it had good results in the hands of my cuirassiers.

When I commanded the cavalry section at Saint-Cyr, I became especially aware how much command one had over the mind of the horse with these rigid reins. In the *manège* there was a grey stallion named *Mameluck* who was exasperated by the vicinity of mares and who expressed this exasperation by whinnying violently. One day when the pupils met for military work, I had *Mameluck* brought to me and provided him with the rigid reins. Lieutenant-*écuyer* Roques, who was riding him, turned around the group where there were only mares and geldings, passing several times between the open ranks. Not only did *Mameluck* not try to stop, but he barely emitted little faint whinnyings. The rigid reins I used then were less bulky than the ones I had used with the 1st Cuirassiers. The sticks were well shaped, enveloped in leather, the latter having replaced the pieces of string.

I had taken one of these gadgets along to Saumur when I became *écuyer en chef*. Two or three days after my arrival, at a meeting of the *écuyers*, I was asked about the rigid reins whose function I then explained. At the end of my explanations, a grey race horse, castrated, named *Capucin*, was pointed out to me as being stubborn, untractable, and who reacted violently against spurs, often getting rid of his rider. It was *lieutenant sous-écuyer* Javey who was burdened with the problems this horse presented. I then told him that, from now on, he would, himself, judge the value of the rigid reins. *Capucin*, provided with these reins, was brought to the *Manège des écuyers*. M. Javey rode him with total success. With many attacks of the spurs and supported by the energetic action of the arms, the horse could only escape forward without defending himself once.

That same year of my arrival at Saumur, *général* de Noue inspected the school. He wanted to judge the efficiency of the rigid reins, about which the commandant of the school, *général* Crespin, had spoken. I had four horses brought to the *manège*, horses known to be most stubborn, known as 'the little group', and composed mostly of vicious horses sent to us by various regiments. These four horses were first ridden and led without any difficulty, by the *sous-maîtres* of the *manège*. *Général* de Noue then asked me if less vigorous riders would have the same success. I had four remount riders, who had brought these horses to the *manège*, get on them. They had to mount bare-legged for their clogs did not fit the stirrup irons. I explained to them that when I told them to move forward, all they had to do was use the sticks as though they were pushing a wheel-barrow. These men had seen for themselves how the horses they were to ride could defend themselves; they only cared for them in the stalls. The concern of these inexperienced riders was quite obvious. They, too, were equally successful in making the horses move from the line. I had recommended that they move their arms energetically if a horse resisted them. The rider on *Carme*, one of the most stubborn horses, not wanting to wait until the horse began to resist, pushed him immediately forward with such force that he almost fell on his knees.

During the whole period as *écuyer en chef*, two pairs of rigid reins were always available in the whip carriers near the pillars so that, if needed, any one could have on hand a means of controlling the horse.

These reins were named after me, but that is incorrect. It is not I who invented them. I only popularized them during the periods I have just mentioned. It was in 1854 that Baucher brought them to my attention, asking me to experiment with them. He showed me the model that had been sent to him from Italy and was of the type I have described. The inventor was Giovanni Sala who had been one of Baucher's pupils when the latter was teaching in Milan. It was the period when the master demanded from the rider the energetic and constant use of his legs. Giovanni Sala lacked strength in his legs and to compensate for this lack, tried to replace his legs by another agent. Thus the idea of rigid reins.

Chapter 11

Military equitation. – The need for simple instruction procedures. – Bases for these procedures. – Advantages of work at undetermined distances. – Work at fixed or determined distances. – Advantages of a marked square on open terrain. – How to mark the track. – Obstacle jumping by cavalrymen. – Jumping over the crossbar by the 18th Dragoons in column formation. – Importance of letting the horses free to follow their instinct. – Some borrowings from the Regulation of 1876: Changes in the regiment; voluntary march; assembly of the troops.

Since military equitation has taken up a good part of my life, it is obvious that I devote some pages to it.

I am considering the Regulations of 1876 on cavalry exercises and am assuming that they are well known. They will bring together the schooling of the troop horse and instruction of the horseman from the ranks, as well as instruction which can be given by the instructors of our regiment. Regiment instructors, with a few exceptions, are not academically oriented. On the other hand, the means used for their instruction must be chosen so as to be within the reach of all horsemen from the ranks. Therein lies the need for simplified methods of instruction.

As the regulation stipulated, the basic essentials of these procedures were to follow straight lines, and turns, linking these lines. I shall first speak about straight lines then about turns.

The straight lines are carefully determined by stakes which delineate the square, linked to those marking the middle of the sides. On the other hand, they are determined by the perpendicular on the side to which the rider moves when he crosses the square, either crosswise or lengthwise. It has been said that to follow a straight line was one of the most difficult things to do in equitation. That is not the case. It is much more difficult to keep a horse on a circle whose radius is accurately determined. What is true, however, is that a straight line, accurately determined, and which gives a direction that is easy to take (whereas this is not the case of a curved line), it follows that as soon as there is a deviation in this direction, the rider senses it immediately. Guided, so to speak, by his instinct, the rider makes use of his hand and legs to bring the horse back into the path or direction he must follow. These repeated rectifications allow the rider to make a correct use of his aids if his attention is maintained. As far as the horse is concerned, he does not follow straight lines of his own accord. The fact that it is necessary to bring him back into the direction to be followed each time he deviates, brings about submission. On the other hand, the instructor sees in the straight lines, delineated for him as precisely as they are for the rider, a definite basis which allows him to make his observations and remind the rider what he must do when he ignores it. That much said of straight lines, let us go to turns.

It is part of the horse's instinct to round off turns as much as possible and, consequently, to reduce them to a single turn; rather, this single turn ought to be two turns succeeding each other at a short distance. Thus the horse, operating on his own, no more follows along the short side of the square any more than he crosses to the other side to turn back. His turn extends from the large side of the square to the other. At no time does the horse follow a straight line and the more a gait is lively, the more the arc (bend) is accentuated.

The progress made by the rider and the dressage (schooling) of the horse is determined by the progressive straightening out of this arc (bend). At first when crossing from one end to the other, probably only a few steps are done in a straight line when the horse arrives at the middle line of the square. But this sort of link, which ties together these two wide turns, must be tightened little by little so that the crossing from one side to the other is done the way the regulation prescribes it.

From the moment when straight lines and turns are executed with precision and regularity at the three gaits, one can then say that the rider has understood the use of his aids and that the horse has become sufficiently submissive so that one and the other satisfy the work that is expected of them. The few movements still needed for the troop horse to complete, are merely additional factors. This indicates that, despite their lack of an extensive equestrian knowledge, the instructors, with attentiveness alone, can further instruction. But their attentiveness must be constant. Generally they do not indicate that they sufficiently possess this requirement. Often the eye of the instructor fails to follow the riders and, although they have been practising for some time, one sees them transform into curves the short sides of the square when crossing from one side to the other. They let the horse's instinct guide them instead of giving him direction. As a consequence neither the rider nor the horse profits. The simpler the procedures are, the more rigorous must be their application. Above all, instruction must not only have execution in mind, but it must envisage *sound execution*.

The instructional procedures I have just delineated and which stand out because of their simplicity and precision, tie in closely with work involving undetermined distances. Their useful application requires this sort of work. And they lose all their value with the resumption of short and fixed or determined distances. Indeed, with this kind of established programme, each rider follows mechanically the one ahead of him, especially with respect to successive movements. And so to render the work more profitable, one resorts to individual movements, which bring about other problems. In that it is absolutely necessary that the riders who must enter the track at the same time, reach it in perfect unison and be able to find their place in the column, this becomes the most important pre-occupation of the riders. The instructor then finds himself forced to pay attention to the total configuration rather than determine how each rider handles his horse.

These inconveniences are avoided when work is conducted at undetermined distances, although each movement is done individually. Some head towards a determined point on the track; others for an undetermined one. But all these movements are performed individually and pre-occupation with the total configuration is never apparent.

Lessons dealing with fixed or determined distances have their use when dealing with skilled riders, when the means of execution no longer requires the attention of the instructor. These lessons introduce variety into the work and also please the spectator.

However, in view of the limited amount of time devoted to the instruction of troops and the degree of skill it is possible for them to acquire, these lessons can only offer preparation for work as a unit, that is, a training unit. Such are the limitations with this kind of work stipulated by the regulation.

It should also be noted that the independence given to each rider with respect to work at undetermined distances takes away from 'optional work' the value that it could have when the lessons were uniformly conducted at determined or fixed distances. Today optional work is considered a means of relaxation for riders and horses.

The square which is marked off in an open area by stakes is very useful to the application of the instructional procedures I have just developed. Their value is greatly diminished when the track goes along the (boot)-rail of the *manège* or the closed rectangle, for the horse will instinctively follow the rail and it will only be at the corners that the riders will be able to make use of the methods of handling the horses at the turns.

To convince oneself of the value and importance of working in open terrain, one has only to examine the impacts made by the horse's hooves on the track of the square, limited only by stakes, and how they reveal the degree of instruction the riders are getting, the attention they are giving to their work, and the attention given by the instructors. If the riders are just beginning their instruction and, if, poorly supervised, they become careless in their work, the track will resemble an elongated oval. When instruction has advanced somewhat the supervision of the instructor is effective, each side of the track will resemble an S. I will explain this later. Eventually, when all four sides indicate that the riders are moving along straight lines, which tie into tight turns, this proves that the horses have become submissive and that the instruction the riders are getting is effective. Every officer who has followed attentively the instruction of a class of recruits can attest to this. When the track takes on the shape of an 'S' for a while during the instruction of recruits, this is due to the fact that the riders are using their aids incorrectly.

As indicated earlier, the horse, left to his own devices, reduces the two tight turns into one wide one at the short side. This happens because he begins the first turn too early; that is why the tracks take on this oval shape. But when the rider begins to use his aids correctly, he prevents his horse from turning too soon. But not yet able to regulate his actions, he exaggerates and, instead of maintaining the horse on the line he should follow, he pushes him out beyond it. Then comes the turn and since the rider is not yet sufficiently in control of his aids to tighten the turn, the horse gains ground outside the line after having passed the stake which marks the turn. The next stake which corresponds to the middle of the side, forces the rider to move towards the centre of the square; and now we already have the formation of the first part of the 'S'. The other half will produce the same effect at the next turn.

Once the track has acquired this incorrect shape, it will remain so all the more since men and horses have a natural tendency to follow the line that has already been marked.

If the square offers any special advantages, the *manège* also has certain advantages of its own. At the beginning of his instruction, the recruit has confidence in the (boot)-rail in that he does not have to concern himself with leading his horse who follows the rail of his own accord. The young horse is calmer and more attentive. Furthermore, when the weather is bad – and with our climate this is often and lengthy – *manèges* become indispensable.

One lessens the shortcomings I have described by frequently marking an inside track at a determined distance from the wall and insisting on work in the opposite direction. But as soon as the degree of instruction permits it and the weather makes it possible, it is important that work be conducted outdoors for the regiments. Instruction will benefit from this, as will the health of both horse and rider.

When I briefly mentioned obstacle jumping, and took into account the limited skill that men from the troops could acquire, I advanced the idea that one had to choose between controlling rather extensively the head of the horse, or, as an alternative, giving it complete freedom. Under these circumstances, one must opt for the latter. I will give my reason for this.

When I was a colonel with the 18th Dragoons, I was already practising at the time what later became part of the Regulation of 1876. There was one exercise which especially interested the officers who came to observe our manoeuvres. This was obstacle jumping conducted by a cavalry troop moving in formation. I must say first that the ordinance of 1829, in use at the time, required that the jumps be conducted row by row. The column had to halt, with the exception of the first row of the troop that led, then each row began to move in succession. One can understand the astonishment on the part of the officers who had always witnessed this procedure when they suddenly saw a column of trainees jump over the obstacles without stopping or slowing down as they moved forward.

This procedure seemed to those who had never practised it as rather dangerous. At Rambouillet *général* Ameil, who was inspecting my regiment, had the procedure stopped after the first group had gone over, not wanting his 'last inspection to be marred by an accident'. The procedure continued when I assured the general that the regiment participated daily in similar exercises. No accidents had ever occurred on the part of the horses in the second row. This is because they were never held back by the hands of the riders and were allowed to follow their instinct.

To prove to those who did not believe in the advantages of giving the horse his head, I asked them to place themselves near the crossbar that was to be jumped, which was made from a tree and had a special sound, and asked them to listen when the horses jumped over the bar. My regiment, moving in troop formation at the trot, was asked to jump twice over the crossbar: once with the riders holding only the snaffle reins, the curb reins lying loose in the form of a ring; a second time by abandoning the reins completely.

This regiment had practised obstacle jumping as much as any other cavalry troop, and the riders held in their hands only the gentlest of brakes, the snaffle; and my last recommendation to them when the formation set out, was for them to lower the wrists and loosen the fingers as they approached the obstacle; yet, when the four squadrons went over the crossbar, one could always hear the hindlegs of a few horses strike the tree. I then made them repeat the exercise, this time completely abandoning the reins. Usually the four squadrons jumped over the crossbar without the horse's feet touching it.

Included in these new principles which I advocated and which emerged from them, there were, among others, three exercises which also surprised the practitioners of the ordinance of 1829 namely:

The conversion of the regiment deployed in battle which the report, placed at the head of the ordinance of 1829, considered 'impractical'.

The voluntary march which allowed a column of a troop of cavalry to cross over any territory and past a narrow area without lengthening out the column, whereas the ordinance of 1829 demanded that the column file off in fours as soon as the width of the area became lower at the head of the troop.

Assembling the troops which made it easier to form promptly for battle, regardless of direction, whereas the regular procedures took too much time or failed. Nothing similar could be found in the ordinance of 1829.

I will not give any further details with respect to the Regulation of 1876; a more complete analysis of its beginnings will be presented when I touch upon the period that has marked my own involvement with the Regulation.[1]

---

[1] Unfortunately *général* L'Hotte was not able to complete this project. The editing of his *Souvenirs* was interrupted by the painful illness which afflicted him and which ended with his death on 3 February 1904. [Editor's note.]

Chapter 12

Programme of a treatise on equitation. – Circus equitation. – Its characteristics as opposed to those of Classical or *savante* equitation. – The artificial airs of our former *manèges*. – Inconveniences of unnatural movements. – Seek the *rassembler* only after the *ramener*. Obligations imposed on circus *écuyers*. – Baucher in the circus and away from the circus. – The passage erroneously considered *haute école*. – The *doux passage*; the *grand passage*. – The passage of *Ourphaly*. The *piaffe*.

If I were to consider equitation as a whole, this study would be presented as a manual and be divided as follows:

(1) *Haute école* equitation,
(2) Cross-country equitation or outdoor equitation,
(3) Horse racing
(4) Military equitation,

Among the pages I have already written can be found a great deal concerning these different kinds of equitation.

High equitation and cross-country equitation were considered under different aspects when my narrative took me to Saumur in 1845 as officer-pupil.[1] These two types of equitation were also developed in my studies on Baucher and d'Aure and can also be found in the questions I put forth inspired by my two masters.[2]

Military equitation and horse racing also feature in my writings.

In that instinctive equitation is not based on any principles and not guided by any rule, I will add nothing more to what I have already said.[3]

In the following pages I will present all I have to say about circus equitation and not return to it. This essay will be terminated by considerations on the passage.

Equitation as practised in the circus and called *haute école* is, by its very nature, the direct opposite of Classical or *savante* or high equitation. This is easy to understand. Circus equitation must strike the crowds visually and thus is far from requiring that, in the course of work, the position of the rider remain unchanging and regular. If the movements of the rider become apparent and express effort, they only impress even further the public who applauds even more loudly when the action it sees appears difficult to obtain. The success increases if the horse seems constrained, is forced to obey, or if it executes movements that are unnatural, especially against nature. The more extraordinary the movements are, the greater is the success. And if there appears to be a battle from which the rider emerges the victor, then the bravos explode.

---

[1] See *Un Officier de cavalerie – Souvenirs du géneral L'Hotte*, Plon-Nourrit, 1906. [2] *Ibid.* [3] *Ibid.*

The characteristics of Classical or *savante* equitation are the opposite of those that contribute to the success of circus equitation. With Classical equitation, the rider must always remain correct, if not flawless. This is the first condition expected of the rider. I have already discussed the care given to the rider's position at the *Ecole de Versailles*,[4] and one wonders what d'Abzac would have thought at the sight of the rider's positions at the circus. The rider must never give the slightest indication of effort; nor should the spectator become aware of the methods of his procedures. The horse must obey at the lightest touch of the aids which must always be discreet, even become a secret. The rider must forget himself and, somehow, become one with his horse. It is even better if the horse seems to function on his own when executing a brilliant movement that is never late or dragging; or if the rider and the horse seem to execute the most simple and easy movements.

The horse's beauty lies in his nobility, his grace, in his proud appearance, in the harmony of his movements, their brilliance, their energy. Equitation that is beautiful, delicate, and tasteful, seeks the development of this beauty by relying on the very gifts of the horse and not by rendering them unnatural. It is nature that this equitation takes as guide and not the extraordinary or the eccentric that is sought.

The exploration of the field is fertile; extension, elevation, the direction given to the natural movements can vary infinitely. Lead changes can acquire a purity, an elasticity, a softness and delicacy, in no way resembling those executed initially.

In Classical or *savante* equitation, movements that run counter to the natural gaits must be checked. In the circus, on the other hand, it is considered particularly skilful to create them, make use of them, or exploit them if the horse takes the initiative.

When the need arises to constrain a horse, the means employed in the circus is quite special, accomplished in hand. But if one accepts that these procedures belong to the domain of schooling, certainly it is not part of equitation as such, for it is only when the rider is mounted that methods of constraint ought to be used.

Our former *manèges*, at a time when equitation was noble and beautiful, included the artificial airs which, on the basis of their nature and elevation, they distinguished between low airs or airs near the ground and high airs. But here one only encountered the perfection of the usual gaits or the natural movements of the horse which schooling regularized. None was unnatural.

In those days, it was customary to say that a horse must be 'powerful in his haunches, generous in his mouth'. That said a great deal in a very few words. On the one hand, these expressions established a base which indicated the means that the horse had at his disposal; on the other hand, it indicated his perfect submission and lightness.

These expressions, used in the past and no longer in use today, had an elegance. Of a horse who had great presence on the forehand, it was said 'he carried himself high'. Certain ways of saying things have also been removed from our equestrian language without being replaced by any equivalent expressions. For example, the expression that indicated the processes that sought lightness was summarized in one word: 'allégir' (to lighten, or make light, the horse), or: 'allégérir'.

Unnatural movements, such as the *jambette* or the Spanish walk, movements which bring about rigidity or a lack of activity in the haunches and put all the action instead on the shoulders, actually hinder the advance of the horse's schooling instead of supporting it and are thus in opposition to the general action; rather, they join together certain

---

[4] See *Un Officier de cavalerie – Souvenirs du général L'Hotte*. Plon-Nourrit, 1906.

joints and muscles and interfere with the diligence of the haunches, which lightness, the harmony of the gaits so imperiously demand. The artificial gaits of the past, on the other hand, as opposed to those practised in the circus, were especially designed to combat inertia of the haunches.

The only merit that these unnatural movements have, if they have any at all, is confined to a difficulty that is won in a special way but whose victory is limited. It is not advisable to broach them unless the horse's schooling is considerably advanced so that they do not introduce too many problems. The true *écuyer*, who wants to be sure that no difficulty is foreign to his art, must act in this manner. As a general rule and in view of his quest for lightness, the experienced *écuyer* knows that he must not seek the *rassembler* before he has introduced the *ramener*. For, should he engage the hocks under the mass prematurely, his hands would never find the necessary opposition with respect to impulsion in order to overcome any resistances in the forehand.

In the circus side reins, using a wooden jockey, or reins attached to the *surcingle*, are often used in the stable to obtain the *ramener*. It is considered successful when the head is maintained in the vertical position or close to it. This position, it is true, assures a certain degree of submission of the head and allows one to appreciate the effect of the bit on the horse in a more accurate manner and to regulate the horse's forces better than if he held his head high. But that is all. But resistances to the hand, even quite energetic ones, can still take place.

The *ramener*, as it is understood in high equitation, has little to do with the position of the horse's head. It lies, first of all, in the submission of the jaw which is the first joint that receives the effect of the hand. If this joint responds with softness to the action that solicits its play, it will bring about the flexibility of the neck and provoke the suppleness of the other joints due to the instinctive correlation that exists between all muscular contractions. If, on the other hand, the jaw resists or refuses to be mobilized, then there is no lightness; it is natural that resistances support each other and will have many echoes. Thus, in Classical equitation what the *ramener* represents is less an unchanging position of the head, but, rather, a general condition of the submission and pliancy of all the joints and muscles.

Circus equitation seeks only the movement in itself and is not actually concerned with lightness. But it is very much the case with high equitation, and if, fortuitously, or in seeking a new movement, the submission of the jaw, this obvious witness of lightness, changes, the first concern of Classical equitation is to re-conquer it as soon as possible. Circus equitation certainly has many skilled riders, but their position alone forces them to practise a kind of equitation that is quite special. This was the case with Baucher. Some people even wanted to link the master's method with the kind of work he did with his horses in public. That is far from being the truth. It was his posture on the horse at the circus that introduced this belief. But Baucher only based his studies on the exploitation of the horse's natural gaits, the only ones he dealt with in his courses and which he revised periodically.

It would be more accurate to characterize circus equitation as eccentric or, if one wishes, fantasy-like, rather than *haute école* which is what the public, and even some riders, usually apply to artificial movements. The term has lost its original meaning. In the past *haute école* meant upper level equitation, as opposed to lower level or elementary equitation.

To have one's horse execute the passage, is, for many riders, the ultimate equestrian prowess. Regardless of how it is executed, they see in it the official stamp of *haute école*. Of the circus, perhaps, but not of the other one, the real *haute école*. They are in error if they do so.

The chief characteristic of Classical equitation is lightness, as I have said many times. Thus – and one can see this daily – if the passage is obtained without fulfilling this condition and the rider is allowed to advance as he wishes, he is far from leading his horse towards lightness; rather, he moves away from it due to the tension that the joints and muscles acquire.

The *écuyer* of the past only acknowledged and practised the *doux passage*, whose characteristic is a marked flexion of the limbs, accompanied by flexibility and suppleness of all the joints and muscles. This kind of passage flows directly out of the piaffe and, quite naturally if, in executing this air, as it should, the horse gives evidence of wanting to move forward, his wish should then be granted.

As far as the *grand passage* is concerned, which is characterized by an energetic and sustained extension of limbs and by a tension of the joints and muscles, and is practised today, it can be achieved in two ways: directly; or flowing out of the *doux passage*, which, in turn, flows out of the piaffe.

In the first instance, it is presented as a particular air, independent of any other air. It can be readily achieved with energetic horses. All that is required is to contain the trot while increasing its energy. Performed in this manner, the passage cannot have a felicitous influence on dressage (schooling) as a whole. Far from that. It is simply executed in a mechanical manner. It has its limits, from which it cannot get out, unless by extending even further its action which has, so to speak, become automatic and, even less, by shortening it.

It is quite different when the *grand passage* is linked to the *doux passage* which, in turn, is linked to the piaffe. Every degree of extension and shortening of movement is at its disposal. To make this fully understood and to complete what I may still have to say about the passage, I remind the reader what I already said about the passage executed by *Ourphaly*, the school horse of *commandant* de Novital, who was *écuyer en chef* when I was at Saumur as pupil-officer.[5] *Ourphaly's* passage was energetic and was by no means the kind of automatic passage one often finds among a number of horses more or less well schooled. With some, the shoulders do all the work and unwillingly drag the haunches along, which, skimming the ground, seem to follow regretfully; the hocks have lost all resilience.

With others, it is the shoulders that do not extend and the haunches' action is simply limited to raising themselves. They seem to want to bring their half-bent knees under them. The lack of power on the part of the rider to extend the movements is all too obvious.

With *Ourphaly*, rather, the haunches, due to their energetic impulsion, pushed the shoulders, forced them to be raised, open up, and extend, giving perfect harmony to all the movements. Nonetheless, I must admit that the passage executed by *Ourphaly* had its limitations. He could not execute all the degrees of extension and lacked this perfection which allows the horse to go, imperceptibly, from the piaffe, to the most extended and energetic passage and then return to the piaffe, always flowing and going through the whole ascending and descending gamut, without ever producing brusque modifications within the movements.

This perfection cannot be achieved without maintaining constantly the play of the joints as well as their resilience. When the passage is carried to its greatest extension, the joints and muscles, while extending, must remain flexible. When the passage is shortened, when it returns to the piaffe, the hocks, while engaging under the mass, must preserve the energy of their play, and the knees, although opening less, must be raised energetically and move forward as though the

---

[5] *Un Officier de cavalerie – Souvenirs du général L'Hotte*, Plon-Nourrit, 1906.

horse wanted to gain ground.

This is how the *grand passage*, the *doux passage*, and the piaffe are united and the rider can, at will, modify the nature of the movements and regulate their extension. But the *doux passage* depends upon the flexibility of the joints and muscles and the results that flow from it are all to the advantage and perfection of dressage. Whereas the opposite consequences could occur if the *grand passage* were asked prematurely. Due to the tension that occurs in the joints and muscles, it should only be practised after their submission has been achieved, that is, after the *doux passage* has been achieved. In that the *doux passage* flows from the piaffe, one must start out by seeking this air which depends upon the rigorously exact opposition of the combined action of haunches and shoulders.

Our former *manèges* facilitated this task by first placing the horse, unsaddled, to piaffe between the pillars to familiarize him with the air. Only later, after he had become familiar with the air, was the horse asked to piaffe when mounted, then to do the passage. One was accustomed to say that 'the pillars gave intelligence to the horse'.

When the passage becomes routine, as is often the case, it brings with it certain difficulties, making the horse respond, by means of this air, to all constraints of the aids that aim at the submission of joints and muscles.

Rather than practise this automatic passage, which is still so frequently disfigured, and when the rider is tossed about, often losing all grace, the natural trot, precise and free, will delight the true horseman who, unlike the crowds, has a feeling for what is beautiful in equitation. Here, as in everything else, it is the approbation of those who know that should be sought without which one would be sacrificing to false gods.

Chapter 13

Methods of dressage. – Basis for the rapidity of work. – Lessons given in the *manège* must be short, but, if necessary, repeated often. – Lessons outdoors can be prolonged advantageously. – The words of Rousselet. – Transformation, but not progress, in equitation. – Similarities and differences between the diverse doctrines. – What can belong to every horseman.

Methods in dressage which emerged from the schools of which my two masters were the leaders, are not the only ones. Others preceded or followed them.

The methods which enable a rider to dispose of a horse's forces are numerous. As a result the methods used in dressage which place them in certain groups, are also numerous. The writings of horsemen, be they of the past or the present, attest to this. These methods proceed in many different ways.

Some methods put the horse in motion right away, devote a great deal of time to the lunge, and seek the total submission of the horse by acting on all his parts simultaneously. Others say that the horse must first be worked when at a halt and achieving his submission must be done successively. Some stress work in hand and some make use of pillars; others use only gadgets.

The actual procedures of each of these methods of schooling vary in their application, depending upon the degree of submission the rider wants, and determined by the requirements made by the uses to which the horse will be put. If properly understood, these methods can serve as a guide in attempting to achieve the different goals one has in mind.

However, no matter how logical and well presented a method is, none is infallible. In order to achieve the desired effect, every equestrian activity must include a special ingredient which no method is capable of imparting, namely 'perfect timing and good measure', that is, *equestrian tact* (equestrian sensitivity). In this connection one can say: 'The value of the means depends upon the worth of the man.'

Regardless of the method employed, progress will advance all the more rapidly if errors are promptly eradicated. And progress will be all the more timely when the rider, forewarned by his equestrian tact, will be able to forestall a false movement by modifying the contractions which give the position which is its precursor.

Dressage lessons in the *manège*, by reason of their constraints on the horse, must be of short duration and the horse must return to the stable in as happy a frame of mind as when he left it. Should there be a reason for hastening dressage, the lessons should not be prolonged; rather they should be repeated once or even twice a day.

Outdoor exercises can proceed differently.

The horse is almost always left to his own devices. And while the rider also is able to function as a free spirit, exercises can be prolonged without causing any problems; on the contrary, outdoor exercises are good for the horse's strength and his health in general. It is also good to combine outdoor activity with *manège* lessons. This will satisfy the needs of the horse, especially the young horse, with respect to movement; but should this outdoor activity be impossible, then it should be replaced by trotting on the lunge.

In the course of the horse's dressage (schooling), one must be content with only a little progress each day, and demand it, but no more. Consequently, with each lesson, the rider should remember the point the horse had reached the day before, but not remember a perfect execution. Progression in the schooling of the horse must, quite definitely, be graduated, because gradual progress is the main road to success. If on a given day an unexpected improvement has been achieved, it should not be taken as something that has been definitely acquired and should not be taken as a basis for the lesson of the following day. If one did so, one would be most surely disappointed.

As far as patience is concerned, which is powerless if used alone, there is no need to call upon it when one knows what one can ask of the horse, and only asks what he is capable of giving. Instead of patience, the rider must have sound judgement and knowledge, and never impatience; he must have perseverance in choosing those methods which result in the daily progress of the horse.[1]

Patience, taken at its face value, is only useful when one is confronted with a recurring problem, diminishing slightly or not at all. Among those are difficulties resulting from physical infirmities, poor eyesight, for example.

Schooling the horse outdoors subdues the horse less and is a way that is much less regularized than schooling him indoors. The duration of the lessons can therefore be lengthened, and would be an asset to the kind of schooling that cross-country equitation requires. In that habit or, if one wishes, routine, influences the horse considerably, placing him in an environment in which he will eventually be employed, he will then become familiar with these areas, calmed and of sound spirit. Thus in an outdoor environment, work will be judiciously graduated, without any excessive fatigue, and the rider will find the means to complete the development of the forces of the horse, increase his breathing, and assure resistance to fatigue.

In this manner the wise words of *commandant* Rousselet will stand out: 'Exercise, instruction, work' which constitute three distinct principles, 'all too often confused', adds the old *écuyer*. Schooling methods have been modified or, to generalize even further, I will add that equitation has been modified, taking into account the needs and tastes of different periods, and the type of horses corresponding to each of these periods. However, contrary to science, one cannot say that equitation, any more than the other arts, has progressed with time.

The vast equestrian truths have come to the fore in all ages and belong to all schools. Comparing the precepts of the different but true masters, one can discern a number of

---

[1] The author's view of the secondary role of *patience* in dressage reminds one of the following anecdote. One day when *général* L'Hotte was riding one of his horses before a prince of the blood who had asked him to do so, His Highness, enthusiastic by the performance, cried out: 'How much patience this must have taken, *général*, to arrive at these results!' 'And also some science, Sire', answered the old *écuyer* with a slight smile. This answer coming from *général* L'Hotte, whose extreme modesty is well known, may astonish one; but is justified when one considers his considerable knowledge in equestrian matters and the excellent long relationship which existed between the Prince and the *général*. [Editors' note.]

connecting points which only prejudices or rivalries have prevented them from being recognized.

It is true that the presentation or form of these equestrian principles or rules may differ and are often the personal expression of the master. But divergences, if they exist, often become apparent to the extent of the principle's application and how this application is interpreted. (In other words, there is a difference in degree and not in kind.) I have proof of this when I was taking lessons from my two illustrious masters, Baucher and d'Aure, these two great rivals.

However, it should be admitted that all horsemen, endowed with the spirit of observation and with considerable practical experience, have been able to make certain statements which have not been made by their predecessors or which escaped them; for the knowledge and use of the horse presents an endless field of research and observation.

Chapter 14

Great artists have stood out at certain periods. – Reasons why the great masters have produced few pupils. – The difficulties of equitation can be found in three kinds of requirements: the practitioner; the horse; the teacher. – At all times have écuyers of value been rare. – They are especially rare outside of France. – Memories of Stuttgart. – Count de Taubenheim. – Writings on equitation are rare in foreign countries. – La Guérinière's book becomes 'the equestrian bible'. – Conclusion.

If equitation has not followed a progressive path, its history teaches us that great artists have stood out at various periods. To this category belong La Broue and Pluvinel; after them comes Duplessis; then La Guérinière, Nestier, Lubersac, d'Auvergne; and belonging to our own period, those who touch us are d'Abzac, Chabannes, and finally d'Aure, this greatly admired centaur, and Baucher, this unparalleled and fertile innovator. Both, each in his own way, have been and continue to be the two great examples of French equitation.

To those few names mentioned, which belong to those who have contributed the most to equestrian art, I could have added other names to complete the gallery of French *écuyers*, who, beginning with the sixteenth century have different claims to fame. But this would not have changed the picture, for the *écuyers* whose names deserve to be in the annals of equitation, are few in number.

I will give the reasons for this and at the same time try to defend the men in charge of equestrian instruction from the reproaches often made against them, that they produced no pupils. It is obvious then when one says pupils one is thinking of écuyers of real worth whose knowledge as teachers corresponds to their talent as practitioners.

There have always been less outstanding men in the equestrian art than in other arts. This has always been the case, even at a time when equitation, not limiting itself exclusively to the usual use of the horse, belonged to an art that was generally widespread and honoured and could even offer to those who practised it, a veritable career.

The reasons can be found in the circumstances that are particular to this art, a complex art, involving three kinds of requirements or special difficulties. They are as follows:

1. The practitioner himself;
2. The instrument, that is, the horse;
3. The means by which the art is transmitted.

My justification for advancing these requirements depends, I hope, on how I will develop it and the points of comparison I will make between equitation and the other arts.

Let us begin with the practitioner. To hope

to make one day a more or less competent *écuyer* out of a horseman, it is absolutely necessary for the horseman to have all the basic and innate qualities, so seldom found in a single individual. These qualities are first to be found in the very structure of the man, a structure which has to satisfy special and well defined demands. The painter and the sculptor are completely free of these demands, all physical, and thus of no interest to them, whereas they weigh heavily upon the rider.

In addition to the rider's conformation, he must have a disposition that is both calm and energetic, so that gentleness without weakness, steadfastness without roughness be his constant guide. Always master of himself, he must dominate his impressions so that he can handle the horse by using opposites, that is, opposing patience with impatience, calmness with violence, energy with laziness as well as refusal to obey. His love of the art must be backed by moral courage of a certain stamp, and that neither discouragement nor difficulty will make him flinch. And perhaps more than with any other artist, perseverance, this foremost quality, is necessary to the *écuyer*. This becomes evident when I shall speak about the horse and show how numerous are the difficulties, as well as the deceptions, which may emerge.

The rider must also possess an intelligence that is particular to his art, which will make him become aware of everything and which will guide him in his own practice and, later, as instructor.

Finally, there is this special feeling, known as the *equestrian tact* which expresses itself as having the ability to discern the disposition of the horse, be it good or bad, the contractions of the horse, and guide the *écuyer* to acquiring perfect timing and good measure. This feeling, which can be developed by work but which the rider must already have within him, is indispensable to the *écuyer*, that is, the *écuyer*-artist, just as the feeling of colour is indispensable to the painter or the sense of the harmony of sounds to the musician.

Although patience is often mentioned as an important attribute of the rider, I can only give it a minor place. First of all, in itself, it is powerless; carried beyond certain limits, it becomes a negative quality. Furthermore, instead of asking the rider to be patient, it would be better to recommend him not to be impatient.

No matter how gifted the rider is, a long period of practice is, in addition, necessary for him to merit the title of *écuyer*. The reasons for this will become obvious when I begin to discuss the horse. For the moment an example should suffice to show that experience is considerably more important and more beneficial to the *écuyer* than to any other artist.

From an equestrian point of view, d'Aure was the most gifted man and he was taught by the best schools. Furthermore, his temperament, overflowing with initiative and feeling, but little given to reflection, was such that it was supposed to profit little from experience. Well! compare his *Traité d'équitation*, published in 1834, written as he emerged from the hands of d'Abzac, and his *Cours d'équitation* of 1853 and one will see what a difference there is between these two works. There is quite a distance separating the pupil from the master. I might add that, in my opinion, the two works of the great horseman give us a measure of his talent as well as his equestrian knowledge during these two periods in his life.

If one examines some of the other arts, I doubt whether one will find in the work of a painter of thirty and some years, and in the work of the same artist some twenty years later, a similar progression, and one as sensitive, as one finds in the works of d'Aure.

From the artist let us go to the instrument that he must handle, the horse. To be an effective rider, one must know the horse well, and to acquire this rational knowledge, the *écuyer* must study and practise a great deal so that he can bring the horse to submission and direct his movements, which is the goal of equitation as such. A similar kind of study does not occur in painting or sculpture. If one considers the horse as raw material that is to be shaped, one sees considerable difficulties emerging which are not found in the other arts. The sculptor, for example, finds in the marble that he fashions or the earth that he moulds, a raw material that is almost always the same; whereas the element with which the *écuyer* practises his art, varies considerably.

Indeed, each horse with which the *écuyer* has to deal, is an individual creature, composed of specific psychological and physical conditions. This requires from the artist a very specific way of proceeding.

How many riders have been discouraged by these initial difficulties, often revealing total failure the very day after experiencing success. With the other arts, the artist can, it is true, have less success on one day than on another, but he does not experience a deception that is as total.

Let us go on and suppose that the horse has been subjected to a long and difficult working experience which consists in obtaining the submission and elasticity of all his joints and muscles. These must be made to play freely; this is when I ask the musician for a comparison.

If we consider the means with which each one of these artists makes use of his instrument, one is right away struck by the simplicity of the mechanism of the musician's instrument, as compared to the mechanism of the rider's instrument. For the rider, indeed, it is not the hands and arms alone which have to demonstrate skill and virtuosity as it is with the violinist. All the parts of the rider's body are asked to act, and in consort, in order to activate the joints and muscles of the horse, to extend or restrict his movements, to harmonize them, just as the musician harmonizes sounds.

The instrument upon which the musician acts is inert in itself. As a result the conditions he presents are invariable and the same action will always produce the same effect. It is quite different with the rider. Life and a will, animate the horse. Therein lie the thousand and one nuances in the way he presents himself and responds to the actions of the one who rides him. The rider discovers a labyrinth of difficulties wherein he could easily stray if he does not have as his guide this special feeling which I mentioned earlier: equestrian tact.

The horseman can experience a very special deception, of which the musician is totally free: that is the loss of an instrument. The musician can immediately replace the lost instrument by another one. The horseman does not have this advantage. If the horse he has ridden for years, his *manège* horse, who represents a living certificate to the *écuyer*, dies suddenly, he will have to spend many years getting a new horse into shape to completely replace the one he has lost, provided, of course, that he possesses to a considerable degree a feeling for his art. For with a committed rider, the progress of the horse is continuous, his movements can be given endless nuances, and the purity of his work does not have any limits. This may seem an exaggeration. But why should the equestrian art differ from the other arts?

In general, the moment an artist believes he has achieved the summit of his art, he actually reveals the extent of his mediocrity. The true artist, on the other hand, who thinks he sees the end of his efforts disappearing as his talent increases, proves thereby the value and range of his sensibility which lets him see his goal move farther away from his reach. This, in turn, gives him more and more the sense of the nature of perfection. Thus it is with the true artist-horseman, the *écuyer*. He becomes one with his horse. He feels that the talent within him and the execution on the part of the horse, are indefinitely perfectible.

Was it not d'Abzac who, at the age of eighty, said that he was still learning something every day? And the research of Baucher was continuous. Does it not indicate that his considerable talent, the schooling of his horses, which, despite achieving perfection, still did not give complete satisfaction to the master? He was filled with a sense of even greater perfection. One day I mentioned to Baucher that I was never quite satisfied with the schooling of my horse. To this he replied: 'But it will always be so. There is always something more that one wants.'

I will now turn my thoughts to teaching. Aside from the problems I have already mentioned, imparting this art to others encounters two special obstacles. One deals with the lack of permanence in equestrian matters; the other deals with the difficulties the teacher experiences in trying to convince the pupil.

To grasp properly the first of these obstacles, I will point to painting as an example. Here we see that the work of the painter remains constantly under the eyes of his pupil, with all its perfections and all the lessons it can give him. If the master makes a stroke of the brush on the pupil's canvas or a pencil mark to his drawing, in that these rectifications are permanent, they will impress themselves all the more on the mind of the disciple. At the same time they will elucidate more easily the artist's feelings. It is different with equitation. The work of the master and the schooled horse, can only be appreciated fleetingly by the pupil. And when attempting to rectify a false position or an irregular movement of the horse, the action of the *écuyer* is replaced for a moment by the action of the pupil he is instructing, and the rectification can only be a fleeting one.

Let us now examine the difficulties the *écuyer* encounters in convincing the pupil of the validity of the principles to which he is being exposed.

It is only with difficulty and with time that the pupil will be convinced, for the means at the disposal of the *écuyer* are insufficient for him to do so. This insufficiency is due to the fact that, as already mentioned, there is a lack of permanency in equestrian matters as well as the variable conditions which the horse presents, for the same actions do not always produce the same results. But these are not the only causes which prevent the pupil from being convinced right away. Another difficulty must be added, namely the difficulty the *écuyer* has making the pupil appreciate, in a more or less obvious manner, the means he, himself, uses; finally, a special and frequent problem, namely, doubt, which I will discuss.

As with all the other arts, so it is with the art of equitation, a demonstration must always be expressed by a physical action, otherwise this demonstration will have no useful goal in that it will have no practical impact. But when the demonstration follows the equestrian action, the latter, no matter how justified it is, will not always bring about the result the master had in mind. To be of any value and produce the expected effect, it is absolutely necessary that all equestrian actions, no matter how simple, be based on 'perfect timing and good measure'. Now, in that this perfect timing and good measure are emphasized to the pupil as a special feeling, they are, to a large extent, missed by the master. Despite the care and careful observation given by the master, it often happens that the pupil will not always be successful in using the means the former has prescribed. And after several fruitless attempts the pupil will quite naturally begin to doubt unless he has absolute confidence in the talent as well as in the words of the master.

How many horsemen, influenced by this doubt, have said about their instructor: 'He does not do what he says.' The *écuyer* worthy of this name, always practises what he preaches, and does better than the pupil. If facts sometimes give credence to this statement made by some pupils, it is because those who have experienced it are not aware that a precept can have a myriad modifications in its application but that it still does not lose its validity.

The master certainly has a sphere of action which is extensive. In his hands can be found all the means which can transform pupils into horsemen, but cross-country horsemen. He can give them the correct posture, regularize their position and see to it that they even act in harmony with their horse and use their aids with precision. By giving them clear and precise demonstrations, he can point out to them the goals they must follow. He can trace for them the means that lead to these goals, regulate indoor and outdoor exercises and, above all, serve as an example. He will talk to his pupils in this manner and enlighten their minds.

But this is where his role more or less stops. To hope to be able to act in a direct manner on the mechanism of the rider, above all, on his sensibility, is aspiring for the impossible. Perfecting the mechanism, developing an equestrian sensibility, is the exclusive domain of the practitioner himself. He alone can give the pupil those qualities which will eventually make of him a great practitioner in his art. He alone has the responsibility of becoming an *écuyer*.

Now that I have discussed the difficulties that involve the practice and teaching of equitation, and to confirm what I have advanced, I shall present some details attesting to the rarity of *écuyers* of worth.

In the course of my career, especially at Saumur, at a time when artistic equitation was fashionable, how often have I seen riders, endowed with advantageous characteristics, and who have a love of horses, progress rapidly at first, then come to a halt at a degree of competence which they could not surpass. The sensitivity of the practitioner now seems incapable of revealing anything beyond the results he has achieved. Furthermore, the sense of perseverance may also be lacking, which is frequently thwarted by pride which often blinds the rider.

When d'Aure and Baucher shone in all their greatness, it was certainly neither masters nor examples that were lacking. Everyone recognized in d'Aure the brilliant horseman. True, some, contrary to my own opinion, felt that he lacked the gift of transmitting his knowledge to others. But with respect to Baucher, apart from his irreproachable and sound horsemanship, nobody could deny him his most remarkable talent as a teacher. There one could discern the most striking side of this learned *écuyer*. True, Baucher was not asked to direct a training school in equitation, but his whole life was spent teaching in France and in foreign countries.

The rivalry that occurred between the schools of d'Aure and Baucher and which impassioned their disciples, gave French equitation an unprecedented boost. Well! If one analyses the situation, one can see how few are the great men who have emerged from this important equestrian movement and who have made their mark in equitation.

The paucity of *écuyers* of merit is not particular to our time. As I mentioned earlier, this has always been so. As further proof, I shall call upon an official document, which I have already mentioned. When the *vicomte* d'Abzac, *écuyer en chef* of the *Manège de Versailles*, died in 1827, the changes that this death brought about in the personnel of the *Manège* motivated an exchange of letters between the duc de Polignac, First *écuyer* of Charles X, and the *duc* d'Anville, minister of the king's household. In a letter to the First *écuyer*, one finds the following statement: 'In connection with the service of the *manège*, M. d'Aure is actually the only person with any real talent'... Thus with the d'Abzacs gone, there was only one man with any real talent among the *écuyers* of the *Manège de Versailles*.

If *écuyers* of merit were a rarity in France, they were of even greater rarity outside of France. While it never occurred in France, other countries were forced, at different periods, to seek men outside of their own countries, for they were unable to find them in their own country.

As an example, during the period of exile, the free town of Hamburg offered, in vain, brilliant proposals to the *vicomte* d'Abzac in the hope that he would accept the direction of the *manège* the town wished to establish. The *vicomte* d'Abzac was also offered the direction of a stud farm in Prussia, which he also refused.

During that same period, King Maximilian of Bavaria made overtures to the *marquis* de la Bigne, who had become famous at the *Manège de Versailles*, asking him to establish in Munich stables and a *manège* modelled after those at Versailles. A salary of fifty thousand pounds was guaranteed. He refused.

At a time closer to us, M. de Sainte-Reine, a well-known French *écuyer*, was approached and then employed in Sardinia. Later, in 1861, the *Grand Ecuyer* of Prussia, who, if I remember correctly, was *général* de Willisen, took, in vain, many steps to lure Sainte-Reine to Berlin. *Général* de Willisen gave him considerable assurances in the hope that he would take over the direction as *premier écuyer* of the king's *manège*.

In an attempt to satisfy a request made by M. de Linden, *commandant* of the Royal Stables of Belgium, the *comte* de Damas d'Hautefort, who had formerly been an *écuyer* of the *comte* de Chambord, wrote to me in 1884 asking me if I knew of an *écuyer* who had the capability and the desired qualities to be placed at the head of the stable of saddle horses of King Leopold.

Three years later, in 1887, I received another similar request from Belgium. *Lieutenant-colonel* Bricou, of the cavalry, commanding the department of the *grand écuyer*, asked me if I could indicate to him a man capable of occupying the position of *écuyer dresseur* in the king's stables which he commanded.

It should also be remembered that during the eighteenth century, France was besieged by foreigners of distinction wanting to further their equestrian training and the possibility of 'going to the academy', an expression used at the time. Included were the English ministers Pitt and Fox. Also Arthur Wellesley, the future Duke of Wellington.

The descendant of the 'iron Duke' brought over to London Henri Baucher, the son of my master, to school his horses, even allowing him to use his *manège* for the purpose of giving private lessons.

If one goes farther back in history, one can see that the English were frequent importers of French *écuyers*. Going back to the reign of Henry IV, the English court sent for Saint-Antoine and, later, Foubert, *écuyer* of the Royal stables of France, for the former to become master of equitation to the heir of the throne, and the latter to direct the Academy that the English sovereign was establishing.

Not to mention solely French *écuyers* sought by foreign countries, I must add that England borrowed Quantin from Germany and asked Meyer from the continent to serve as First *écuyer* in her army. The Austrian court, later the court of Prussia, borrowed Campen from Hannover. I must also state that the Count de Taubenheim who became the *grand écuyer* of the king of Wurtemberg, not having available in his own country men to develop his equestrian instruction, had to seek them elsewhere: from Goettingen, the School of Hannover, founded in 1737, and long since disappeared after having experienced a period of fame, and from the Spanish *manège* of Vienna, still in existence today.[1]

In 1885, I was in Stuttgart as chief of the French mission charged with observing German manoeuvres. It was then that I met Count de Taubenheim who talked about his equestrian background. During dinner, then

---

[1] Among the papers of *général* L'Hotte we found a note written in his hand on the *Spanish Manège of Vienna*. We are publishing this note at the end of the present volume. [The editors.]

during several visits to the *manèges* and stables of the king, which the *grand écuyer* showed me in great detail, he entertained me with interesting questions regarding his service, equitation, *écuyers*, and German horses.[2]

At the time I knew Count de Taubenheim he held the position of *Grand Ecuyer* for forty years and was eighty years old. The day he reached that age, as though to prove that he was still vigorous, he jumped over the crossbar of the *manège* which was in its highest position. Tall and thin, he was still a handsome rider. His fine presence as a horseman reminded one of Laurent Franconi for whom he had great admiration.

Not only is there a rarity of outstanding *écuyers* in foreign countries, but writings on equitation are not that common abroad. One has only to remember how greatly admired is the work of La Guérinière. In the various *manèges* beyond the Rhine, and as tribute to French equitation, this book has become the 'Equestrian Bible'.

To conclude the question I raised and discussed so lengthily, I return to my point of departure by saying: it is the extensive demands of the equestrian art itself that is responsible if *écuyers* of merit are rare exceptions.

---

[2] The details regarding German horses which *général* L'Hotte was supposed to have included in his *Souvenirs*, were written upon his return from Germany. We were lucky to have found these notes which we reproduce later in form of an Appendix. [The editors.]

Appendix
Austria
Schools of equitation – The Spanish School

Although equitation is widespread in Austria, outstanding horsemen are rare. Thus a 'school of equitation' was established for the purpose of creating a 'nursery' and preserving the equestrian tradition in the army.

This is not the only school that Austria possesses. Another school, even more special and whose activities occur in a more restricted area, has been established in the imperial palace and is called *The Spanish School*. This school goes back to Charles VI. It is there that the low and high airs of our former equitation are practised. It also holds our La Guérinière in high esteem. It is placed under the direction of a *grand écuyer*. His personnel, directed by M. Niedermeyer[1] is civilian. Young men of good social position, some officers, receive special instruction; those managing the stables also receive instruction. The school functions very much as did our own *Manège de Versailles* during the Restoration when the *comte* d'Abzac was at its head. But other procedures are followed. One peculiarity is that all the horses represented are of Andalusian breed from which the school got its name. These horses are the descendants of five stallions: *Majestoso, Conversano, Napolitano, Pluto, Favori* which were introduced into Austria during the reign of Charles VI. The five families descending from these stallions are kept completely separate in the stud farm of Lippiza, which belongs to the emperor.

In the *manège* where equestrian festivities are held, one can find the portrait of Charles VI on *Favori*. When one sees the descendants of this horse one realizes how much care was given in preserving the breed, for their resemblance to the head of this family is perfect. These horses have a rounded action which makes them perfect for *manège* riding. Their hallmark is their strength and suppleness. They are close to the ground, vigorous, with sound limbs, the neck high and arched, the head curved, they remind one of the former Spanish breed. I say 'former' because ten years ago I saw a horse who had been sent from Spain and was considered the most beautiful horse one could obtain. But while resembling closely the breed so carefully preserved in Austria, he was far from possessing, to the same degree, those qualities which these Spanish horses raised in Lippiza embody.

The interior of the *manège* of the Spanish School includes a gallery of loges decorated with sculptures which resembles a spectator hall. Under the loges there is a large corridor in which the horses can circulate. A spectator gallery with a fire-place, a sort of salon, occupies the section along the short side. The floor of the gallery is about 75 cm above the ground which allows the rider to place his foot in the stirrup iron without having to walk along the dusty ground of the *manège*. A corridor is located under this

---

[1] Written in 1884.

spectator gallery and makes it possible for the horses to be brought in without having to cross the *manège*. Brilliant equestrian festivities are presented in this building which is richly lit with gas lighting.

Germany
I
The School of Hanover

The School of Hanover of today[2] in no way reminds one of the former School of Hannover which featured prominently in the annals of equitation. The goal of the former school was to perpetuate the traditions of equestrian art which expressed itself in all that was of a high and delicate nature, and geared only to a restricted personnel. Nothing remains of this former school. Since 1866 much of it has been dispersed. The buildings, constructed in the centre of the town, were sold and given another purpose. And a new school was established.

Today's School of Hanover is the school of the German Cavalry and has consequently taken on a completely different complexion from that of the past. Situated at the edge of one of the suburbs of the town, it is on the edge of the countryside and can easily expand should the need arise. The school has a vast open space in its centre which serves as a *carrière*. It is surrounded on either side by living quarters, *manèges*, and stables.[3]

There are seven enclosed *manèges*, one of which is circular. The rectangular *manèges* do not have a uniform architecture. Some have a gallery, situated on one of the short sides; others have a small gallery in the middle of one of the large sides. With respect to the design and its use, the gallery located on the short side is preferable. But actually to be able to judge the kind of work that is being conducted in the centre of the *manège*, it is on the large side that the gallery should be located. From this central position one can see the ensemble of the movements and above all, each rider, and be able to follow the whole length of the line from a short distance. Seeing the work presented in profile is much more advantageous.

Two of these *manèges* are linked by a hangar which protects the horses as they wait to enter the *manèges*.

The floor of the *manèges* is provided with sand. Wood shavings would have been preferable.

The horses are divided into several categories:

(1) The horses of the officers. Each officer has two horses: a war horse supplied by the state and a horse actually belonging to the officer;

(2) Horses of remount, schooled by the officers and NCOs. The less distinguished horses are schooled by the latter;

(3) About one hundred horses are maintained by the school; of these twelve are considered 'school' (*manège*) horses, which I will discuss later; twelve horses belong to the grooms. The tails of horses of the grooms are cut short, whereas those of the others are cut below the hock.

Should the horses belonging to the school no longer be of service, which is usually at the age of ten, they are sold to infantry officers for the modest price of 200 or 300 marks.

Two so-called 'school' horses were exhibited to me ridden by two NCOs specifically put in charge of their schooling. Work at the

---

[2] Written in 1885.
[3] Here follows in great detail information dealing with the regulations of the school, its framework, its buildings, stable management, etc. We therefore publish only that which deals specifically with *manèges* and equitation; the remainder has only a limited connection with *Questions équestres*. [Editors' note.]

canter was executed sometimes on the correct lead, sometimes on the wrong (counter?) lead. The schooling of these horses does not include flying lead changes but only lead changes on the ground, that is, they take one step to go from the canter on one lead to a canter on the other lead.

Along the walls of the *manège* were exhibited large charcoal sketches of horses executing the raised airs such as the courbette. I asked if these *manège* airs were actually practised. They said yes, they were. I then asked them to execute a courbette. One of the two horses absolutely refused to do so. The other one did not execute a courbette, but reared, pivoting on his hindlegs, which is quite different.

What characterizes especially the work of these horses, is the passage at a sustained extension, that is, a trot that is energetic and very elevated and when the horse cadences slowly. But executing this *manège* air which, by the way, is brilliant, the horses showed no flexibility in their joints and muscles. Their stiffness, especially the stiffness in the neck, was obvious and I asked if these horses went from the passage to the piaffe, that is, from the cadenced trot to the trot in place. Their answer was no. Indeed, with horses so contracted, the transition from the passage to the piaffe would be impossible.

The passage, as I have seen it executed, offers a brilliance that may strike the public. But I ask myself in what way does this *manège* air, wherein the horses seemed so automatic, and which they executed in an automatic manner, serve as a way of perfecting the equestrian instruction of officers. If that is an example of what is known as *haute école*, that is certainly not an application of academic equitation and the two must not be confused.

At the School of Hanover the hunt occupies a large part of their equestrian instruction. At a special time of the year, this training occurs three times a week and is graduated from a course of two km to the length that a hunt demands and lasts sometimes hours.

At first to regulate the duration of the course of a hunt as it is understood, and to train progressively men and horses, one uses the drag which allows one to determine precisely the path to be followed and the limits of the hunt. The drag is preferable to those little pieces of paper which do not give the kind of excitement that dogs give. Furthermore, instead of looking down on the ground, as it is necessary when the track to be followed is marked by little bits of paper, the riders, when they follow dogs, look far ahead and get used to seeing the terrain and judging it. To preserve a certain degree of order during the hunt, the riders are placed eight abreast, but this arrangement is not rigorously kept. A captain is in charge of the hunt. He has occupied this position for six years. Four NCOs are employed as grooms. One of them, their direct chief, has been occupying this position for eight years and must retain it.

The pack is composed of eighty dogs, most of them of English breed. Wild boar is hunted, as are the fox and deer. When the courses are completed and the officers go on leave or return to their regiments, the pack is divided and loaned to the nearby regiments.

In short, on the basis of what I have seen and especially heard say of Hanover, equitation is given a sound direction with respect to exterior equitation, obstacle jumping, especially the hunt. But I cannot say the same for *haute école*.

II

An outline of some princely stables

The stud farm of Trakehnen furnishes almost all the horses to the Imperial stables. In 1848 when the stud farm of Trakehnen, Graditz, and Bebereck passed from the administration of the Crown to that of the State, the sovereign could reserve for himself, each year, the choice of forty horses from these centres to stock his own stables. Last year,[4] of the forty horses, thirty came from the stud farm of Trakehnen. This says much about the superiority of its production.

The carriage horses for the German emperor are all black. Saddle horses of the Imperial stables are of various colours.

The Imperial stables are under the direction of His Excellency the *vice-Grand Ecuyer* von Rauch. It is Count Pückler who is the *Grand Écuyer*.

Almost blind, he retains the title of *grand écuyer*, although he is no longer able to perform his duties.[5]

His Excellency M. de Rauch is a tall and handsome rider, riding, even outdoors, his horses with a cadence and a tempo which characterizes the *manège* work of this *écuyer*. His reputation indicates that he is a great connoisseur of horses. He visited France to study the organization of the imperial stables at a time when *général* Fleury was *grand écuyer* and he established the stables of the court of Prussia in a similar fashion.

I visited the stables of the king of Wurtemberg which ought to have contained one hundred and fifty horses, but which contain today only one hundred and twenty. These stables no longer live up to the reputation they had reached in the past, but they still retain certain of its aspects. The former king, who died when he was more than eighty years old, had a passion for horses and a marked predilection for the Arabian. The stud farm of the crown, situated not far from Stuttgart, furnished almost exclusively, the horses for the king's stables. Of these six stallions that I examined, all beautiful creatures, only one comes directly from Syria. The five others are from the stud farm of the king. These five, by their supreme distinction, the harmony of their conformation, remind one in every detail of their noble ancestors. In addition to the mark of distinction of this breed, one of these stallions has a very special trait, his size, which is seldom part of this breed's heritage. All the qualities found in this horse make of him a stallion of great value. These stallions are small, but their off-spring are much larger, and justify the proverb: 'It is better to consult the size of the sack of oats than the size of the stallion.' In the stables of the king I saw two thoroughbred stallions which were bought in England. These two horses stood out because of their size rather than their distinction and were only stallions that had been cross bred. Their coat is black, whereas the Arabian stallions are all grey. All the horses of the king's stables are either black or grey. I asked the *Grand Ecuyer* why horses of different colour were absent. He answered that it was so because of colour harmony, for the royal livery was scarlet.

All the horses of the king's stables are distinguished by their extreme gentleness. One alone is the exception, also by reason of the colour of his coat, which is chestnut. He is an English thoroughbred and came to the royal stables under special circumstances. He belongs to the stables of the royal heir.

The *Grand Ecuyer* of the court of Wurtemberg, Count de Taubenheim, has three *écuyers* under his immediate command. He has held this position for forty years and is now over eighty years of age. He is still an outstanding horseman whose posture reminds one of Laurent Franconi, now dead for over thirty years and who is remembered by the *Grand Ecuyer* of Wurtemberg as an accomplished horseman.

The Count de Taubenheim is a pupil of the famous School of Equitation of Goettingen (Hanover) which was then Germany's first school of equitation and whose reputation was unequalled in Europe except by our own *Ecole de Versailles* directed by the comte

---

[4] Written in 1885.
[5] Shortly after these lines were written, Count Pückler, due to his infirmities, had to give up his duties as *grand écuyer*. M de Rauch succeeded him.

d'Abzac. The *manège* of Goettingen, which was later moved to Hanover, became famous because it possessed some of the most outstanding *écuyers* of Germany: Ayrer, *général* Mayer (whose son, a Captain, is in charge of the schooling of the emperor's saddle horses), the *majors* Kampe and Schweppe. The latter, the most remarkable of all, is still living. He resisted the many advances made, urging him to become part of the stables of the king of Prussia. He now lives in retirement in Hanover, faithful to the memory of his king, whose last *écuyer* he was. The Count de Taubenheim went from Goettingen to Vienna, where, for a year, he frequented the *manège* of the Spanish School which I have discussed elsewhere.

The *manège* of the Royal stables of Stuttgart in some ways reminds one of the Spanish *manège* of Vienna, although it is less luxurious than that of Vienna. There is a gallery for the spectators that goes along the whole length of the *manège*. Below this gallery there is a corridor in which the horses can move about. But this *manège* does not have a salon-gallery as does the one in Vienna. Chandeliers make festivities at night possible. One of these feasts, held several years ago, had their riders perform opposite Moorish riders, which had considerable repercussions in the country. One of the singularities of the *manège* at Stuttgart is the height of the boot-rail which corresponds to the shoulders of the riders. The boot-rails of the *manèges* at Hanover are also noticeable because of their height, but they do not go beyond the shoulders of a man on foot.

In Hanover I saw horses whose coats are almost unknown in France. They come from the late king's stables. They are white, that is, the purest milk white, without any hairs of other colours mixed with the white. There are also horses whose coats are the colour of a very light *café au lait*. Some are void of any hair at the natural orifices, especially above the eyelids. Their eyes are of light hues and, to some extent, they are the albinos of the species. They were originally destined to become carriage horses to be used on gala occasions. They have the size, the build, the bearing that this kind of service requires. The white horses are much more beautiful than the *café au lait* horses; their mane and tail are long and silky. The mane falls below the knees and the tail touches the stable bedding. These horses are the off-spring of Arabian stallions and Danish mares. It should be mentioned that this cross-breeding eventually brings with it a change in the colour of their coat which loses its brilliant white, taking on a lightly yellowish hue. To give the coat its original brilliance, the blood has to be rejuvenated by introducing other Danish mares. The stable I visited, which is the one connected to the palace of the king of Hanover, contains ten white horses, two of which are used as stallions, and eight *café au lait* horses. One of these is twenty-four years old and is still used for breeding. All these horses have the most gentle disposition. Other horses of the same breed are distributed on neighbouring farms. I was unable to visit them. All of them, like everything else that belongs to the duc de Cumberland in the kingdom of Hanover, are kept sequestered.

When I was in Vienna and visited the Imperial stables, there was a row of these *café au lait* horses given to the emperor by the king of Hanover. Not a single stallion was among them, for the king did not want this breed to perpetuate itself outside of Hanover. The Imperial stables of Austria also contain white horses who resemble considerably those I have just discussed. They have the same origins but seem to possess less nobility and their mane and tail are less fine and silky. These stables also contain horses who are completely black, similar in build to the white ones, but less distinguished looking; their mane and tail are long and abundant, but are not fine. These horses pull funeral carriages.

Like the white horses, they also come from the stud farm of Kladrubb, located in

Bohemia, and belong to the emperor. The other stud farm that also belongs to His Majesty, the Lippiza stud farm, which is situated near Trieste, does not provide horses of this type. This latter stud farm is strictly reserved for the Arabian and for this Spanish breed which is preserved with such great care and which I discussed earlier when discussing the Spanish School of Equitation. Not only do the Lippiza horses furnish remounts to the Spanish School, but they are also used in other capacities in the Imperial stables, especially in the Horseguard Squadron, which uses primarily horses from this region.

Bibliography

d'Aure, Antoine Cartie, *Cours d'équitation*, Paris, Bureau du Journal des Haras et des Chasses, 1853.
 Cours d'équitation, Paris, Emile Hazan, 1962.
 Observations sur la nouvelle méthode, Paris, Leneveu, 1842.
 Traité d'équitation, Paris, Leclère, 1843.
 Traité d'équitation et Histoire illustrée de l'équitation, Paris, Jean-Michel Place, 1987.
Barbier, Dominique with Mary Daniel, *Dressage for the Age*, New York, Prentice Hall, 1990.
Baucher, François, *Méthode d'équitation et réponse aux observations de M. d'Aure*, Oeuvres complètes, Tome Premier, Paris Jean-Michel place, 1988.
 Oeuvres complètes, Paris, Dumaine, 1854 and 1859.
Beudant, Etienne, *Extérieure et haute école*, Paris, Jean-Michel Place, 1987.
 Mains sans jambes . . . suivi de Dressage du cheval de selle, Paris, Jean-Michel Place, 1987.
Belasik, Paul, *Exploring Dressage Technique*, London, J. A. Allen, 1994.
 Riding Towards the Light, London, J. A. Allen, 1990.
Decarpentry, Albert, *Academic Equitation*, London, J. A. Allen, 1987.
 Baucher et son école, Paris, Lamarre, 1948.
 Baucher et son école, Paris, Jean-Michel Place, 1987.
 Equitation académique, Paris, Henri Neveu, 1949.
 Equitation académique, Paris, Emile Hazan, 1972.
 La Méthode de haute école de Raabe, Paris, Emile Hazan, 1980.
 Maîtres écuyers du Manège de Saumur, Paris, Emile Hazan, 1954.

Decarpentry, Albert et Jacques Perrier, *Les Maîtres écuyers du Manège de Saumur*, Nouvelle Edition de 1674 à nos jours, Paris, Charles-Lavauzelle, 1993.
De Kunffy, Charles, *The Ethics and Passions of Dressage*, Middletown, Maryland, Half Halt Press, 1993.
Etreillis, Baron d', *Ecuyers et cavaliers, d'autrefois et d'aujourd'hui*, Paris, L. Badouin, 1883.
Faverot de Kerbrech, *Dressage méthodique du cheval de selle, d'apres les derniers enseignements de F Baucher*, Paris, J. Rothschild, 1891.
 Dressage méthodique du cheval de selle, Paris, Emile Hazan, 1958.
 Dressage méthodique du cheval de selle, suivi de Dressage du cheval de selle, Paris, Jean-Michel Place, 1990.
Fillis, James, *Journal de dressage*, Paris, Flammarion, 1903.
 Principes de dressage, Paris, Jean-Michel Place, 1991.
Froissard, Jean, *Equitation*, N. Hollywood, Wilshire Book Co., 1978.
Gerhardt, Adolphe, *Manuel d'équitation analyze raisonnée du bauchérisme*, Paris, Jean-Michel Place, 1987.
Harris, Charles, *Riding and Dressage*, London, Harris, 1981.
Henriquet, Michel, *A la recherche de l'équitation*, Paris, Crépin-Leblond et Cie., 1968.
 Les Maîtres de l'équitation classique, Paris, André Gérard, 1974.
Henriquet, Michel et Catherine Durand, *Gymnase et dressage*, Paris, Maloine, 1991.
Henriquet, Michel et Alain Prévost, *L'Equitation, un art, une passion*, Paris, Seuil, 1972.
Herbermann, Erik, F. *Dressage Formula*, London,

J. A. Allen, 1989.
L'Hotte, Alexis-François, *Questions équestres*, Paris, Plon, 1906.
  Questions équestres, Paris, Emile Hazan, 1960.
  Questions équestres, Paris, Jean-Michel Place, 1991.
  Un Officier de cavalerie – Souvenirs, Paris, Plon-Nourrit, 1906.
  Un Officier de cavalerie, Paris, Emile Hazan, 1958.
  Un Officier de cavalerie, Paris, Jean-Michel Place, 1991.
Joussaume, André, *Dressage*, Paris, Editions du fer à cheval, 1951.
  Progressive Dressage, J. A. Allen, 1978.
Licart, Jean, *Dressage*, Paris, Charles-Lavauzelle, 1989.
  Basic Equitation, London, J. A. Allen, 1968.
Loch, Sylvia, *Dressage, The Art of Classical Riding*, North Pomfret, Vermont, Trafalgar Square Publishing, 1990.
Molier, Ernest, *L'Equitation et le cheval*, Paris, Pierre Lafitte, 1911.
Monteilhet, André, *Les Maîtres de l'oeuvre équestre*, Paris, Odège, 1979.
Morand, Paul, *Milady*, suivi de *Monsieur Zéro*, Paris, Gallimard, 1936.
Musany, F. *L'Amazone: au manège – à la promenade*, Paris, J. Rothschild, 1888.
Nelson, Hilda, *François Baucher, The Man and his Method*, London, J. A. Allen, 1992.
Oliveira, Nuno, *Classical Principles of the Art of Riding*, London, Howley and Russell.
  Haute école, London, J. A. Allen, 1965.
  Reflections on Equestrian Art, London, J. A. Allen, 1976.
  Réflexions sur l'art équestre, Paris, Crépin-Leblond, 1965.
Perrier, Jacques, *L'Epopée du Cadre Noir de Saumur*, Paris, Charles-Lavauzelle, 1992.
Podhajsky, Alois, *Die Klassische Reitkunst*, Munich, Nymphenburger, 1965.
  Die Spanische Hofreitschule, Vienna, Hans Hammar, 1948
Racinet, Jean-Claude, *Another Horsemanship*, Cleveland Heights, Ohio, Xenophon Press, 1994.
  Racinet explains Baucher, Cleveland Heights, Ohio, Xenophon Press, 1997.
Salins, Jean de, *Epaule en dedans*, Paris, Emile Hazan, 1957.
Saunier, Gaspard, de, *L'Art de la cavalerie*, Paris, C. A. Joubert, 1756.
Saurel, Etienne, *Histoire de l'équitation*, Paris, Stock, 1971.
  Pratique de l'équitation d'après les Maîtres français, Paris, Flammarion, 1964.
Seunig, Waldemar, *Horsemanship*, New York, Doubleday, 1956.
  Meister der Reitkunst, Heidenheim, Erich Hoffmann, 1960.
Steinbrecht, Gustav, *Le Gymnase du cheval*, Paris, Epiac, 1963.
  Le Gymnase du cheval, Paris, Elbé, 1985.
  The Gymnasium of the Horse, Cleveland Heights, Ohio, Xenophon Press, 1995.
Thomas, Jacques-Léonard Clément, *De L'Equitation militaire de l'ancienne et de la nouvelle école*, Paris, Pagnerre, 1846. (First published in *Le National*, 6, 10, 16 and 23 September, 1845.)
Van Schaik, H. L. M., *Misconceptions and Simple Truths in Dressage*, London, J. A. Allen, 1986.
Vaux, Baron de, *Ecuyers et écuyères*, Paris, J. Rothschild, 1893.
  Les Femmes de sport, Paris, C. Marpon et E. Flammarion, 1885.
Weyrother, Max Ritter von, *Hinterlassene Schriften*, Hildesheim, Olms Presse, 1977.
Wynmalen, Henry, *Dressage*, N. Hollywood, Wilshire Book Co., 1972.
  Equitation, London, Country Life, 1938.

Index

Abzac, *chevalier* d' 55
Abzac, *Vicomte* Pierre-Marie d' (*écuyer cavalcadour and écuyer ordinaire*, trained D'Aure) 7, 10, 37, 51, 54, 55, 56, 59, 61, 62, 63, 78, 80, 89, 136, 137, 138, 139, 143
Académie des Tuileries 1
Academy of Equitation 4
Age of Absolutism 107f
aids xiii, xv, 13, 21, 29, 37, 39f, 45, 50, 65, 68, 70, 72, 73, 80, 86, 89, 92, 93, 94, 95, 96, 97, 100–1, 106, 107, 124, 128, 130, 138, 144
   hand 77, 83, 86, 101
   leg 72, 77, 83, 86, 103
airs 109, 145
   airs relevés 129
   artificial 29, 32, 49, 67, 85f, 107, 108, 124, 140
   high airs 9, 116, 124
   low airs 9, 116, 124
   natural airs 29, 107
Alembert, Jean Le Rond d' (French philosopher) 42f
Allarty, Blanche 118 (port.)
amazone(s) (pleasure riders) 43, 62, 63, ch. 8: pp. 111–34
ancien régime 10, 20
Angoulême, Marguerite d' (sister of King François I) 2
Anne of Austria (mother of Louis XIV) 7
Archer, Frederick (steeplechase jockey) 104
Artois, *comte* d' (future Charles X) 55

Association pour l'Académie d'Art Equestre de Versailles 11f
Astley, Philip 111
Aubert, P.-A. 7, 54, 95, 95f, 96, 119, 121
Aure, *Vicomte* Antoine Cartier d' 7, 10, 16, 21, 23, 24, 25, 26, 28, 32, 33, 35f, 41, 43, 44, 47, ch. 4: pp. 52–73, 53 (port.), 56 (port.), 58 (port.), 58 (port.), ch. 5: pp. 75–81, 83, 84, 87, 88, 89, 93, 96, 109, 118, 119, 131, 136, 138, 140, 141, 142, 143, 144
Auvergne (also Dauvergne), Jaques-Amable d' (especially influential in introduing military equitation) 9, 17, 55, 83, 85
Avril de Pignerolle 16

balance(d) 70, 104, 130
ballotade 129
Balme *see* Mottin de la Balme
Balzac, Honoré [de] 111
Baracé, M. de 104
Barail, *géneral* du 29, 30
Baucher, François 13, 16, 18, 24, 25, 28, 29, 32, 35, 38, 39f, ch. 3: pp. 41–51, 42 (port.), 48 (port.), 52, 54, 57, 59, 63, 64, 68, 73f, ch. 5: pp. 75–81, 85–86, 87, 88, 93, 95f, 96, 103, 103f, 108, 109, 117, 119, 124, 127, 129, 130, 131, 132, 136, 137, 138, 140, 141, 142, 143, 144, 144f
Baucher, Henri 139

Beauregard, *Colonel* François de xiii, xv, 11f
Bernhardt, Sarah 120 (port.)
Bigne, *marquis* de la 139
Bishoffsheim, *madame* 121
bits 9, 13, 60, 83, 103, 108, 116
   curb-chain 67, 102, 130
   pelham 116
   snaffle 60, 72, 102, 116, 130
bloodline 89
Bohan *see* Loubet de Bohan
Boideffre, Jean-Baptiste de 55
Boisfoucard, *comte* de 63
Borghese, prince 78
Boulanger, *général* 33
Bourgelat, Claude (French veterinarian) 19
Brack, *général* de 60
breeding, horse 63
bridle 70, 103, 105, 129, 130
   double 60
Broue, Solomon de la 95, 136, 142, 143
Brun, Louis-Auguste (painter) 114
Brunet *see* Neuilly, Brunet de
Buraud, *capitaine* 23

Cadets-Gentilshommes 16, 17
Cadre Noir 11, 16, 38, 40, 142
Calvin, Jean (French theologian) 2
Calvinist Reformation 2
Cambis, *comte* de 69
Camposelice, *duchesse* de 121
canter *see* gaits
capriole 129
Carabiniers de Monsieur 4, 17

Index

Carrière du Chardonnet 4, 5 (il.), 11f, 21, 84
Carrières, *général* 25
carrousel(s) 25
cavalry equitation, *see* equitation, military
Chabannes *see* Ducros de Chabannes
Chambord, *comte de* 31
change(s) of lead *see* lead changes
Chanzy, *général* 32, 33
Charles II 117
Charles IX 3
Charles X (king of France during the Restoration) 10, 20, 55
Charles of Lorraine, Prince 1, 11
Chartres, *duchesse de* 119, 121
Choiseul, *duc de* (after the Seven Years' War established several military schools of which Saumur is the sole survivor) 4, 5
circles 105
circus(es) *see also* equitation, circus 28, 33, 43, 46, 47, 49, 59, 66, 68, 69, 75, 78, 118, 119, 127, 130, 131, 132, 144
  covered 111
  Renz 128, 129
Cirque des Champs-Elysées 127
Cirque d'Eté 129
Cirque d'Hiver 127
Cirque Franconi 132
Cirque Molier 117 (il.), 118 (il.)
Cirque Nouveau 129
Cirque Olympique 124
Clemenceau, Georges 33
Clément-Thomas, *général* Jacques Léonard 75f
Coligney, Gaspard de (French admiral, Huguenot leader) 3
collected, collection 13, 32
Comité de Cavalerie 24, 33, 41, 132
Compagnie de l'Ouest 72
conformation 71, 76, 89, 98, 110, 129, 135
  natural 99
coordinated effects *see effets d'ensemble*
Corbie, de 129

Cordier, J.-B. 11
Cornieu, *baron de* 43
Coubertin, baron Pierre de 112, 113
Council of Tours (May 1881) 32
Courtivron, *captain* Paul de 80
Covent Garden 129
cross country equitation *see* equitation, cross country
croup 90
curb-chain *see* bits
Cuzent, Pauline 124, 127, 126 (port.), 129, 144

Danloux, Pierre 142
Decarpentry, *général* Albert-Eugène Édouard xiii, xv, 14, 15, 44, 81, 117, 132, 132f, 139, 141–2
Delacroix, Eugène 47, 119
Delherm de Novital 21, 82, 83, 86, 109
Delton, Jean-Louis (photographer) 121
Descartes, René 42f, 44, 45
descente de l'encolure (yielding of the neck) 39f
descente de main, la (surrender or yielding of the hand) 13, 39f
Deshayes, *colonel* 20–21
Deshorties, *lieutenant* 70
deuxième manière 13, 50, 129
diagonal 99
Diderot, Denis (French philosopher) 41
displacement 99
Domfront 15, 36
Don Carlos (duke of Madrid) 31
doux passage see passage, doux
dressage (schooling) 10, 25, 65, 80, 85, 89, 91, 107, 109–10, 131f, 135, 140, 141
Dreux, Alfred de 119, 123, 125
Drouin, Adèle 124, 129, 130, 144
Drumont de Melfort 9
Du Plessis, Vernet 1, 10, 136
Ducros de Chabannes, *marquis* 55, 83, 85, 136
Dumas, Alexandre 47, 119
Dupont, Diane 124, 129, 144
Dupuis, *commandant* (L'Hotte's first equitation teacher) 18, 144f
Durand, Catherine 11f
Durand, *général* Pierre 13, 83f
Durrell, Lawrence 16
Dutilh, François (Barada) 32, 140

Ecole d'Application de l'Arme Blindée [et de la] Cavalerie (established in 1946) 11
Ecole de Cavalerie (Saumur) (became *Ecole d'Application de l'Arme Blindée [et de la] Cavalerie*) 1, 2, 3, 5, 6, 7, 10, 11, 13, 15, 19, 20, 24, 25, 26, 31, 32, 60, 64, 67, 68, 73f, 83, 84, 85, 86, 133, 139, 140, 142, 143
Ecole de Versailles 1, 2, 6, 7, 10, 11, 57, 81, 118, 119, 133, 143
Ecole d'Etat major 132
Ecole d'Instruction des Troupes à cheval 83
Ecole Militaire (Paris) 1, 11, 25, 83
Ecole Nationale d'Equitation (established 1972) 11, 13, 14, 142
Ecole spéciale militaire 83
écuyère(s) (women specializing in *haute école*) 111–34
Edit of Nantes (13 April 1598) 3, 4
  Revocation of (1685) 3, 4
effets d'ensemble (coordinated effects) 13, 45, 50
Eisenberg, *baron* Reis d' 16
elasticity 56, 65
elementary equitation *see* equitation, *basse école*
elevation 107
Embrun, Mathilde d' 124
Enghien, *duc d'* 8 (port.)
équilibre rassemblé 13
equilibrium 43, 60, 65, 66, 67, 73, 80, 88, 90, 94f, 98, 105, 124
  artificial equilibrium 46, 50
  horizontal equilibrium 7
  natural equilibrium 50, 67
equitation 1, 4, 11, 22, 24, 33,

Index

42, 50, 52, 55, 62, 63, 64, 73, 75, 78, 83, 90, 124, 138, 141, 142, 143
basse école (elementary equitation) 101, 103, 108
circus 103, 106–108, 109, 119, 124, 127, 131, 132, 135, 142
Classical 7, 9, 11, 14, 15, 23, 55, 79, 106–8, 92, 94, 97, 100, 103,106, 107, 108, 109, 116, 118, 127, 129, 142, 143
cross-country (exercises, riding, equitation) 21, 32f, 54, 55, 57, 63, 65, 73, 78, 79, 80, 83, 91, 94, 97, 106, 121, 132, 133, 135, 138, 140
direction changes 49, 69, 73, 77, 90, 93, 94, 95, 97, 100
exterior (*l'équitation d'extérieur*) 7, 9, 10, 13, 14, 21, 54, 55, 56 (il.), 66, 68, 79, 103, 106, 110, 111, 116, 118, 119, 132, 138, 140
for ladies 63
haute école 7, 10, 27, 28, 29, 32, 33, 59, 66, 67, 68, 85, 92, 94, 95, 101, 106, 107, 108, 121, 124, 127, 130, 132, 135, 140, 142, 143
la manière française (the French manner) 13
manège 7, 9, 10, 13, 14, 21, 28, 29, 49, 55, 57, 68, 79, 80, 83, 85, 87, 110, 116, 119, 124, 132, 133, 135, 138, 140
military 6, 9, 10, 11, 13, 14, 15, 19, 21, 49, 55, 65, 79, 80, 85, 87, 91, 103, 105–6, 135, 140
principles of 23, 25, 43, 73, 78, 79, 80, 81, 83, 86, 88, 135
race horse 103–4
savante 7, 27, 51, 79, 115, 116, 118, 127, 128
teaching 88–9
theory 1, 13, 16, 65
women 112–13
Étreillis, *baron* d' 47, 65, 130, 131, 132, 144
Eugénie, Empress 72, 119
extension 107

Faverot de Kerbrech, Baron François de, *général* xiii, xv, 13, 28, 38, 39, 124, 129, 130, 130f, 131, 140, 141, 142, 143, 144
February Revolution of 1848 21
Fénélon, François de Salignac de La Mothe 4
Feray, *général* 24
Fiaschi, Cesare 143
Fillis, Anna 124, 127–9, 130, 133
Fillis, James 33, 35, 127, 129, 131, 132, 144
First Empire 5, 20, 78, 83
Fitz-James, *duchesse* de 121
Fleury, *général* 26, 27, 29, 72
flexibility, flexion 13, 16, 39f, 44, 45, 51, 66, 86, 90, 91–2, 108, 109, 137, 144
Fontenelle, le Bovier de 4
forehand 93, 96, 104, 107, 108, 127
 heavy 66, 67
 light 66, 144
Fox, Charles James (British statesman) 2
Franco-Prussian War (1870) 24, 29, 113f, 131
Franconi, Laurent 28, 68, 69, 131
Franconi, Victor 68–9, 121
François I (1515–47) 2
Franz-Josef (emperor of Austria) 31
Froissard, Jean 102f
Fronde, Frondes 6–7

gaits 49, 56, 59, 65, 66, 70, 73, 89, 90, 98, 99, 106, 107
 artificial 27, 32, 80, 108
 canter 32, 49, 59, 60, 67, 68, 73, 77, 82, 84, 93, 96, 97, 100, 101, 128; left 97; right 97; strike-offs 130
 extended, extension 7, 21, 14, 32, 65, 68, 71, 80, 90, 92
 extended trot 130
 fast trot 68
 gallop 66, 84
 natural 7, 56, 108, 109
 racking gait 22, 82
 sitting trot 22, 23, 24
 trot 59–60, 63, 65, 66, 70, 73, 77, 109
 trot écouté 95
 trot enlevé (rising trot) 22, 23–4, 54, 68, 98, 99–100, 116 (*aka trot à l'anglaise*)
 walk 70, 73, 77, 82, 84, 90, 110
Galliffet, *général* de 33, 35
Gaussen, Maxime 26, 29, 41f, 47, 75, 76, 129, 131, 144
Gautier, Théophile 47, 114, 119
Gazaux *see* Nestier, Louis de Gazaux de
Gendarmes Rouges 17
Ghyga (or Ghika), Countess Fanny 124, 130–1, 133, 134
Gide, André xiii, xv
Gilly, *vicomtesse* de 119
Glorieux 15, 36
Goyon, de, *général* 24, 25
grand passage *see* passage, grand
Grande Armée 6, 18, 20, 83
Grande Ecurie (Versailles) 6, 9, 11, 63
Grandjean, Edmond (painter) 122
Greek ideal (sound mind in sound body) 4
Grisone, Frederico 81, 101, 101f, 116, 143
Guérin, *colonel* Etienne 32
Guérinière, François Robichon de la 1, 10, 11, 13, 39f, 55, 90, 95, 135, 135f, 136, 139, 142, 143, 144f
Guides d'état-major (cavalry detachment serving as the Armée des Alpes) 22, 23, 25, 52

hack, hacking 29, 54, 57, 68, 85, 99
half pass 49
half turn 73, 130
halt 130, 132
Hamilton, Duke of 72
hand without legs *see main sans jambes*
hand(s) 54, 71, 79, 80, 92, 94, 96, 97, 99, 100, 101, 104, 105, 108, 124
harnessing 72

— 219 —

Index

haunches 13, 57, 66, 68, 71, 72, 73, 84, 88, 90, 91, 92, 93, 94, 95, 96, 97, 98, 99, 101, 102, 103, 107, 108, 109, 127, 144
head with tail movement *see tête à queue, le*
heel(s) 81, 90, 92, 93, 94, 97–8, 103
   function of 101–2
   inside (direct) 95, 97, 101
   outside (opposing) 95, 97, 101
Helena Charlotte, princess 116 (port.)
Helvetius, Claude Adrien (French philosopher) 42f
Henriquet, Michel 11f, 44f, 144f
Henry II 3
Henry III 3
Henry IV 3, 4
Henry de Navarre 3
hindquarters 66, 127, 130
hippodrome 104, 129, 130
hock(s) 72, 92, 95, 97, 100, 101, 104, 105, 108, 109, 131, 132
Holt, Richard 111
horseman, horsemanship 4, 6, 10, 16, 21, 33, 43, 52, 54, 55, 61, 65, 66, 79, 85, 98, 111, 116, 119, 133, 135, 140
horizontal equilibrium *see* equilibrium, horizontal
Hugo, Victor 47, 111
hunting 7, 10, 54, 57, 135

impulsion 13, 21, 39f, 45, 46, 51, 54, 56, 65, 69, 79, 80, 88, 90, 91–2, 93, 99, 102, 103, 109, 141
Insensé 36

Jacquemin, *colonel* 64
Jauemire, *général* 30
jambes sans main (legs without hand) 13, 46, 50
jambette 107
Janin, Jules 119, 124
jaw, flexibility of 44, 45, 80, 92, 108
Joan of Arc 113, 116
Jockey Club 47, 62
Joinville, Prince de 119

July Monarchy (aka Bourgeois Monarchy) 1830–1848 10, 18, 20
jumper at liberty *see sauteur en liberté*
jumping, obstacle 10, 29, 54, 55, 57, 65, 85, 93, 100–1, 104, 106, 121, 135
June Revolution of 1848 21

Kant, Immanuel (German philosopher) 42f
Kerbrech *see* Faverot de Kerbrech
knees 54

La Lance *see* Menessier de la Lance
l'epaule en dedans (the shoulder in) 13, 44f, 101
Lafont, *général* 142
Lamartine, Alphonse Marie Louis de Prat de (French statesman) 117
Lamplugh (jockey with whom L'Hotte was acquainted) 104
Lancosme-Brèves, *comte* Savary de 47
Laruns 29, 30 (port.), 129
lead changes 29, 49, 59, 60, 67, 71, 77, 78, 84, 96, 97–8, 101, 130
   at the canter 46
   flying 77, 128, 130
   single 97
   successive 97
   tempi, tempo 29, 59, 97, 128, 130
Lefèvre d'Etaples, Jacques 2
lêgèreté, la (lightness) 11–13, 15, 16, 37, 39f, 43, 44, 45, 46, 50, 51, 57, 67, 79, 88, 90–2, 94, 104, 108, 127, 128, 130, 131, 135, 137, 144
legs 54, 79, 80, 96, 100, 101, 102, 103, 124
legs without hand *see jambes sans main*
Leibnitz, Gottfried Wilhelm von (German philosopher) 42f
Léopold, *duc* de Lorraine 16, 17 (port.)

levade 129
L'Hotte, *général* Alexis-François, iv (port.), xiii, xv, 10, 13–14, chapter 2: 15–40, 30 (port.)
L'Institution chrétienne 2
lightness *see lêgèreté, la*
Loisset, Antoine 134
Loisset, Emilie 130
Lorentz (caricaturist–2 caricatures appear in Nelson's book on Baucher) 41, 44
Loubet de Bohan 17, 85
Louis XIII 4, 116
Louis XIV 1, 3, 4, 6, 7, 107f
Louis XVI 10
Louis XVIII 10
Louis Napoléon *see* Napoléon III
Louis-Philippe 10, 68
Loyo, Caroline 124, 127, 132, 134, 144
Lubersac de Livron, *comte* (*écuyer* at Versailles for a while, then cavalry officer; one of the initiators of Military riding) 9, 11, 55, 136
Lunéville (birthplace of L'Hotte) discussed primary in ch. 2
lunge 39f, 62, 72, 110
Lyautey, Hubert (Marshal of France) xiii, xv

Maillé, *marquis* de 31
main sans jambes (hand without legs) 13, 46, 50
Manège de Saumur 63, 64, 69
Manège de Versailles 1, 6, 7, 9, 10, 11, 18, 35f, 43, 52, 55, 57, 59, 61, 62, 63, 64, 83, 138, 139, 143, 144f
Manège des Ecuyers 1, 5, 7, 20, 23, 60, 64, 67, 70, 142, 143
Manège royal de Paris 47
Manège royal des Tuileries 1
Margot, Colonel George 14, 35, 48, 84
Marialva, *marquis* de 144f
martingale 66
Massacre de Saint Barthélemy (August 1572) 3
Maturin, Charles III
Maupin, Madeleine de 114

Index

Mazarin, Jules (French cardinal/statesman) 7
Mazuchelli, Frederico 51, 78, 143
Meaux, Bishop of 2
Meaux Circle 2
Médicis, Catherine de (Queen Mother) 3, 113
Melfort *see* Drumont de Melfort
Mendès, Catulle 119
Mennessier de la Lance, *général* xiii, xv, 142
Middle Ages 113
Molier, Ernest 114–15, 115f
Monet, *général* de 25, 26
Montaigne, Michel Eyquem, Seigneur de 4
(16th century essaysist, Humanist)
Montesquieu, Charles Louis de Secondat, Baron de la Brède et de (French philosophical writer) 41
Montfaucon de Rogles 9, 55
Montigny, *comte* Louis-Xavier de 133, 144
Montjou, Gaborit de 142
Mottin de la Balme 17
movement 56
  multiple movements 107
Musany, F. 119, 121, 121f, 124

Napoleon I 5, 6, 55, 83
Napoleon III 25, 27, 55, 72, 119
Neapolitan Riding School 143
neck 66, 67, 93, 94, 97, 98–99, 100, 102, 103, 105
  bend (curvature, inflexion) 94–5
  elevation 98
  extension 32, 54, 72, 98, 102, 104
  equilibrium 39f
  flexibility 65, 127
Nelson, Hilda 73f, 75f, 95f
Nemours, *duc* de 29, 43, 68, 69, 119
Neneu, Le (d'Aure's editor) 73
Nestier, Louis de Gazaux de 1, 136
Neuilly, Brunet de 2
Newcastle, Duke of 117, 143

Nodier, Charles 111
Noë, *comte* Pierre de la 10
noseband 67, 67f
Nouveau Cirque 129 (see Cirque)
nouvelle méthode (introduced by Baucher) 13, 25, 35, 38, 41, 43, 44, 57, 64, 76, 81, 85, 86, 87, 127, 132, 140
Novital *see* Delherm de Novital
Nyss, Yola de 117 (port.)

obedience 89
Oliveira, Nuno 144, 144f
oppositions 43, 72, 77
Orléans, *duc* d' 43, 48, 68, 69, 119
Orléans, *duchesse* d' 48
Oudinot, *général* 23, 47, 83, 85, 86

Palais d'Industrie 29
Parlement of Paris 2, 3, 6
parole, sur (on parole) 13, 29, 89, 107
Pascal, Blaise 44f
passage(s) 32, 46, 67, 96, 127, 128, 130
  doux 108–9
  grand 108–9
pelham *see* bits
Pellier, Charles 26
Pellier, Jules-Charles 26, 119, 127
Percherons 72
Perrier, Jacques 15, 83f, 86, 139, 142, 144f
Petite Ecurie 6
Petzolf, Elisa 121, 124, 129, 130, 133, 144
piaffe(s) 46, 96, 108–9, 127, 128, 130
Pignatelli, Giovani Battista 116, 143
pirouette(s) 90, 101
  at the canter 46
Pitt, William (went to Angers to study horsemanship) 2
placer, le 94
Pléiades 142
Plinzner 131
Pluvinel, Antoine de (author of *Le Maneige Royal*) 4f, 19, 116, 142, 143
Poincaré, Raymond (president of France, 1913–20) 33f
Poitiers, Diane de 113
pommel 113, 124
Pompadour, Madame de 4
Pons d'Hostrum, L. de 121
Pope Gregory VII 113
position 71, 97, 98, 99
  of rider 7 100–1, 138
posture 7, 21, 25, 63, 77, 80, 102, 129, 138
Prizeluis, J.G. 116 (il.)

Raabe, Charles-Hubert 140, 144
Rabelais, François (monk, doctor, Humanist, author of *Gargantua and Pantagruel*) 4
Racine, Jean Baptiste (French dramatist) 145
Racinet, Jean-Claude 144f
racing, races 10, 57, 59, 68, 105
racking gait *see* gaits
Radcliffe, Anne 111
ramener, ramené 38f, 92, 98, 108
Randon, *maréchal* (Minister of War) 23
rassembler 92, 108, 124
Regulations of 1876 105
rein(s) 54, 72, 85, 93, 94, 97, 101, 102, 105
  fixed 108
  rein change 77, 78
  rein of opposition 68, 72, 102
  reinback 130
  rigid 102–3
  side 108
Renaissance 116
Renaissance man 4
reprise(s) 25, 27, 29, 32, 59, 60, 65, 67, 84, 140
resistance(s) 43, 45, 50, 57, 67, 98, 100, 102, 103, 108, 128, 130
Restoration of 1815 10
Revolution of 1789 5, 112
Revolution of 1830 10, 62
Revolution of 1848 112
riding, outdoor *see* equitation, exterior

rising trot *see* gaits: *trot enlevé*
Robichon de la Guérinière, François *see* Guérinière
Roche, Daniel 11f
Roger, A. 121
Rogles *see* Montfaucon de Rogles
Rothschild, *baronne* Laure Alphons de 121
Rothwiller, *baronne* 121
rouler, le (circular race track) 104, 105
Rousseau, Jean-Jacques 41, 42, 11, 139f
Rousselet, *monsieur, commandant* 7, 11, 16, 28, 54, 60, 61, 62, 80, ch. 6: pp. 82–7, 88, 110, 117, 135, 144
Rul, Louis Joseph 144

saddle(s) 11, 13, 27, 68, 71, 99, 100, 104
    English saddle(s) 23, 27, 28
    French saddle(s) 27
    side-saddle 113, 115–16, 124
Saint-André, *colonel* Jean de 15–16
Saint-Cyr 15, 16, 19, 23, 25, 26, 52, 59, 72, 105, 142
Saint-Phalle, *capitaine* Jacques de 38–40, 141, 142
Saint-Phalle, Madeleine 38
Saint-Vual, *monsieur* de 4
Salles, *comtesse* R. de 119
Salvert, François de 1–2, 9, 11
Saunier, Gaspard de 9, 10
Saurel, Etienne 142, 142f, 143
sauteur en liberté (jumper at liberty) 61
schooling *see* dressage
seat 7, 21, 25, 63, 68, 71, 77, 80, 98, 10, 101, 129
Second Empire 25, 72
Second Republic 21, 25, 55
Seeger, Louis 131
Selve, *colonel* (aka Soliman Pacha) 20
serpentines 25
Seven Years' War (1756–63) 4

Seymour, Lord Henry (Jockey Club founder) 47, 59, 61, 62
Shelley, Mary 111
shoulder in *see l'épaule en dedans*
shoulder(s) 91, 93, 95, 96, 97, 98, 100, 103, 104, 109
Sicambre 27, 28 (port.), 29
sitting trot *see* gaits
snaffle *see* bits
Societé hippique française 26
Spanish Riding School 131f
Spanish walk 107, 122(il.), 128
speed 56, 65
spurs, use of 39f, 45, 61, 69, 77, 83, 102, 103, 104
Stanislas Leszczinski (father-in-law of Louis XV) 16
steeple chase 21, 25, 55, 68, 104
Steinbrecht, Gustave 130, 131
stiffness 68, 69
Stirling-Clarke, Mrs. J. 121
stirrups 7, 9, 11, 54, 83, 98, 99, 104, 116
straight, straightness 88, 90–1, 94, 97, 99, 101, 105, 106, 130
strength, control of 88, 108
stride 56, 98
Stubbs, George 119
submissiveness 88, 93, 100, 103, 105, 110, 137, 144
Sue, Eugène 47, 119
supple (supples, suppling) 13, 39f, 56, 67, 89, 90, 94, 141, 144, 145

tabula rasa 44f, 45
tête à queue, le (head with tail movement) 59
thighs 54
Toulouse-Lautrec, Henri Marie Raymond de (French painter) 113
Tournon, *vicomte* de 47
tracks
    one 100
    two 90, 97, 100, 101
trot enlevé (rising trot) (aka *trot à l'anglaise*) *see* gaits

turn(s), turning 92–5, 96, 100, 101, 103, 104, 105, 106, 132
Tuscany, Mathilda, Countess of 113

Van Walberg, Camile 133
Vaux, *baron* de Ch.-M., 65, 75–6, 112, 113, 117f, 119, 121, 124, 124f, 127, 128, 130, 131, 132, 133, 144
Vendeuil, Antoine de 1, 10, 11
Voltaire, François Marie Arouet (French philosopher) 16, 41
volte(s) 49, 78, 90

walk straight 70
Walpole, Horace 111
Warner, Marina 116f
Wattel, Jean-Charles-Edmond 142
Weber, Eugen 112, 112f
weight distribution 66, 72, 73, 80, 89, 90, 94f, 97, 98–100, 103, 104
Wellesley, Arthur, 1st Duke of Wellington (went to Angers to study horsemanship) 2
whip, use of 104
women
    equitation 112–13
    horseback 113; astride 113, 115, 116
    manége 113
    society 111
    sports 111, 112
work in hand 13, 39f, 45

Xenophon 81, 117

yielding of the hand *see descente de main, la*
yielding of the neck *see descente de l'encolure*

Zégris 26, 27 (port.), 29, 80
Zidler 129, 130

Xenophon Press Library

www.XenophonPress.com

Xenophon Press is dedicated to the preservation
of classical equestrian literature.
We bring both new and old works to English-speaking riders.

30 Years with Master Nuno Oliveira, Henriquet 2011
A Journey Through the Horse's Body, Fritz 2012
A Rider's Survival from Tyranny, de Kunffy 2012
Another Horsemanship, Racinet 1994
Austrian Art of Riding, Poscharnigg 2015
Broken or Beautiful: The Struggle of Modern Dressage, Barbier/Conrod 2020
Classic Show Jumping: the de Nemethy Method, de Nemethy 2016
Classical Dressage with Anja Beran, Beran 2017
Divide and Conquer Book 1, Lemaire de Ruffieu 2016
Divide and Conquer Book 2, Lemaire de Ruffieu 2017
Dressage for the 21st Century, Belasik 2001
Dressage in the French Tradition, Diogo de Bragança 2011
Dressage Principles and Techniques: A Blueprint for the Serious Rider, Tavora 2018
Dressage Principles Illuminated, Expanded Edition, de Kunffy 2021
Dressage Sabbatical: A Year of Riding with Classical Master Paul Belasik, Caslar 2016
École de Cavalerie Part II, Robichon de la Guérinière 2015
Elements of Dressage, von Ziegner 2016
Equestrian Art: The Collected Early Writings (1951-1956), Master Nuno Oliveira 2022
Equestrian Art The Collected Later Works, Nuno Oliveira 2022
Equine Osteopathy: What the Horses Have Told Me, Giniaux 2014
Equitation, Bussigny 2021
Fragments from the Writings of Max Ritter von Weyrother, Fane 2017
François Baucher: The Man and His Method, Baucher/Nelson 2013
General Chamberlin: America's Equestrian Genius, Matha 2020
Great Horsewomen of the 19th Century in the Circus, Nelson 2015
Gymnastic Exercises for Horses Volume II, Eleanor Russell 2013
H. Dv. 12 German Cavalry Manual of Horsemanship, Reinhold 2014
Handbook of Jumping Essentials, Lemaire de Ruffieu 2015
Handbook of Riding Essentials, Lemaire de Ruffieu 2015
Healing Hands, Giniaux, DVM 1998
Horse Training: Outdoors and High School, Beudant 2014
I, Siglavy, Asay 2018
Horsemanship & Horsemastership Volume 1, US Cavalry 2021
Horsemanship Training Films 3 DVD set, US Cavalry 2021
Learning to Ride, Santini 2016
Legacy of Master Nuno Oliveira, Millham 2013

Lessons in Lightness: Expanded Edition, Mark Russell 2019
Methodical Dressage of the Riding Horse, Faverot de Kerbrech 2010
Military Equitation or, A Method of Breaking Horses, and Teaching Soldiers to Ride, Pembroke, and *A Treatise on Military Equitation*, Tyndale 2018
My Horses Have Something to Say, de Wispelaere 2021
Principles of Dressage and Equitation, a.k.a. Breaking and Riding, Fillis 2017
Racinet Explains Baucher, Racinet 1997
Releasing the Jaw, Poll, and Neck DVD, Mark Russell 2021
Riding and Schooling Horses, Chamberlin 2020
Riding by Torchlight, Cord 2019
Riding in Rhyme, Davies 2021
Schooling Exercises In Hand, Hilberger 2009
Science and Art of Riding in Lightness, Stodulka 2015
Sketches of the Equestrian Art, Barbier/Sauvat 2021
The Art of Riding a Horse, D'Eisenberg 2015
The Art of Traditional Dressage, Volume 1 DVD, de Kunffy 2013
The Chamberlin Reader, Chamberlin/Matha, 2020
The de Nemethy Method: A training seminar, 8 DVD set, de Nemethy 2019
The Ethics and Passions of Dressage Expanded Edition, de Kunffy 2013
The Forward Impulse, Santini 2016
The Gymnasium of the Horse, Steinbrecht 2018
The Horses, a novel, Walker 2015
The Italian Tradition of Equestrian Art, Tomassini 2014
The Maneige Royal, de Pluvinel 2010, 2015
The New Method of Dressing Horses a.k.a. A General System of Horsemanship, Cavendish 2020
The Portuguese School of Equestrian Art, de Oliveira/da Costa 2012
The Quest for Lightness in Equitation and Equestrian Questions, Nelson/L'Hotte 2021
The Spanish Riding School & Piaffe and Passage, Decarpentry 2013
The Spanish Riding School: The Miracle of the White Horse DVD, US Lipizzan Association 2021
To Amaze the People with Pleasure and Delight, Walker 2015
Total Horsemanship, Racinet 1999
Training Hunters, Jumpers, and Hacks, Chamberlin 2019
Training Your Foal, Ettl 2011
Training with Master Nuno Oliveira, 2 DVD set, Eleanor Russell 2016
Truth in the Teaching of Master Nuno Oliveira, Eleanor Russell 2015
Wisdom of Master Nuno Oliveira, de Coux 2012

www.ingramcontent.com/pod-product-compliance
Lightning Source LLC
Chambersburg PA
CBHW060500240426
43661CB00006B/859